IN PEACE
AND WAR

This book is dedicated to the officers, soldiers and horses of all seven cavalry regiments with which it is concerned. Some were killed in action, many were injured and others became prisoners-of-war, suffering all manner of privations. All did – and in the case of the Queen's Royal Hussars (The Queen's Own and Royal Irish) continue to do – their duty. Living or dead, they are not forgotten.

IN PEACE AND WAR

The Story of
The Queen's Royal Hussars
(The Queen's Own and Royal Irish)

Robin Rhoderick-Jones

**Foreword by
HRH The Prince Philip,
Duke of Edinburgh**

Pen & Sword
MILITARY

First published in Great Britain in 2018 by
PEN & SWORD MILITARY
An imprint of
Pen & Sword Books Ltd
47 Church Street
Barnsley
South Yorkshire
S70 2AS

ISBN 978-1-52674-695-5

Typeset by Concept, Huddersfield HD4 5JL.
Printed and bound in England by TJ International Ltd, Padstow, Cornwall.

Pen & Sword Books Limited incorporates the imprints of Atlas, Archaeology, Aviation, Discovery, Family History, Fiction, History, Maritime, Military, Military Classics, Politics, Select, Transport, True Crime, Air World, Frontline Publishing, Leo Cooper, Remember When, Seaforth Publishing, The Praetorian Press, Wharncliffe Local History, Wharncliffe Transport, Wharncliffe True Crime and White Owl.

For a complete list of Pen & Sword titles please contact
PEN & SWORD BOOKS LIMITED
47 Church Street, Barnsley, South Yorkshire, S70 2AS, England
E-mail: enquiries@pen-and-sword.co.uk
Website: www.pen-and-sword.co.uk

CONTENTS

LIST OF PLATES

LIST OF MAPS

Soldiers mounted on horses formed an essential part of armies for hundreds, if not, thousands of years. Then along came the tank and everything changed. Everything, that is, except the officers and soldiers of the cavalry regiments. Although my father was a cavalry officer, I spent thirteen years with the Royal Navy, so my appointment in 1953 as Colonel-in-Chief of The 8th King's Royal Irish Hussars was a challenge to both of us. However, I am happy to say the most cordial relations were very soon established. I am glad to say that this has continued through The Queen's Royal Irish Hussars from 1958 until 1993, when I became Deputy (to Queen Elizabeth) Colonel-in-Chief of The Queen's Royal Hussars. In 2002 I became Colonel-in-Chief of The Queen's Royal Hussars.

Over the years, I have become associated with a wide variety of military formations from the Royal Marines to the Royal Electrical and Mechanical Engineers and the Intelligence Corps and I have been struck by the unchanging unique character of each organisation. This is particularly true of the cavalry regiment. I am quite sure that readers of this book will see what I mean. Cavalry regiments have always been different and, as this book will testify, their mechanisation has barely made any difference to their generally light-hearted approach to their profession. Needless to say, this does not in any way affect their military qualities and achievements.

In some ways, this is rather a sad story. A shrinking Army, and the inevitable amalgamations have removed a large number of famous regiments from the order of battle. It is therefore timely to record the achievements of all the predecessors to The Queen's Royal Hussars. It's quite a story.

ACKNOWLEDGEMENTS

The writing of this book has been a delight and I need very much to thank those responsible for its completion. First is the Colonel of the Queen's Royal Hussars (The Queen's Own and Royal Irish), Lieutenant General Sir Tom Beckett, who has supported the project from the very beginning. He and the regimental trustees, particularly Colonel Nigel Beer who has carried the commercial burden, have entered enthusiastically into the processes necessary to bring the book to publication. Major Jim Austin and his team at regimental home headquarters have been unfailingly helpful in responding to my frequent cries for help for which I am truly grateful.

I thank, too, those past colonels, commanding officers and regimental sergeant majors of the Queen's Royal Hussars who answered my appeal for personal reminiscences of their time in office and provided much useful material, as did a number of others serving at regimental duty. Members of the Regimental Association also got in touch and contributed their own memories. David Botsford put all the images, maps and captions on to disc which saved a huge amount of work for the publishers. To all of them I am grateful.

I have the greatest pleasure in singling out my old friend Peter Donovan, an old comrade of the 4th Queen's Own Hussars, who has kindly contributed towards the cost of the production of *In Peace and War* – one of several hugely generous donations he has made to regimental charities. Finally I thank my most assiduous editor, George Chamier, and Henry Wilson and Matt Jones of Pen & Sword for their help and encouragement.

All proceeds from sales of this book go to the Regimental Association.

Robin Rhoderick-Jones
St Patrick's Day 2018

INTRODUCTION

In 1685 several regiments were raised by King James II to fulfil his long-held dream of possessing a standing army. Two of these were The Queen Consort's Regiment of Dragoons (later the 3rd King's Own Hussars) and The Princess Anne of Denmark's Regiment of Dragoons, which eventually became the 4th Queen's Own Hussars. Six years later the 7th Queen's Own Hussars were created in the shape of Cunningham's Dragoons for service in Scotland and three years after that came Conyngham's Regiment of Dragoons, which was later to become the 8th King's Royal Irish Hussars, raised in Ireland at the behest of King William III. All four regiments have been the subject of detailed histories, but this book weaves them together, highlighting the instances in which they fought alongside each other at Dettingen, Balaklava, the Peninsula, in India and during the First and Second World Wars. In 1953 His Royal Highness The Prince Philip, Duke of Edinburgh, was appointed Colonel-in-Chief of the 8th and has been closely associated with this and its successor regiments ever since – as illustrated by his foreword to this volume.

In 1958 the 3rd and the 7th became the Queen's Own Hussars and the 4th and the 8th were amalgamated to form the Queen's Royal Irish Hussars. Brief accounts of their activities appeared in 1985 to mark their respective tercentenaries, illustrating their service in far-flung conflicts in Aden, Malaya, Korea, Borneo and the Gulf as well as tours in Northern Ireland and more sedentary postings in Germany and the United Kingdom. This book brings them all together and tells the stories of these two parent regiments leading to the birth of the Queen's Royal Hussars (The Queen's Own and Royal Irish) in September 1993.

Since that day the Queen's Royal Hussars have been busy, seeing action in Bosnia-Herzegovina, Kosovo, Iraq and, most recently in Afghanistan, where the regiment provided the first cavalry-led ground-holding battle-group, and where a squadron was part of the last battle-group to deploy before British withdrawal. Back in Germany at Athlone Barracks, Sennelager – their home for the last twenty years – they are, in 2018, the only cavalry regiment equipped with tanks. Retaining their Challengers, the regiment expects to move to Tidworth in the summer of 2019 as the British presence in Germany comes to an end. The chapters describing life in a cavalry regiment over the last twenty-five years illustrate vividly the complexities which face officers and men – vastly different in scale from those experienced by their predecessors in the last 300 years. It is evident, however, that at least some aspects of life have not changed – the dedication, bravery, commitment, sporting endeavour and sense of humour of those who choose to join the Queen's Royal Hussars.

Robin Rhoderick-Jones
St Patrick's Day, 2018

CHAPTER ONE

EARLY DAYS

There must be a beginning of any great matter, but the continuing unto the end yields the true glory. (Francis Drake)

James VII of Scotland and II of England and Ireland had much in common with his father of whom he was the youngest surviving son. Both firmly believed in the primacy of the monarchy and distrusted, indeed despised (in the case of Charles I, fatally), Parliament. Was James, as is still believed by his most ardent critics (mostly Protestant) an egotistical and tyrannical bigot plotting, against the supposed wishes of the 98 per cent of his subjects who were not Roman Catholic, to restore the throne to the 'old religion', or was he, as is advanced by his apologists, simply a stupid man – well intentioned, even enlightened – who failed to grasp political realities? The truth, no doubt, lies somewhere between these extremes, but what cannot be questioned is that his behaviour led to bloodshed in all three of his kingdoms and personal disaster for himself. The trigger that led to his fleeing his realms and his *de facto* abdication was the birth of a son in June 1688, an event at once supposed by the overwhelming bulk of the population to be a preposterous deception.

James had already decisively survived two armed rebellions. In 1685 two exiles, James Scott, Duke of Monmouth, a bastard son of Charles II, and Archibald Campbell, 9th Earl of Argyll, returned simultaneously to England and Scotland respectively from Holland, where they had enjoyed the protection of the Dutch Stadholder, William, Prince of Orange. Their declared aim was to mobilize the '*Protestant forces of the kingdoms*' and achieve Monmouth's '*legal and legitimate*' right to the Crown. Both men were woefully over-optimistic: Monmouth failed to raise more than a rag, tag and bobtail force in the South-West after his landing at Lyme Bay, and Argyll was not even supported by most of his own clansmen. Both were captured and executed within barely a month. In order to meet these rebellions and deter any recurrence, James was galvanized into realizing one of his dearest dreams – the raising of a substantial standing army. Among those units brought into being on 17 July 1685 were two regiments of dragoons: the Queen Consort's Regiment, eventually to become the 3rd The King's Own Hussars, and the Princess Anne of Denmark's Regiment, which in due course became the 4th Queen's Own Hussars.

The Queen Consort's Regiment of Dragoons was named in honour of James' wife, Mary, daughter of Alfonso IV, Duke of Modena, a staunch Roman Catholic, and had been originally formed from three troops detached from the Duke of Somerset's Royal Dragoons sent to guard the northern approaches to London against any incursion by Monmouth's forces, a role in which they saw no action. The regiment wore the Queen's livery with Garter-blue feathered hats – an association with the colour which has survived into the twenty-first century. Princess Anne of Denmark's Regiment of Dragoons was so-called after the King's younger daughter, who like her sister Mary was a devoted Protestant and married to Prince George of Denmark. The regiment was raised by a professional soldier, the Honourable John Berkeley (later 4th Viscount Fitzharding), who had served in the army of Charles II and later commanded the right wing of the First Foot Guards against Monmouth, and was thus popularly called Berkeley's Dragoons. In their first few years neither regiment was called upon to do any fighting but both were troubled by religious differences among both the officers and their men. In 1688 their loyalty to the Stuart king was severely put to the test when, on 5 November, William of Orange landed in Torbay at the head of an army numbering some 14,000 and began his advance on London. King James had assembled his army at Salisbury, but as news of the invasion spread to the Queen Consort's regiment there were immediate defections. Lieutenant Colonel Richard Leveson and several of his officers led a majority in support of William to Devon, where it adopted the title Leveson's Dragoons. The remainder, under Colonel Alexander Cannon, remained loyal and joined in James' retreat to his capital, after which he fled to Ireland. Similar ructions were occurring in Berkeley's Dragoons: Berkeley himself, together with many senior commanders including John Churchill (later to become the first Duke of Marlborough), deserted the King. Princess Anne's Regiment, now under command of Thomas Maxwell, who although a Catholic was not regarded as reliable, was ordered out of the line and sent to Burford in rural north Oxfordshire out of harm's way. It had not fought for James and it remained to be seen whether it would do so for William. It soon had its chance: in 1689 Viscount ('Bonnie') Dundee rallied the Highland clans to the Stuart cause and Berkeley's Dragoons were despatched north to join the Scots Brigade under Major General Mackay, who was charged with putting down this latest manifestation of resistance to the Williamite cause. On the banks of the Spey near present day Grantown, and later at Forfar, the regiment was commended by the *London Gazette* for its role in speedily defeating the highlanders and chasing them home. And home, too, having proved its loyalty, went Berkeley's to quarters in the English Midlands. Origins of the regiment which, after the introduction of Hussars into the British order of battle in 1807, eventually became the 7th Hussars, have never been clear. The earliest reference to its birth appears in 1690 when six troops of Scottish cavalry militia were given to Colonel Robert Cunningham and became known inevitably as Cunningham's Dragoons. Cunningham was a veteran soldier, having served in the Scots Brigade in the Netherlands as a captain in a regiment of foot, and was one of the first of William's entourage to step ashore at Torbay. His new regiment had a quiet couple of years engaged in internal security, dispersed to widely scattered troop locations in the Highlands. Light relief came when it was brought together at Leith on the outskirts of Edinburgh to quell '*a multitude of women*' who, in the words of the Scottish Secretary of State in an agitated despatch to King William, '*come here to infest and threaten Major-General Mackay; more of this is feared, the poor people are not able to give the soldiers subsistence for many of them have difficulty to subsist themselves*'. The lack of barracks and the evils of the billeting system which compelled households to take in soldiers (and their horses), often with delayed, inadequate or no compensation, had come home to roost. The versatility of the Dragoons must have been sorely tested as they tried to pacify this monstrous regiment of women with whom, no doubt, their sympathies lay.

Vastly more troublesome than Scotland's highlanders and the women of Edinburgh were the Irish. Overwhelmingly Roman Catholic in religion (other than in the northern province of Ulster where transplanted Protestants prevailed), most of the population of Ireland retained its allegiance to James II. Leveson's Dragoons were transported to Ulster in August 1689 to become part of the 30,000-strong army led by William and were in action as that army moved south to counter James's Catholic forces – largely composed of French troops provided by Louis XIV, from whom he had sought sanctuary – as they advanced north from Cork and Kinsale. The ensuing clashes – hitherto mainly minor in nature – came to a decisive conclusion in

Battle of the Boyne, 1 July 1690.

July 1690 at the Battle of the (River) Boyne at Oldbridge near Drogheda, where the Jacobite army, now some 25,000 strong, was decisively beaten and James fled back to France, whence he was never to return.

Despite the absence of their preferred king, Catholic forces continued to resist and Leveson's continued to campaign until, in September 1691 at Limerick, peace of a sort descended on Ireland. William, however, was now determined to confront Louis XIV, who had been a sharp thorn in his side, not only in Ireland but on the mainland of Europe. To continue his struggle with France, William needed more troops and in 1693 he commissioned Colonel Henry Conyngham *'our well-beloved Cousin and Counsellor ... to raise one Regiment of Dragoons within our Kingdom of Ireland'*. And so was created Conyngham's Regiment of Dragoons, the last of the four regiments who were, precisely 300 years later, to metamorphose into The Queen's Royal Hussars (The Queen's Own and Royal Irish).

If the practice of changing the titles of regiments in the British order of battle to conform with the names of their commanders caused some confusion in the seventeenth and eighteen centuries, it is even more of a challenge for historians. For reasons of simplicity this account will usually ignore the frequent changes of name as colonels or commanding officers changed, so that Leveson's, Berkeley's, Cunningham's and Conyngham's Regiments of

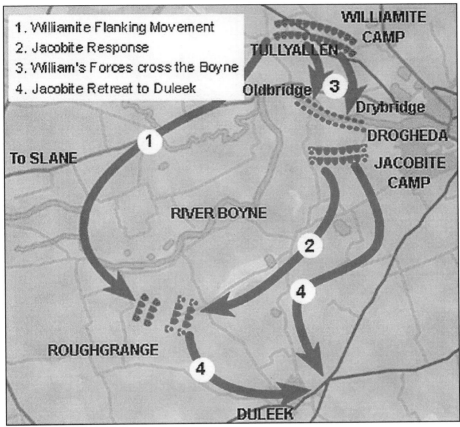

1. Williamite Flanking Movement
2. Jacobite Response
3. William's Forces cross the Boyne
4. Jacobite Retreat to Duleek

Battle of the Boyne, 1 July 1690.

Dragoons will be referred to mostly as just the 3rd, 4th, 7th and 8th Hussars respectively.* The first of these regiments into battle during the Nine Years War between France and a coalition of armies from various nations including the Netherlands and England was the 4th, who were engaged in 1692 in the disastrous (from William's point of view) action at Steinkirk, some 30 miles south-west of Brussels.

Severely mauled, the regiment under Lieutenant Colonel Hawley lost 160 men killed or wounded in a desperate attempt to rescue five hard-pressed infantry battalions, an action in which Hawley lost his life as did the

* All changes of names and designations are shown in Appendix A.

veteran General Mackay. The 3rd fared as badly: arriving in Flanders in 1694 they were engaged in July of the following year in garrisoning the city of Diksmuide where, much to their dismay, the Danish general commanding the force decided to surrender to the investing French. Colonel William Lloyd did his best to persuade the general to change his mind, but when his protestations went unheeded the whole regiment became prisoners of war. Released in late autumn, they spent the next two years skirmishing with the enemy until the war was concluded with the treaty of Ryswick and they returned home. The 4th, too, embarked for England, landing at Harwich in January 1698 before being deployed on garrison duties in Ireland.

The 7th had also been in Flanders, being quartered on arrival with the 3rd, the first meeting of two regiments who were destined, 264 years later, to become one. No detailed records exist of their actions during the Nine Years War, but in December 1697 the 7th landed in England and were immediately despatched to Berwick-upon-Tweed under Lord Jedburgh, a hard-riding cavalryman contemporaneously described as '*having abundance of fire, is brave in his person, loves his country and his bottle; a thorough libertine*' – a character template which could be applied accurately to many cavalry officers down the ages. Back, as it were, home in Scotland, the regiment spent the next dozen years in routine patrolling and internal security. Little is known either of the 8th during their first ten years, during which they remained in Ireland under Conyngham's command. Their second decade was, however, to prove momentous.

The death in 1700 of the childless Charles II of Spain and the attempt by Louis XIV to secure the succession for his grandson, Philip of Anjou, so uniting France and Spain under a powerful monarch with territories spread all over the known world, alarmed the other European powers. England, the Dutch Republic, Austria and their allies in the Holy Roman Empire formed an association which became known as the Grand Alliance and in May 1702 declared war on France – the so-called War of the Spanish Succession. The 8th, still under the command of the enduring Conyngham were deployed first to Lisbon, where their duties were little more than showing the flag. Five years later and now in Spain, the regiment was joined by half (three troops) of the 4th, now called Essex's Dragoons and the 3rd (The Queen's Own Dragoons); they had the great misfortune to find themselves under the command of the immensely incompetent Earl of Galway at the battle of Almanza where, as components of a 15,000-strong Allied army, they took on 25,000 French and Spanish troops with the inevitable result, Colonel

Conyngham losing his life. In 1710, however, at Almenara, the 8th over-threw a corps of Spanish cavalry and adorned themselves with the sword-belts worn by the enemy in addition to their own, thus earning themselves the nick-name 'The Crossbelts Dragoons', a soubriquet which lives on in the twenty-first century as the name of the regimental journal of The Queen's Royal Hussars. Meanwhile, in contrast to this feverish activity on the continent, the 7th soldiered on in Scotland on humdrum internal security duties, led by a new Colonel, the Hon William Ker, younger son of the Duke of Roxburghe, and did not reach the Iberian Peninsula until 1712, barely a year before the war ended with the peace of Utrecht.

As has always been the way, the cessation of hostilities in Europe was seized upon by politicians in England to justify a reduction in the Army. After their brief stay in Spain the 7th were sent to Ireland where, on arrival, Ker was ordered to hand over all their horses to *such person or persons as shall be appointed to receive them; your regiment to continue unmounted until further orders*. Those 'orders' followed almost immediately and, dismay-ingly, resulted in disbandment. A similar fate awaited the 8th as they arrived back in England after nine years of campaigning. Because of their seniority the 3rd and 4th were spared this ignominy, but the former had been so reduced by its campaigning that when it landed in England it could muster only 150 all told, so that its first priority was recruiting. The 4th, on the other hand, having been reunited as Evans's Dragoons, had sailed to Ireland to replace the disbanded units on internal security duties. Salvation came within a year to both the 7th and 8th, saved from permanent oblivion by their old enemy the Jacobites who, under the leadership of the Earl of Mar, raised the Stuart standard at Braemar and summoned the clans on behalf of the Old Pretender, marching to make his headquarters in Perth. Three of our regiments were sent to Scotland to join George I's army mustering at Stirling under the Duke of Argyll, while the resurrected 8th remained in England with the task of mopping up pockets of Jacobites wherever they broke cover – during which operation they arrested four would-be rebels in Oxford who were duly executed at Tyburn. In Scotland, battle was joined on 13 November on the bleak heathland of Sheriffmuir, some 3 miles north of Dunblane. The result was tactically inconclusive but it put an end to the rebellion as the clans melted back into the Highlands. By the time that the Old Pretender landed at Peterhead in January 1716 his cause had once again been lost, and he returned to France, never to return. The 7th had not fared well at Sheriffmuir: placed by Argyll on the left flank, they and the infantry met the most ferocious of the clansmen and were routed. Colonel Ker, as he desperately tried to rally his men, had three horses shot from under him before he was forced to order a full and disorganized retreat. The day on the left was partially saved by a counter-charge by the 3rd (now known as the King's Own Regiment of Dragoons), while the 4th, together with the Royal Scots Greys on the right flank, were able after initial setbacks to put the enemy to flight, their final charge taking them to the banks of the River Allan. All the regiments at Sheriffmuir with the word 'King's' in their title were awarded the White Horse of Hanover to be worn as a badge – a forerunner of the battle honour system and carried still by the Queen's Royal Hussars.

During the best part of the next three decades the four regiments led a largely peaceful existence (the 8th was again disbanded from 1716 to 1719), so boring at times that there was much scope for mischief. In 1724, Cornets Oliphant and Lewis of the 4th went further than youthful high-jinks by engaging in such a violent quarrel at the Mitre Tavern in Charing Cross that Oliphant ran Lewis through with his sword, killing him. Astonishingly, the killer was allowed to remain in the 4th for a further fifteen years before leaving to command a regiment of foot. The regiment's official duties now centred on smuggler-hunting as it moved about the country from station to station, ranging from Kent to Cumberland, until in 1738 they were sent to Scotland as little more than mounted policemen. The 3rd, having remained in Scotland for a while, were posted to southern England where, as an understrength garrison force it, too, did little other than track down smugglers. Chasing the importers of contraband ('*brandy for the parson and baccy for the clerk*') was not popular with the locals, as the 7th also found when they were similarly engaged, troop by scattered troop, in East Anglia. Constantly on the march in all weathers, rarely in one place for more than a month, they, in common with most of the Army were victims of the paranoid attitudes of both politicians and populace to large concentrations of troops such as would be found in permanent barracks or garrisons, a posture given a voice by Rudyard Kipling over a century later: '*It's Tommy this and Tommy that an' chuck him out, the brute.*' Not until the end of the century and the rise of the Napoleonic threat did this position change: '*But it's saviour of 'is country when the guns begin to shoot.*' The 8th spent the years of peace in Ireland, emerging only when, in 1745, the Jacobites made their final bid for power.

The War of the Austrian Succession fought from 1740 to 1748 has a claim to be the first of the world wars. In addition to the battles fought on the European mainland, related campaigns took place in India, North America, the Mediterranean, and on the North and Caribbean seas as well as the Indian Ocean. It all started with the death in 1739 of the Hapsburg Emperor Charles VI, who had, with the prior agreement of some European powers including England and Holland, specified that his daughter Maria Theresa was to succeed him. The ever troublesome French, together with their principal allies, Prussia, Spain and Bavaria, challenged her eligibility on the grounds that Salic Law precluded women from royal inheritance. The belligerent Frederick II of Prussia also had territorial ambitions and seized the Austrian province of Silesia, further alarming the British, who feared that his next target might well be Hanover. So once again Britain and France were at war, and in 1742 the 3rd (Bland's), 4th (Rich's) and 7th (Queen's Own) Dragoons sailed for Ostend as part of the British expeditionary force under the elderly veteran, John Dalrymple, Earl of Stair. Stair was an undoubtedly competent commander but was not universally popular among his men, being a stickler for discipline, demanding of his troops that all their uniforms, accoutrements and horses should be well cared for, not to mention spick and span to a degree which his soldiers recognized uneasily as 'bull'. But he was also a canny strategist and experienced tactician, and had matters been left to him outcomes could well have been different; but in the spring of 1743 King George II arrived in Flanders to take personal command. He ordered Stair to advance into Germany and by June he and his army, around 40,000 strong, were massed in the valley of the River Main near the village of Dettingen, some 20 miles east of Frankfurt. Order, counter-order and a consequent descent into disorder emanated from the King, who against the advice of Stair managed to mass his troops in a strip of boggy land bounded on one side by the river and the other by wooded hills, a trap set for him by the French commander, Marshal Noailles. George prepared to lead his army into battle, but his horse, sensibly taking the view that affairs should best be left to Stair, set off towards the rear at the gallop carrying the hapless King with him. George, not lacking courage, eventually returned to the front, dismounted, drew his sword and, to the cheers of his men, remarked that at least his legs would do as he asked them.

Skirmishing and some often comedic manoeuvring followed, until the French cavalry under an impatient commander, and against Noailles' orders, charged the British left flank, being eventually repulsed with heavy losses by British cavalry, notably the 3rd, who had been hastily switched from the

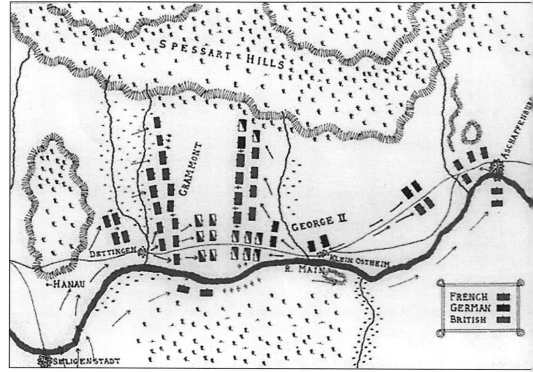

Battle of Dettingen, 27 June 1743.

right to make charge after charge until reinforced by others, including the 4th and 7th. The French broke and Stair saw that the rout could be completed by ordering the cavalry to continue the chase, only to be thwarted by the King – perhaps not unwisely, as losses had been heavy. The 3rd had suffered particularly badly during their three charges, losing three quarters of their number killed or wounded. But it was not in vain: the French infantry had failed to support their mounted colleagues, and the victory – if it can be called a victory – belonged, in spite of George's blunders, to the British. The affair at Dettingen threw up its share of heroes but none was as singular as Mary Ralphson, wife of a trooper of the 3rd. She had accompanied her husband to the battle and even into it, so that when one of her husband's comrades fell wounded by her side she equipped herself with his uniform and weapons, mounted his charger and joined the fray. Mary had a taste for action, accompanying her husband on other campaigns including Fontenoy in 1745, and the life obviously agreed with her as she lived to the age of 108. Two more regulation troopers, George Daraugh of the 4th and Thomas Brown of the 3rd, distinguished themselves by rescuing their respective regimental standards as they were carried from the field by the French. Both men were immediately decorated by the King, who was so elated that he honoured Brown by dubbing him a Knight Banneret (a decoration awarded by the Sovereign only on the field of battle) and rewarded Daraugh by handing him a purse of guineas as well as promotion to cornet. Brown, whose heroism when badly wounded was to be remembered by a silver statuette subscribed to by the officers some forty years later, was also given a pub in Yorkshire, where sadly, according to a regimental comrade-in-arms John Andrews, '*he did kill himself drinking*'. The 3rd, 4th and 7th were awarded the battle honour *Dettingen*, and all three regiments saw further action on the continent until, in 1748, another fragile peace was achieved.

The 3rd left Flanders in 1745 as part of an army being assembled by King George's son, the Duke of Cumberland, to deal with yet another Jacobite rising in Scotland, led this time by the Young Pretender, Prince Charles Edward Stuart, sometimes called Bonnie Prince Charlie, whose avowed aim was to win the throne for his father, whom he regarded as James III of England and Ireland and VIII of Scotland. Charles had calculated that the war in Europe so occupied the British that he would have a relatively easy time of it – at least in Scotland. And so it proved, but only for a while. The Pretender landed on the island of Eriskay in the Outer Hebrides on 2 August and within a month had reached the mainland and gathered a force of 1,600 men, which grew to around 2,500 by the time he entered Edinburgh in mid-September. Cumberland's hastily assembled troops had headed north and by 1 November had made camp at Lichfield to await developments. Charles' progress south was swift: Carlisle, Penrith, Kendal, Lancaster, Preston, Manchester and finally Derby put up little or no resistance, and the rebels paused only 24 miles from Lichfield. At this point the Young Pretender's advisers took fright: the promised French support, although safely ashore at Montrose, were in no position to join the advance, and furthermore, English Jacobites had not turned out to join the revolutionary cause in the way the highlanders had done. Despite these disappointments, Charles was all for pressing on but, eventually, persuaded otherwise, he reluctantly ordered a retreat and the 3rd were in the vanguard of Cumberland's forces as they set off in pursuit. At Clifton Moor near Penrith the loyalists were ambushed in darkness, forcing the 3rd to dismount, upon which they found their muskets to be no match for claymores. They suffered heavy casualties and although they continued to be part of the chase through Scotland it is not certain that the regiment was still with Cumberland at Culloden. Reports of its presence at the battle on 16 April 1746 are vague and remain unsubstantiated, but its loyalty to King George II was marked by His Majesty giving the officers the twin privileges of never drinking the loyal toast in their mess and remaining seated after dinner as the band played the national anthem.

Compared with the intensity of the campaigns to be fought by the four regiments over the next 200 years, the second half of the eighteenth century was a relatively peaceful affair. A number of administrative changes were wrought in uniform, equipment, regimental titles and, perhaps most important, living arrangements. In 1756 the 3rd, 4th and 7th all saw the addition of light troops to their establishment. These were the forerunners of the reconnaissance sub-units which were, in various forms, to remain a feature of cavalry regiments for the next two and a half centuries. Made up of three officers, two sergeants, three corporals and upwards of sixty private soldiers, and trained to fire from the saddle, they were mounted on light, fast ponies, whose speed was nevertheless constricted by the fact that each rider had to carry a carbine, bayonet, pistol and sword as his personal kit. Occasionally, as in 1758, the light troops were detached from their parent regiments and banded together for special operations as part of a much larger force of 13,000 commanded by the 3rd Duke of Marlborough. A raid on St Malo, Cherbourg and St Luniare was launched in June of that year with mixed results. Shipping, privateers, men-o'-war, munitions and merchant ships were destroyed at St Malo and Cherbourg, but St Luniare proved a raid too far, and it was only after losing some 800 men killed or wounded that a Dunkirk-style withdrawal was ordered. In 1760, during the Seven Years War, the 7th embarked to reinforce the Hanoverians and distinguished themselves against the French at Warburg under the Marquess of Granby (who minus his hat and wig went '*bald-headed at the enemy*'), but then spent two miserable years skirmishing up and down Germany, so badly supported by the supply chain that they ran out of boots, having to bind bundles of straw to their legs and suffering the indignity of being referred to as *Straw-boots*. It was with great relief that they returned home in 1762.

Home for most cavalry regiments meant being posted almost anywhere in England and Scotland, engaged in anti-smuggling duties, keeping the peace, and putting down the occasional local riot while being split up into troops far removed from each other while billeted on the local population; not a recipe designed to endear them to civilians. Home for the 8th was in Ireland where, as the 8th King's Royal Irish Dragoons, they had an uncomfortable four decades trying to keep the peace against a background of agrarian unrest fuelled by unpopular (and blatantly unjust) landlord-tenant laws aggravated by periods of famine. In 1780, the 3rd and the 4th were brought together in London to deal with the anti-Catholic riots sparked by the rabble-rousing head of the Protestant Association, Lord George Gordon, who wanted repeal of the Papist Act which was designed to further emancipate Roman Catholics. So violent were the mobs that Newgate Prison was destroyed, embassies were attacked and Catholic homes and churches set on fire. The Army shot and killed some 285 rioters and 450 were arrested, of whom up to 30 were later tried and executed.

Towards the end of the 1780s the government belatedly decided that it was no longer practical to expect its Army to live piecemeal off the country. A building programme was started which, when complete, saw some 200 barracks built in England, Wales, Scotland and Ireland, capable of housing and fettling up to 70,000 cavalry and twice that number of infantrymen. Troops were still scattered across the country as situations demanded, but as garrisons were completed at, for example, Colchester, Aldershot, York and Chichester, more permanent centres were established at which regiments could train as an entity in preparation for more serious business in continental Europe. One such opportunity occurred in the spring of 1794, when the British chose to limit the threat posed by the French revolutionaries by sending a force to Holland under the command of the Duke of York. His cavalry included four troops of the 7th under Major William Osborne, and at battles fought at Beaumont and Willems in Flanders the British horsemen, together with their allies from Austria, put to flight vastly superior numbers of enemy infantrymen (said to be 25,000 at Beaumont and even more at Willems), so earning the unstinted praise of their commander, the admiration of the British infantry and two battle honours.

For one regiment, however, far more exotic adventures beckoned: in the autumn of 1796 the 8th embarked from Dublin for the Cape of Good Hope, where for the next five years they kept order among the Boer settlers, some of whom were sympathetic to French aspirations in Europe. Despatched on a secret mission to Egypt in 1801, the regiment briefly engaged with the French before the fall of Alexandria put an end to that nation's expansionist activities in the region. In June 1802, the now peripatetic 8th embarked from Suez for Madras, where it joined the East India Company's Bengal Army which had launched a war against the Marathas, the great military confederation of Hindus who were supported by the French. At *Leswarree* the 8th received its first battle honour and for twenty years they were involved in a number of actions, including the suppression of Sikh uprisings and the putting down of the sepoy mutineers at Vellore who had massacred all the Europeans in the vicinity. In 1814 they met for the first time the Gurkhas of Nepal who had taken to raiding Indian territory. The 8th had never encountered such a skilled enemy, nor one so brave, and the campaign led to such mutual respect that, at its conclusion, Gurkhas were recruited into the Bengal Army, thus beginning a tradition of loyal service to the British crown unbroken for over 200 years. In 1823 the regiment, having been awarded a further battle honour, *Hindoostan*, and re-designated The 8th King's Royal Irish Hussars, returned to the United Kingdom.

While the 8th struggled, not only with the enemy but also with the oppressive heat and ever-present diseases affecting both men and horses in India, the other three regiments found themselves suffering similarly in the Iberian Peninsula. First to embark were the 7th, who landed at Corunna on the north-west tip of Spain as part of a cavalry brigade sent to reinforce Sir John Moore's army in its attempt to stem a French invasion. The regiment was placed on a war footing of eight troops and 749 all-ranks, but from the start there was confusion and chaos. On 8 November 1808 they arrived at Corunna harbour to find no arrangements for their reception. Horses were lowered into the water to swim a quarter of a mile to shore and then were forced to stand shivering in the streets for four hours until barns were eventually found as shelter for them. Fodder was both scarce and poor in quality – many horses wouldn't touch it. The men, too, were shamefully neglected by the commissariat, Captain Edward Hodge recording that '*the meat was stinking & the wine so infamous that the men would not take it*'. On their 150-mile march to join Moore's army the 7th almost disintegrated: their horses' feet, softened by weeks on board ship, could not cope with the stony roads, and the incessant rains made conditions nigh-on unbearable. By December Moore's plans had crumbled: Madrid was lost and the Spanish army had fallen apart; the French, unhindered and 200,000-strong, were free to take on Moore's 38,000 interlopers. Sir John ordered a general retreat and in Hodge's words: '*An army is sent to the assistance of Spain, advanced 150 miles . . . and then before a man is within 10 miles of the enemy, not only retreats but evacuates the country they came to protect.*' By 11 January 1809 the 7th, now mustering only around 150, staggered into Corunna to find the majority of their troopships had been sent to Vigo, so that there was enough room for only a few of their remaining horses. The rest had to be shot, and only a tenth of the 700 animals which had left Portsmouth returned to

England. One further disaster was in store: within sight of Cornwall, one of the ships was wrecked on rocks, sixty men were drowned and all the regimental silver was lost. Home at last in a new cavalry barracks in Weymouth, the regiment rested, recruited up to strength and was then sent to Ireland for three years.

The reputation·of the British Army in the Peninsula was in tatters, and it was down to General Arthur Wellesley to restore it with victories at, among other battles, Talavera, Albuera, Salamanca, Vittoria and Toulouse. With this general who apparently could do no wrong marched the 3rd or King's Own Dragoons and the 4th Queen's Own Dragoons. First to arrive in Portugal were the 4th, who sailed up the Tagus and disembarked at Lisbon in April 1809. Within three months they were in action in a supporting role at Talavera, where 40,000 French clashed with half that number of British, supported by inadequately trained Spanish forces. Wellesley won the day tactically and was created Viscount Wellington, despite the fact that strategically the French had probably retained an advantage. At Albuera in May 1811 the regiment played a more prominent part in what turned out to be something of a pyrrhic victory, the British losing more than half of those engaged. Wellington now resumed his march north and east through Cuidad Rodrigo and Badajoz and on to the great battle at Salamanca on 22 July 1812, when the cavalry was to win more glory and fame than had hitherto been the case in the Peninsula.

Playing a full part were the 4th and, having been in Portugal and then Spain since April 1811, so were the 3rd, both regiments being in General John Le Marchant's brigade which successfully charged the French left for which they were awarded the *Salamanca* battle honour. For the 4th there was a very special postscript to the battle: the regiment captured some of Joseph Bonaparte's (Napoleon's elder brother) silver from his fleeing baggage train. Much was subsequently melted down and fashioned into cutlery still used by officers of the Queen's Royal Hussars, while on the dining-room table can often be seen a silver donkey with panniers which formed part of the loot. The brigade of which both regiments were a part advanced by way of encounters at Vittoria in the Basque heartland, and then into France itself where, after Napoleon Bonaparte had abdicated, the British fought one of their bloodiest battles, eventually triumphing at Toulouse. The war with France was now over – at least for a spell. When it was resumed the following year, following Napoleon's escape from exile on Elba, only the 7th of our four regiments was to be engaged.

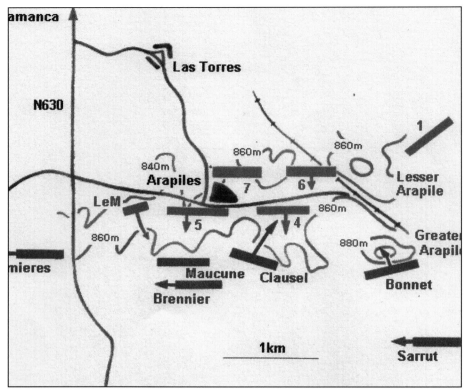

Battle of Salamanca, 22 July 1812.

The regiment which, since 1807, had rejoiced in the unwieldy title of the 7th (or Queen's Own) Regiment of Light Dragoons (Hussars) returned to England in the spring of 1813, and after a spell of ceremonial duties embarked for Bilbao in September to join the Hussar Brigade. In October, having crossed the Pyrenees, they went into winter quarters near Bayonne and in February of the following year were engaged in the Battle of Orthes, at which they carried out the only effective cavalry charge, taking 200 prisoners, gaining a battle honour and being singled out for praise by Wellington. Returning to England after the break in hostilities which followed Toulouse, the regiment found itself again furnishing unpopular revenue patrols, punctuated by a brief period of more active service taking on the Corn Law rioters in London. Napoleon's re-emergence from captivity brought about a great deal of hasty British mobilization, during which the

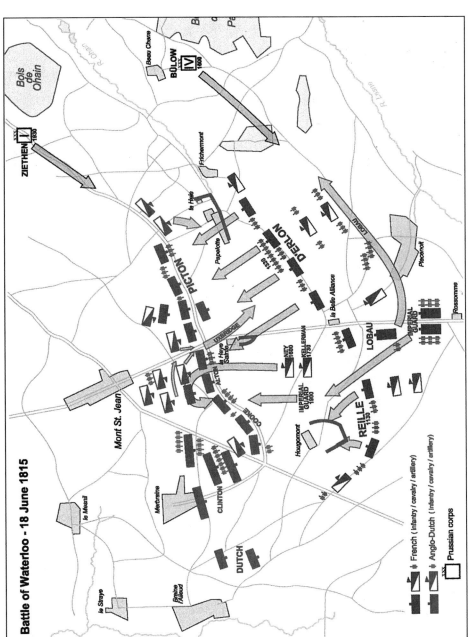

Battle of Waterloo, 18 June 1815.

7th embarked from Dover for Ostend, landing on 20 March 1815. Brigaded with the 10th and 18th Hussars, and concentrated with the rest of the Allied armies in Belgium, they were subject to an irritating regime of reviews, inspections and field days right up to the eve of Waterloo. At four o'clock in the morning of 16 June, the regimental trumpeters sounded reveille and the 7th were reassigned to Grant's Brigade, joining the 13th Light Dragoons and the 15th Hussars. Riding at ease through a wonderfully sunny day, they eventually arrived at Quatre-Bras and camped among the debris and corpses of the battle of which they had no knowledge – but the sight of which greatly sobered both officers and men. Torrential rain followed and the ground turned into a quagmire.

During the twenty-four hours of 18 June, known ever since as the Battle of Waterloo, the 7th had little to do until about 3.00pm when they were called upon to charge repeatedly the enemy's advancing cavalry until finally joining in the general advance and pursuit. The regiment, while being awarded the *Waterloo* battle honour, lost two officers killed and eleven wounded, while sixty-two soldiers died and over a hundred were wounded. As usual, equine casualties were even greater: eighty-four were killed and 116 had wounds from which some would not recover.

CHAPTER TWO

COLONIAL CAMPAIGNS AND THE GREAT WAR

There is many a boy here today who looks upon war as all glory,
but boys it is all hell. (William Sherman)

The end of the Napoleonic threat to the United Kingdom marked the beginning of a period of nearly a hundred years during which the Army was not once called upon to cross the English Channel under arms. Garrison and peace-keeping duties at home provided our regiments with little excitement other than the occasional riot in England and the more frequent disturbances in Ireland. During these years of relative peace, the Army suffered again from the general neglect of parliament and hostility from those of the general public whose grievances (often both real and justified) were suppressed by military action. This was particularly the case in Ireland, where both the 3rd and the 8th were engaged in sometimes violent action against insurgents such as the Whiteboys of Munster and the Ribbonmen of Connaught, with occasional light relief in the form of ceremonial duties when, for example in 1821, the 3rd escorted the corpulent King George IV, the first peaceful visit of a reigning monarch to Dublin for over four centuries, and in 1849 when the 8th escorted Queen Victoria and Prince Albert on their first visit to Ireland – an occasion during which the Queen expressed the view that lance corporals (wearing one stripe) were not of sufficient seniority to command any section charged with guarding her person. The regiment met this royal command by adorning all their lance corporals with two stripes – a military curiosity which has stood the test of time.

The British government, assured that there was no threat of invasion, now turned its attention to far off lands, and its expansionist ambitions were never more evident than in India. Following the earlier tour of the 8th, the 4th sailed to the sub-continent in 1821, followed by the 3rd in 1837. The 7th, however, were a year later despatched in the opposite direction to deal with a little local difficulty occasioned by a French republican rebellion in Canada, and the regiment remained in and around Montreal for four years. But it was India that became the prime diplomatic and military focus as the 4th disembarked in Bombay in May 1822. There they were to spend the next twenty years, based successively in Kaira and Kirkee but taking part in only one major campaign, Afghanistan in 1838–39, when two squadrons were ordered to join the so-called Bombay Column and set out from Karachi (now in Pakistan) to march to Kabul to dethrone the warlord Dost Mohammed. At Ghuznee, some 100 miles south of the Afghan capital, the Column encountered stiff resistance, but in a largely infantry and artillery battle, the 4th were virtual spectators. Kabul was then taken without a fight, after which the regiment was ordered back into India, thus avoiding the catastrophic retreat from Kabul three years later. Complete with two new battle honours, *Ghuznee* and *Affghanistan 1839* (spelt then with double f), the regiment sailed home in late 1841.

The 3rd had landed at Calcutta, marched to Cawnpore in January 1838 and were to experience a hugely more difficult time: of the 420 non-commissioned officers and men who had arrived at their new station only forty-seven were to return to England sixteen years later. The first few years were, apart from the pestilential diseases which afflicted both men and their horses, trouble-free, but then in early 1842 rumours of an appalling disaster in Afghanistan began to reach the regiment. An Anglo-Indian army of some 4,500 fighting men and three times that number of camp followers, including women and children, leaving Kabul for Jalalabad under promise of safe-conduct, had been massacred in ambush or left to die in the deep snow. Only one man, a Scottish surgeon, William Brydon, had survived to stumble into Jalalabad badly wounded. It was now necessary to relieve Jalalabad, and the 3rd were part of the force commanded by General George Pollock sent, by way of Peshawar and the Khyber Pass, into Afghanistan. Once there they garrisoned the city until, after months of tedium and choking dust storms, it was decided that Afghanistan should be evacuated in its entirety – a decision that over the years was to be repeated more than once by those who sought to impose their political and military will on this ungovernable country. The march back to India via Kabul, where they were joined by a force from Kandahar, was not without incident, for the 3rd were in the thick of the fighting as Akbar Khan – son of Dost Mohammed – made his last stand, the regimental records remarking that the 3rd were *'actively engaged in cutting up and dispersing several parties of the enemy . . . who left behind a thousand killed, all their guns and three standards'*. For this action the regiment was awarded the battle honour *Cabool 1842*.

Within three years the 3rd were in action again, this time against the Sikh army of the Punjab, separated at that time from India by a frontier on the Sutlej river. Driven by the prospect of plunder from the coffers of the East India Company, 60,000 Sikhs crossed the river in December 1845, taking the British by surprise. The 3rd from their barracks at Ambala, some 100 miles away, were turned out in a hurry to meet the threat and joined the army assembled by General Sir Hugh Gough. Within two months it was all over. Aided not a little by the equivocation of the Sikh commanders, Tej Singh and Lal Singh, who were secretly supplying the British army with useful intelligence, four battles were fought, of which the 3rd were involved in three, the first of which was at Moodkee, where the enemy began to call them the *'Moodkee Wallahs'* – a nickname which was to stick. Later, at Ferozeshah, the regiment distinguished itself to such an extent that Sir John Fortescue in his *History of the British Army* wrote:

> *The heroes of the action were beyond doubt the 3rd Light Dragoons. It is rare for cavalry to charge entrenched artillery and only troopers of rare devotion and discipline would have faced such a trial. The Third lost nearly one hundred men and one hundred and twenty horses on the 18th of December and one hundred and fifty-two more men and sixty horses on the 21st. Yet they charged without hesitation and defeated superior numbers of Sikh cavalry. Few regiments of horse in the world can show a finer record of hardihood and endurance.*

Following the final battle, Sobraon – 'the Waterloo of India' – a formal peace treaty was concluded at Lahore, but three years later the Sikhs were at it again, this time supported by the ever troublesome Dost Mohammed. The rival armies met at Chillianwallah, deep within the Punjab. Gough's army hardly distinguished itself, for despite the commander-in-chief's claim that the *'enemy was signally overthrown'*, the general consensus both in India and in London was that this was an inglorious defeat, exemplified by the whole-sale desertion of one Indian mounted regiment and the precipitous with-drawal of the bulk of two British cavalry regiments, all in the same brigade. In contrast, the 3rd's behaviour was exemplary, Captain Walter Unett's squadron particularly distinguishing itself in a charge which penetrated half a mile through a dense mass of Sikh infantry. The price, though, was high: the squadron lost nearly half its number. A month later, the final battle of what became known as the Second Sikh War was fought at Goojorat, and this marked the end of Sikh aggression: their army was destroyed, the Punjab was annexed and Dost Mohammed and his Afghans were sent scuttling home through the Khyber Pass. The 3rd remained in India for another four years, basking in the well-deserved plaudits of the government and the Army (but dying of disease in horrific numbers) before, in February 1853, they set sail for home accompanied by a galaxy of battle honours to add to that awarded at Kabul: *Moodkee, Ferozeshah, Sobraon, Chillianwallah, Goojorat* and, finally, *Punjab*.

Few military campaigns in British history can have begun with such unbelievable ineptitude as that against Russia in the Crimea. The underlying reasons for this war were in themselves bizarre, pitting ourselves and our old enemy France, two Christian nations, in alliance with the Muslim Ottoman Empire, against Christian Russia. Alarmed at the possibility of a Russian threat to the Mediterranean and their route to India, Britain and France moved fleets to the Dardanelles and, following the defeat of the Turkish navy by Russia, declared war on the Tsar in March 1854. The allies were woefully unprepared: the neglect of the Army at home in Britain ensured that the 50,000 men who set sail for the Crimea lacked tents, suitable clothing, medical supplies and appropriate commissariat, while the French had no cavalry because of a shortage of horses. As part of this expeditionary force both the 4th Light Dragoons and the 8th Hussars had landed in May at Varna, the major Bulgarian port on the Black Sea. There cholera struck, so that by the time they reached Kalamita Bay in the Crimea around a third of both regiments were either ineffective or dead. The allies' objective was Sevastopol, home of the Russian Black Sea fleet, the base from which the Tsar's navy could threaten free passage of the eastern Mediterranean. But before this prime target could be taken, several battles were fought, the first beside the River Alma, where both the 4th and the 8th were largely spectators. Heavy losses were inflicted on the Russians but still Sevastopol was out of reach and, worse, the Russians in the garrison in attacking the investing Turkish troops had captured some of their English gun batteries. It was this that was to lead to the calamitous charge of the Light Cavalry Brigade at Balaklava on 25 October 1854.

The circumstances surrounding the Charge have been written about more than any other episode in British military history – with the possible exception of Waterloo – and will not be rehearsed here. The misunderstandings, brought about by the incompetence at three levels of command

The Charge of the Light Brigade, Balaklava, 25 October 1854.

represented by the Commander-in-Chief, Lord Raglan, and the brothers-in-law Lieutenant General Lord Lucan and Brigadier General Lord Cardigan, are well known. Lucan's command was the Cavalry Division comprising both the Heavy and the Light Brigades, while Cardigan had been given command of the latter, consisting of five regiments.

As they drew up before the Charge, the 13th Light Dragoons, 17th Lancers and 11th Hussars made up the first line, with the 11th slightly in rear of the other two, while the 4th and the 8th – in which Cardigan had been a cornet – made up the second line under the command respectively of Colonels Lord George Paget and Frederick Shewell. These two redoubtable soldiers were cast in different moulds: Shewell was a martinet who reprimanded his men as they formed up still smoking their pipes as *'disgracing the regiment in the presence of the enemy'*, while the more eccentric Paget, whose regiment had become known as *Paget's Irregular Horse*, lit a cigar and continued to smoke it throughout the charge. All five regiments were at a strength far removed from the muster when they began the campaign. Disease and the lack of medical care had taken their toll; the 4th began the charge with 127 all ranks (one troop was detached) while the 8th were scarcely better off. When Cardigan famously and audibly muttered, *'Here goes the last of the Brudenells'* followed by the order *'The Brigade will advance. Walk March, Trot'*, 673 men started down the valley towards the Russian guns a mile and a half away. When they returned, a total of only 195 answered the regimental roll-calls. The 4th had lost four

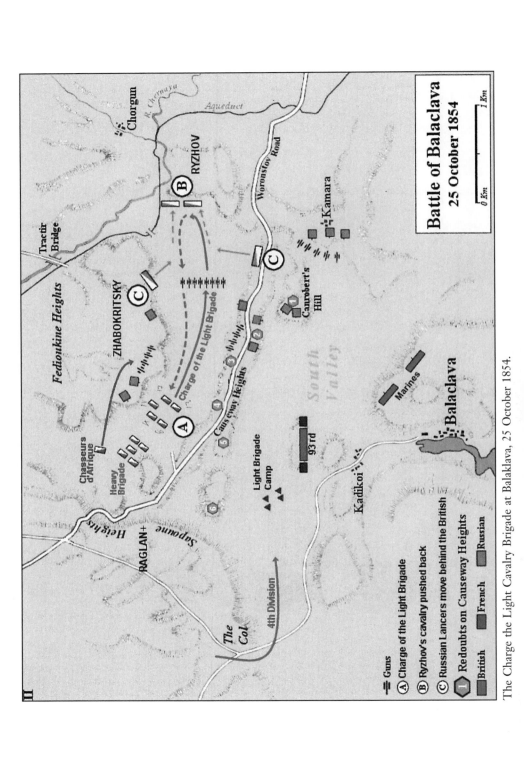

The Charge the Light Cavalry Brigade at Balaklava, 25 October 1854.

officers and fifty-five men and the 8th, four and fifty-three. Private Samuel Parkes of the 4th, in rescuing his trumpet major from being hacked to pieces during the return, was, after a year in Russian captivity, to be awarded the Victoria Cross. Captain Robert Portal, also of the 4th, in a letter to his mother a month later, summed up the general feeling when he wrote:

> *As to Lord Cardigan, he has as much brain as my boot, and is only equalled in want of intellect by his relation Lord 'Look-On'. Two bigger fools could not be picked out of the British Army to take command.*

'Look-On' comes in for further scathing comment, notably from Fanny Duberley, wife of the Paymaster of the 8th, who accompanied her husband

Officers of the 4th Light Dragoons, Crimea, 1854.

throughout the Crimean campaign. In her *Journal Kept during the Russian War* she wrote of Lord Lucan:

> *A most officious man in his late forties brimming over with that spurious brand of military energy which drives subordinates almost mad. His one virtue in the reckoning of those whom he commanded was that, carried away in the torrent of orders and instructions he daily poured out in happy gusts, he usually forgot in the days following to ensure that his directions had been obeyed, being so busily employed in inventing new ones.*

Two more battles were to be fought until, after a siege of 349 days, Sevastopol fell in September 1855, bringing an end to Russian expansionist policies in the Near East. Every man who had served in the 4th and 8th in the Crimea received a medal with four clasps reflecting the battle honours awarded to both regiments: *Alma*, *Balaklava*, *Inkerman* and *Sevastopol*. A number of Distinguished Conduct medals (DCM) were awarded to soldiers of both regiments and, most unusually, Lance Corporal Gillam of the 4th was made a Chevalier of the Legion of Honour in circumstances never recorded. In May 1856 they embarked for home, to be welcomed at Portsmouth by the Queen, Prince Albert and the Princess Royal. Also disembarking was 'Jemmy', a rough-haired terrier who ran with the 8th as they charged at Balaklava and although wounded in the neck survived. The regiment made him a collar on which were attached the four clasps of the medals worn by his human comrades after the Crimean campaign. He later travelled with the regiment to India, where he was awarded a fifth.

The second half of the nineteenth century was to prove a relatively quiet time for both the 3rd and the 4th, the former having provided a draft of 253 men and 300 horses for the 4th in Varna to help make good the losses caused by cholera and the intense heat. During the rest of Victoria's long reign the 3rd spent a total of fourteen years peacefully in India (now, post-Mutiny, a British possession) and about the same in Ireland, until they were deployed to South Africa at the tail end of the Second Boer War. For the 4th, too, there was little fighting to do, but two events were of some significance. In 1861 Light Dragoon regiments disappeared from the army and the 4th became the 4th (Queen's Own) Hussars. More important in historical terms was the appearance in 1895 of the most distinguished man ever to serve in the regiment, Second Lieutenant Winston Leonard Spencer Churchill.

The young 4th Hussar subaltern – Winston Churchill, 1895.

At Sandhurst the young cadet applied himself in a way he had singularly failed to do at Harrow and passed out a creditable eighth of an intake of 150. When he was commissioned, the regiment was at Aldershot under the formidable Lieutenant Colonel John Palmer Brabazon – known (but not to his face) as Bwab because of an inability, real or affected, to pronounce his r's. The lack of opportunity for active service in the last decades of the nineteenth century frustrated the young 4th Hussar officers: scarcely a captain and hardly ever a subaltern sported any campaign medals. Churchill, impatient to get stuck in, had discovered that in Cuba there appeared to be a promising war between the Spanish colonialists and Cuban rebels. Through a connection of his father's and with Bwab's blessing he and Lieutenant Reginald Barnes found their way to the island where, as guests of the Spanish government, they found a taste of the action they craved, marching with General Suarez Valdez's flying column – and forming the strong impression that the Spanish could never win this war – before returning to England, where at Hounslow the 4th Hussars were preparing to sail for India, described by Bwab in his farewell speech as '*that famous appendage of the Bwitish Cwown*'.

In Bangalore, a station set at 3,000 feet above sea level, the climate was excellent and Churchill made the most of the abundant amount of time available to a young cavalry officer, educating himself with, among other books not regarded by his fellow officers as light reading, Gibbon's *Decline and Fall* and the four volumes of Macaulay's *History of England*. He also passed out top of a musketry course (much to the surprise of Sergeant Hallaway, his Troop Sergeant) and was a constant contributor to the officers' mess betting book and even more frequently to the complaints book – usually about the standard of the food. But again he found the lack of action irksome. On leave in England he read that a force of three brigades was to be formed to deal with a revolt of Pathan tribesmen on India's North-West Frontier. It was to be commanded by Brigadier General Sir Bindon Blood (a descendant of the self-styled Colonel Blood, an Anglo-Irish desperado who in 1671 had attempted to steal the crown jewels from the Tower of London), with whom he had a slight acquaintance. Hastening back to India, Churchill persuaded his commanding officer – now Lieutenant Colonel William Ramsay – that he should be seconded to Blood's brigade, which had become known as the Malakand Field Force. Churchill's time on the frontier provided him with as much action as he could have wished for, fighting hand-to-hand with the rebels in the Mamund valley and dragging the wounded to safety under heavy fire. But still he was not done. A new campaign had opened in the Sudan, where Major General Sir Herbert Kitchener commanded a British and Egyptian force of 20,000 men about to advance to Khartoum against a vastly numerically superior force of *ansars* (servants of Allah) led by the Khalifa Abdullahi. Again Churchill persuaded his commanding officer that he should take leave from the regiment and head for the Sudan, but this time he came up against formidable opposition in the shape of Kitchener himself. The general had heard about Churchill's exploits in Cuba and the North-West Frontier – largely from newspaper despatches filed by the young officer and from reading *The Malakand Field Force*, a book he had written – and Kitchener strongly disliked such unorthodoxy, considering Churchill to be a medal-hunting, publicity-seeking nuisance that he could well do without. He told Colonel Ramsay that he had no vacancies. But the Prime Minister, Lord Salisbury, had also read the book, and when young Winston was in London, asked to see him, warmly applauding the young officer's adventures. Churchill persuaded Salisbury to send a telegram to Kitchener asking that he should be seconded to the 21st Lancers, a regiment already in the Sudan. Kitchener acquiesced with not a little ill-grace, and thus it was that on 2 September 1898 the 4th Hussar subaltern charged with the Lancers at Omdurman, the decisive and bloodiest battle of the campaign, and at the same time sent reports on proceedings to the *Morning Post* at £15 a column – a sum equating to £1,700 in 2018.

In his accounts of his early life Churchill makes light of his active service experiences, writing on his return to India, '*We have now to turn to other and more serious affairs*', by which he meant the 1899 All-India Polo Tournament taking place in Meerut and never won by a regiment stationed in the south of the country. He played in the first two rounds with a dislocated shoulder which much limited his contribution, but the team felt that even if he could not hit the ball hard, his knowledge of the game and of their teamwork would give them a better chance of success than playing a reserve. In the eight-chukka final they were up against the formidable 4th Dragoon Guards, and despite his injury Churchill, playing at No. 1 with his right arm strapped closely to his side but well mounted, managed to mark the opposing back (who later became an English international) almost out of the game. He also managed to tap in three goals, thanks to the superbly accurate hitting of his team-mates, Albert Savory, Reginald Hoare and Reggie Barnes, so that the regiment won by four goals to three, a fitting climax to his service.

4th Queen's Own Hussars Polo Team India, 1899. (L to R) Albert Savory, Reggie Barnes, Winston Churchill and Reginald Hoare.

Although he had stayed with the 4th for only four years – three of them at Bangalore – he never broke the connection, becoming Honorary Colonel in 1941 and remaining so until his death in 1965. After his departure for the life of, first, a journalist and then a politician, the regiment moved to Secunderabad and thence to Meerut. In 1905 they shipped to South Africa, taking over from the 7th Hussars at Potchefstroom, some 60 miles south-west of Johannesburg. While there the commanding officer, the now Lieutenant Colonel Hoare, learnt that his petition to King Edward VII that the regiment should officially be allowed to adopt as its motto *Mente et Manu* (literally *By Mind and Hand*) had been successful. The motto had in fact been in use since at least 1748 and probably earlier, but had never been authorized, despite previous applications to Lancaster Herald, the Inspector of Regimental Colours. In 1909 the regiment returned to England to be stationed at Colchester until moving to the Curragh in Ireland two years later.

In bleak contrast to the largely agreeable experiences of the 3rd and 4th, the second half of the nineteenth century opened for the 7th and 8th with the horrors of the 1857 Indian Mutiny. On 10 May the cantonment and city of Meerut erupted in an orgy of rape, slaughter and looting as the sepoys

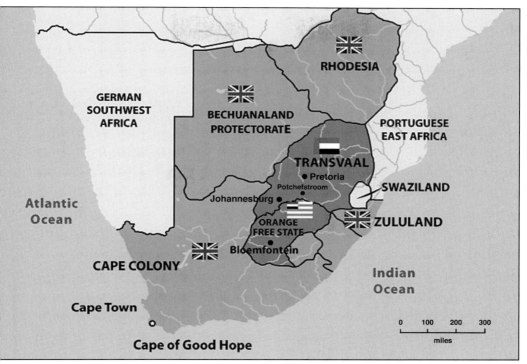

Southern Africa during the period of the Matabele and Boer Wars (1893–1902).

he volunteered to be attached to the 21st Lancers as they advanced towards Omdurman in the Sudan, where he joined Lieutenant Winston Churchill, also an attached troop leader but busy too as a war correspondent. The 7th, through no fault of its own, was also late for the Second Boer War, arriving in early 1902 to be engaged only in final mopping-up operations until peace terms were signed in June. The regiment remained in South Africa for three further years before handing over to the 4th Hussars and returning to join the 1st Cavalry Brigade in Aldershot. In 1911 the regiment sailed again for India, not imagining for one moment that it would be languishing in Bangalore when, within three years, the greatest war the world had ever seen was about to engulf Europe and beyond. The 3rd also arrived in Cape Town in time only for the final stages of the second Boer rebellion, but saw plenty of action centred round the conjoining frontiers of Natal and the erstwhile Boer republics of Transvaal and the Orange Free State, where they were in company for some of the action with the 8th Hussars who had arrived in March 1900. The 8th, who had sailed from England with 600 men and 500 horses, had been engaged constantly in mobile operations, leading to the taking of Bloemfontein and the subsequent advance to Johannesburg and Pretoria. By May they had crossed the Vaal River – the first regiment to do so. In February 1901, however, this progress had come to a virtual halt because the appallingly incessant rains had rendered bridgeless rivers impassable. Rations for both men and horses were reduced to a quarter, and General Sir John French, the Divisional Commander, was moved to apologise for the dreadful conditions his troops found themselves in. When the regiment was able to resume the advance, its role changed from that of operating as a complete regiment to being divided into detachments deploying temporarily with different all-arms columns or carrying out an independent role. Attacks by Boer formations, sometimes as large as 400-strong, were frequent until in May 1902 the Peace of Vereeniging was signed and an uneasy truce prevailed. In this arduous campaign the 8th had lost three officers, seven non-commissioned officers and forty-four men, coming away in October 1903 with the battle honour *South Africa*. In March 1905 a memorial to the fallen was dedicated in St Patrick's Cathedral in Dublin.

The 3rd left South Africa almost immediately after the peace, returning to India to be stationed peacefully at Sialkot where, according to letters home written by young Lance Corporal Seed, they led a '*sort of gentleman's life*', the even tenor of their ways being disturbed only by two ceremonial visits to Rawalpindi, the second of which was in order to take part in one of the greatest military displays ever seen in India as the Prince and Princess of Wales arrived at the camp of the Commander-in-Chief, Lord Kitchener. In 1907 the regiment returned to South Africa for garrison duties in Pretoria, being stationed at Roberts Heights, before returning to England in time for Christmas in 1911. The 4th Hussars completely missed the Boer War, soldiering on in India until arriving in South Africa in 1905 where they remained for four years, taking over from the 7th Hussars at Potchefstroom. In October 1911 the regiment moved to Ireland and was stationed in barracks on the Curragh in County Kildare as part of the 3rd Cavalry Brigade commanded by Brigadier General Hubert Gough. There, in 1914, they found themselves involved in one of the most extraordinary and distasteful episodes ever to afflict the peacetime Army.

The so-called 'Curragh Incident' was sparked by a decision of the United Kingdom Liberal government that, as a step towards full Home Rule for Ireland, the largely Protestant province of Ulster would, after five years, be able to vote itself out of control of the Dublin parliament. This measure was not acceptable either to Ulster or to the Conservative opposition in London. Under the unofficial leadership of Sir Edward Carson, a firebrand Protestant lawyer, an Ulster 'army' was formed and supplied with substantial quantities of smuggled weapons – mainly from Germany. Rumours of civil war abounded, and in particular it was forecast that the Army would be sent to disarm Carson's irregulars. On a Friday afternoon in March 1914 Gough was summoned by the General Officer Commanding in Ireland, General Sir Arthur Paget, who ordered him to establish whether the officers of his brigade would obey orders if deployed to Ulster to deal with the armed threat. Paget then added that any officer who would not give this undertaking would have to resign immediately or be dismissed. Officers who lived in Ulster were excluded from this draconian measure; they would be allowed to slip away quietly and be re-instated later. In vain did Gough protest; eventually he put the matter to his brigade which, as well as the 4th Hussars, comprised the 5th Lancers and the 16th Lancers, saying as he did so that he himself would resign. The officers went to their own messes to consider. They were shocked and bewildered; they were being asked either to give up their careers and prospects as professional soldiers or to fight men whose religious beliefs and loyalties they largely shared. The 4th made its collective decision: out of the nineteen officers at regimental duty, seventeen decided to accept dismissal, the other two had homes in Ulster. Seventeen out of twenty officers in the 5th Lancers made the same decision, as did all twenty in the 16th. Colonel Ian Hogg, the 4th's commanding officer, wrote to Paget and to Winston Churchill, at that time First Lord of the Admiralty. General Paget talked to the officers and threatened to court-martial those who refused the conditions imposed upon them. Gough and the three cavalry commanding officers travelled to London to meet Sir John French, the Chief of the Imperial General Staff – the head of the Army. Word got out and there was an outcry in the newspapers and in both houses of parliament; eventually, the Army Council agreed that a mistake had been made: the government did not, after all, intend to use the Army to coerce Ulster. Interested spectators of these unedifying events were the German Kaiser and his government, who concluded that as Britain's Army was on the brink of mutiny, its government would be too busy to concern itself in what was happening on the continent of Europe. They were wrong.

The 3rd Cavalry Brigade sailed for France on 18 August 1914 – three weeks after the outbreak of what was to become known as The Great War – and was also in action when the Armistice was declared on 11 November 1918. In the intervening years the 4th lost 500 men killed (including, within days, Colonel Hogg during the retreat from Mons) or wounded, won almost 100 awards for gallantry and had been awarded 22 battle honours.

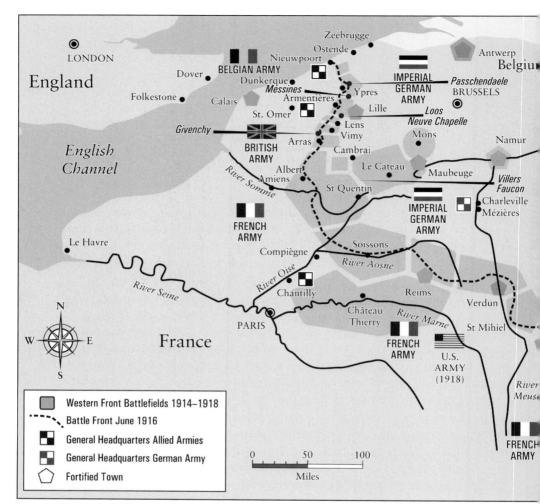

The Battlefields of the Western Front, 1914–1918.

The regiment fought most of the war from trenches, moving from deployment to deployment on their horses and accompanied by wagons carrying the heavy equipment, notably their machine guns. They fought at Ypres and in September 1915 at Loos, after which the regiments of the brigade were ordered to furnish a dismounted infantry battalion whereby each provided eight officers and 300 men and, in turn, the commanding officer and battalion headquarters. The winter of 1916/17 was particularly severe and the horses suffered terribly, but by the spring the regiment was once again fighting fit. Deployed on a hill overlooking Vimy Ridge, they saw, for the first time, tanks in action and were suitably both astonished and impressed. Captain H.S.L. Scott was, however, less than happy when, while leading his squadron in the resumed advance the next day, he came upon one of these

The 4th Hussars move up, France, 1918.

mechanical monsters out of which an officer climbed and shot at him with a pistol. Luckily, the tank officer was as bad a shot as he was at own-troops recognition and quickly apologised. After a blessedly peaceful summer in excellent billets near Amiens, the 4th marched north-east, ending up near Cambrai, where on 18 November they received a warning order for an offensive to begin the next day.

Cambrai was planned to give the new Tank Corps its first major opportunity: 400 tanks were to advance upon the Hindenburg Line in three waves, followed by six divisions of infantry. The Cavalry Corps was to exploit the hoped-for resulting gap. At the beginning all went well – even brilliantly – but the advance could not be sustained and the waiting cavalry were hardly deployed, the 4th fighting only one brisk action before once again becoming dismounted and settling down to trench warfare. The following spring saw the final German offensive between Arras and St Quentin. Here the 4th fought their most costly battle of the war: between 23 and 31 March the regiment lost 129 all-ranks of which 33 were killed. In the autumn, as the final Allied advance got under way, the regiment was broken up, the three squadrons being deployed with three different infantry divisions. Regimental Headquarters were with A Squadron and at 11 o'clock on 11 November they found themselves at Villerot, only 10 miles away from their first action in August 1914.

The 3rd Hussars arrived for the war on precisely the same date as the 4th, but as part of the 4th Cavalry Brigade, in which they were joined by a composite Household Cavalry Regiment and the 6th Dragoon Guards (Carabiniers). The regiment was commanded throughout the conflict by Lieutenant Colonel Walter Willcox, whose book *The 3rd (King's Own) Hussars in the Great War* covers the whole span of the regiment's involvement from August 1914 to the autumn of 1919. The regiment's first actions were during the great retreat from Mons, during which A Squadron found themselves fighting the 3rd German Hussars – a Prussian regiment with which they had been in the habit of exchanging Christmas cards during the years of peace! The 3rd's war ran along broadly similar lines to the 4th's: periods of trench warfare in morale-sapping conditions interspersed with mounted movement into reserve, rest in relatively comfortable billets and then deployment back again to the trenches. Often the regiment was given orders to advance or withdraw this way or that without even the commanding officer being told either their destination or their fate when they got there. '*The fog of war*', wrote Colonel Willcox, '*was upon us pawns in the game ... officers and men hungry and exhausted and their equally tired and hungry horses.*' When the initial German tidal wave was turned and Paris was seen to be safe, morale rose as the allies set about pursuing the enemy over the rivers Marne and Aisne. And then, on the Aisne, both sides fought almost to a standstill, until the race – with the newly designated Cavalry Corps in the van – resumed north-west towards Antwerp and the Channel ports. The 3rd were in the thick of it at the Messines ridge (arguably the most successful local operation of the whole campaign in Flanders), Armentières and Ypres, where effectively the dismal routine of trench and siege warfare which characterized most of the rest of the war began. It was still only December and the 3rd had won nine battle honours.

In the spring of 1915, at Neuve Chapelle, the 3rd Hussars experienced their first gas attack; greenish-yellow smoke began to drift across their lines, followed by masses of retreating French soldiers who were staggering blindly towards them. Regimental Sergeant Major Smith, on his own initiative, left the trenches under heavy fire, rounded up the dazed infantry and shepherded them into trenches behind the regiment's lines – an act of heroism rewarded by the Distinguished Conduct Medal. The rest of the year was spent in preparing for a much heralded offensive around Loos, during which it was expected that a hole would be punched in German lines allowing the cavalry to exploit a gap. It didn't happen, and in November the regiment moved into winter quarters. At the Somme in 1916 the 3rd were in reserve, providing administrative labour behind the lines but, like the 4th, the following year found them at Vimy Ridge poised yet again to exploit a gap made by the infantry; in common with the remainder of the massed cavalry, they were disappointed to be foiled once more. But this was not the last time; in September another concentration of cavalry at Passchendaele was not, despite the forecasts, provided with a passage through the German trenches – just as well, reflected a frustrated but resigned Colonel Willcox, *'for the ground, churned into a morass by shells and pelting rain, was no place for horses'*. At Cambrai in November the regiment was again denied the chance to exploit a breakthrough, and when they did go into action it was as infantry, attacking as part of the now dismounted cavalry brigade a vital wooded feature called Bourlon Hill. It was shortly after this action that Troopers Knowles and Gurnham, who between them ran B Squadron's officers' mess, bicycled off in search of rations. Crossing a canal and entering a town which turned out to be Cambrai and was still occupied by the Germans, they realized that they had probably travelled a bridge too far. However, despite curious glances, no one tried to stop them, and they eventually located a food store which they relieved of as many goodies as could be carried on their bikes before pedalling off back to B Squadron unmolested. Their officers dined well that night – as, of, course did Knowles and Gurnham and their mates! The last year of the war proved the bloodiest for the 3rd: at the Somme they lost six officers and 122 soldiers killed or wounded, and before the gates of Amiens at Rifle Wood their casualties were again heavy, losing nearly half the leading squadron and carrying the

The taking of Rifle Wood, 3rd Hussars, 1918.

dead and wounded down the hill in the aftermath. Before the armistice was signed, they were to gain seven more battle honours, finishing – as did the 4th and the 8th – with *France and Flanders 1914–18*.

The 8th King's Royal Irish Hussars entered the trenches for the first time in December 1914 as the cavalry component of the Indian Army's Ambala Brigade, with whom they served for most of the war. In support of the Indian Corps they saw their first action – and gained their first battle honour of the campaign – at *Givenchy*. In common with our other two regiments, the 8th passed the next few months marching to and fro, caring for their horses and, above all, digging. They, too, had their first whiff of gas during the second battle of Ypres in 1915 and were among the first to marvel at the appearance of 42 tanks at Flers-Courcelette in September 1916 during the battle of the Somme, the first use of armoured shock action which was to play such a major role in the lives of our regiments during the Second World War. Crossing the Somme the following year, B and D Squadrons were ordered to take the heavily defended village of Villers Faucon with the assistance of two new-fangled armoured cars which mounted a heavy machine gun. This they did with great panache – a description applied to the squadrons by a captured German officer, but one which sadly could not be employed in relation to the unfortunate armoured cars, both of which fell into a shell hole and were put out of action. Their undignified predicament did, however, draw a lot of enemy fire which enabled D Squadron to enter the village virtually unscathed. For this action, Major Van der Byl (D Squadron Leader) and Trooper Garvey were awarded the DSO and MM respectively.

The year 1917 saw Russia leave the war after its revolution and the United States enter it. The successful battle of Arras had been fought, and the Hindenburg Line lay seemingly at the feet of the allies and the 400 tanks which had been assembled to smash through it. Like the 3rd and 4th, the 8th stood by to exploit this victory. The Ambala Brigade was now a part of the 5th Cavalry Division and bore the brunt of a German counter-attack, the 8th losing one officer and fifteen men before the situation could be restored. The regiment was in action again in the spring of 1918 as Ludendorff launched an offensive during which the 8th suffered 66 casualties and Captain Adlercron was awarded the DSO. This was by no means their last action, involved as they were in chasing the enemy down, through and beyond the now shattered German defences, and at the armistice they counted that during the last four years ten officers, twenty-three non-commissioned officers (NCOs) and seventy-two soldiers had died. Three

The Somme, 1918 (3rd, 4th and 8th Hussars).

DSOs, seven MCs, three DCMs and eight MMs had been awarded to them, and among the major battle honours were those at *Givenchy 1914*, *Somme 1916–18*, *Cambrai 1917–18*, *Bapaume 1918*, *Amiens*, *Albert 1918*, *Beaurevoir*, *Pursuit to Mons* and *France and Flanders 1914–18*.

In 1914 the 7th Hussars, having spent three years basking in the luxuries attendant upon service in the Empire, were enjoying life. The officers had their polo, their pig-sticking and, for those of flexible morals, their poodle-faking. A young soldier, for a very modest sum, could share the services of an Indian bearer who would relieve him of the dreary round of cleaning, polishing and blancoing his quarters and his equipment. As a sahib he was exempt from all menial duties, including mucking out the stables. He could even have a shave in his bed and a peremptory call of '*Char wallah!*' would immediately conjure up a mug of tea. There was little to do except to make the most of what facilities there were, including those offered by the many brothels in the local bazaar – almost always followed by the need for remedial medical attention. There was certainly no military action and very few ceremonial parades other than those which celebrated the Royal Proclamation of King George V as King-Emperor held on 1 January each year. Peace-keeping was of a level which could be dealt with easily by a junior NCO and a few Indian policemen armed with the wooden clubs called *lathis*. And then in August 1914 came the news that the United Kingdom of Great Britain and Ireland was at war. The 7th imagined that it would be but a little time before they, as an efficient, fully trained regiment, were dispatched to France. But it was not to be, and for three frustrating years they

kicked their heels and watched with ever-increasing bewilderment the departure of other regiments – British and Indian and including the 7th Dragoon
Guards, the other cavalry regiment stationed in southern India – for
Europe. A new commanding officer was necessary before the lethargy that
now threatened to overcome the regiment became irreversible. Such a man
was Lieutenant Colonel Charles Norton, whose first act was to sweep away
the afternoon siesta and institute a daily physical training parade led by
himself in the searing midday sun. Then in 1917 an urgent telegram arrived
from Simla to warn the regiment for service in Mesopotamia. Why this
missive was marked *Urgent* was not immediately apparent, as the instruc-
tions which followed merely led to squadrons being dispatched to Benares
and to Delhi in aid of the civil power who expected armed clashes of Hindu
and Muslim mobs during their disparate festivals. The appearance of the
7th riding through the bazaars with swords drawn was, however, enough to
dissuade the would-be belligerents, who went quietly home. Days turned
into weeks, and then in early November 1917 – at last – the regiment sailed
away from their frustrations and, a fortnight later, disembarked on the Iraqi
banks of the Tigris, a few miles upstream from Basra.

Mesopotamia, a geographical term now consigned to history, was the
name given to the landmass encompassing the river valleys of the Euphrates
and Tigris, mostly in present-day Iraq but taking in bits of Syria, Lebanon
and Kuwait and also areas of the Turkish-Syrian and Iran-Iraq borders. It
was a territory of the Ottoman Empire which, from its capital Constan-
tinople (now Istanbul) had been for six centuries the centre of interaction
between the eastern and western worlds. At its height the Empire stretched
from Algiers in the west to Baku, on the Caspian Sea in the east, and from
Budapest in the north to beyond Mecca in the south. By the beginning of
the twentieth century, however, it had for some years been in decline, but by
allying itself with Germany at the beginning of the Great War it hoped to
regain some of its lost lands. Mesopotamia was, however, a low priority
for the Ottoman armies, who were heavily engaged in Palestine, Gallipoli
and the Caucasus. By the time the 7th Hussars arrived, Basra had been taken
by the British but the advance to Baghdad had been delayed by a humili-
ating defeat on the River Tigris at Kut, some 100 miles to its south. The 7th
spent little time in Basra – rather less than that spent there by their successors in the Queen's Royal Hussars some ninety years later. The regiment
had joined the 11th Indian Cavalry Brigade together with the Indian Army
regiments, the Guides and the 23rd Cavalry, and leaving Basra in December

they rode the 500 miles north up the Euphrates in six weeks. There they remained until March before resuming their advance, fighting a number of actions, notably at Khan al Baghdadi, north of Fallujah, before the enemy – the Turkish 50th Division – disintegrated. Portents of the future came in the form of support from a Light Armoured Motor Battery (Lanchester armoured cars armed with Vickers machine guns) commanded by a 7th Hussar in the shape of Major Sir Thomas Thompson, and two reconnaissance aircraft, one of which was piloted by Lieutenant Devonshire of the regiment.

Having returned to Baghdad, the regiment was on the move again in October 1918, this time north up the Tigris. The Turks were concentrated in the area of Sharqat, and it was there that the 7th suffered their heaviest casualties of the campaign, losing either killed or wounded eight out of thirteen officers and nearly half their effective strength. The attack was nevertheless wholly successful, and at the end of the month all Turkish forces on the Tigris surrendered and an armistice was signed. Internal security duties in Mosul in the far north of the country followed, in conditions reminiscent of those on the Western Front in Europe as constant torrential rain fell on the regiment who had perforce left all their tents, bivouacs and groundsheets some 100 miles to the south. Wet, cold and miserable, with the horse lines a quagmire, men and animals found little to rejoice in their victory. They were now down to 290 all ranks and 335 horses – a loss, including widespread sickness, of more than 40 per cent. What was left of the regiment after further depletions to a composite regiment formed by the army of occupation, arrived at Southampton in May 1919, bearing the battle honours *Sharquat, Khan Baghdadi* and *Mesopotamia 1917–18.*

CHAPTER THREE

MECHANIZATION AND PEACE IN EUROPE

If the changes we fear be thus irresistible, what remains but to acquiesce with silence, as in the other insurmountable distresses of humanity? (Samuel Johnson)

The two decades between the World Wars brought to cavalry regiments the biggest changes in their existence. The 1920s opened with a severe reduction in the strength of the Army: infantry regiments lost countless battalions, while in the cavalry sixteen regiments of the line were reduced by amalgamation to eight and even the household cavalry was affected, having to accept the merging of the 1st and 2nd Life Guards. None of our regiments was involved as they settled down to a welcome spell of peacetime soldiering in exotic (India and Egypt) and not so exotic (York and Aldershot) stations. The threat of mechanization however cast its shadow over all – despite the efforts of Field Marshal Earl Douglas Haig (a former 7th Hussar) and others to shut out the awful possibility. At a lecture given to that most prestigious of military bodies, the Royal United Services Institute, in 1922 Haig pronounced that he was all for using aeroplanes and tanks but that they were only accessories to the man and his horse. '*I feel sure*', he pontificated, '*that as time goes on you will find just as much use for the horse – the well-bred horse – as you have ever done in the past.*'

Fatuous as now seems this Canute-like declaration, the case for mechanization of reconnaissance on the battlefield was far from proven. Reconnaissance had often been the forte of hussar regiments, but in the Great War they had found it increasingly difficult to carry the up to 20 stone (127kg) required of the horse if it and its rider were to be self-sufficient. The advent of mechanical transport to ease this problem by carrying tents, rations, spare ammunition and clothing, and also to bring up the machine guns – now an integral part of the weaponry of a cavalry regiment – was only partially successful, the vehicles being slow, inclined to get stuck in the mud in wet conditions and, even more frequently, break down. In France and Flanders the introduction of armed and armoured Rolls-Royce reconnaissance vehicles – provided initially at his own expense and led by the Duke of Westminster – proved ineffectual, but when they were sent to North Africa to join the fight against the Turkish-led Senussi tribesmen they were a spectacular success, combining mobility, protection and firepower under, as it were, one roof. Sadly, neither this experience nor the battle-winning shock action demonstrated by the tanks at Cambrai was absorbed entirely by the War Office. Lessons learnt were soon forgotten, and it was the Germans who wholeheartedly seized the baton of armoured warfare which was to lead to devastating results barely twenty years later.

After the war 3rd The King's Own Hussars spent a couple of years in Aldershot – a tour notable mainly for equestrian triumphs at the International Horse Show and winning accuracy at rifle events – before in 1921 joining the army of occupation in Turkey. There, on the banks of the Bosphorus, their role was to police the neutral zone set up by the Allies to dissuade the Greeks from invading, and also to prevent Kemal Ataturk's Turkish nationalist forces from upsetting the agreed peace terms. In 1923 the regiment was in Egypt, taking over from the 8th Hussars in their barracks at Abbassia on the outskirts of Cairo, where they stayed for four largely trouble-free years before sailing to India to take over from the 4th Hussars at Lucknow. The 4th, having been first stationed in Colchester, had been in India since 1921 – nine years in which militarily they were hardly taxed but were able, instead, to concentrate on the sporting opportunities on offer. Prominent among these activities was pig-sticking and its premier competition, the All-India Kadir Cup. Between 1923 and 1930 Captain John (Scotty) Scott-Cockburn of the regiment and his horse *Carclew* won the Kadir Cup three times and reached the semi-final on a further four occasions. *Carclew*, who took part in his first event aged eighteen, achieved country-wide fame as did *The Bishop*, the show-jumping mount of Sergeant Major Watts who beat all-comers at the Imperial Delhi Horse Show between 1923 and 1929. In 1930 the 4th sailed home to be stationed at York (followed by the 3rd two years later), then moving on to Aldershot.

The 7th Queen's Own Hussars, having been away from home for seven and a half years, arrived briefly at York in 1919 before a short three-year tour of India. The twelve years between 1923 and 1935 were spent first in

Carclew and Captain John (Scotty) Scott-Cockburn, 4th Hussars. Three times winners of the Kadir Cup.

Edinburgh and then in Aldershot, where they were reorganized into two mounted sabre squadrons and a Vickers Machine Gun Squadron of eight guns carried in six-wheel vehicles. Comically, two baby Austin Seven cars also arrived for – the War Office insisted – *'reconnaissance purposes'*. Life, though, for most of the regiment still revolved around the horse and there were some spectacular sporting successes: in 1934 the polo team won the Inter-Regimental tournament at Hurlingham, while Lieutenant Arthur Talbot-Ponsonby hit the equestrian headlines by winning the King George V Gold Cup for show-jumping in both 1930 and 1934 on a troop horse called *Chelsea*. In 1935 the regiment embarked, with its horses still intact, for Egypt, where it joined the 8th Hussars.

At the end of the Great War the 8th had been despatched to Lucknow and then, within a year, to Mesopotamia where, almost treading in the footsteps of the 7th, they landed near Basra. Their task was first to move up the Tigris in boats, with barges carrying the horses lashed to the sides, and then to disembark at Kut and march the 100 miles to Medali on the Persian (Iranian) border. Some of the Iraqi people had not accepted the imposition

The last mounted parade of the 8th Hussars, Aldershot, 1932.

of British mandated rule after the defeat of the Ottoman Empire with anything approaching equanimity, and there had been a general revolt helped along by a religious *fatwa* issued by the most eminent of Shia clerics which declared that, on pain of death, it was forbidden to work for the British. The unrest was short-lived, thanks in great part to bombing operations carried out by the newly fledged Royal Air Force, and by the time the 8th arrived there was little to do other than to mop up. By December 1921 the regiment was staging in Egypt on its way to York. The next nine years were spent both in England (York, Aldershot and Hounslow in turn) and for the three years from 1926 to 1929 in Wiesbaden in Germany as part of the first British Army of the Rhine. In 1933 they marched from Aldershot to Hounslow with 400 horses in preparation for another spell in Egypt, where they arrived a year later, taking over at Abbassia from the 14/20th Hussars.

On 11 November 1935 the regiment held its last mounted parade, a magnificent spectacle as Lieutenant Colonel Decimus Pope led three squadrons and the mounted band, first at the trot-past then at the gallop, for the last time in 242 years. In January of the next year the same fate befell the 7th as they too sent all their horses to the remount depot and prepared to train with their newly-issued Mark VIB Light Tanks.

At Tidworth the 3rd Hussars had been instructed to carry out mechanization trials since 1934, being equipped for this purpose with a variety of

The 8th Hussars – Abbassia, Egypt, 1939.

The Mark VI Light Tank – 3rd Hussars, 1938.

A Squadron 3rd Hussars, Tidworth, 1936.

15cwt and other wheeled trucks pretending to be tanks, and by 1936 a similar pantomime was being conducted by the 4th Hussars in Aldershot.

It would be idle to pretend that morale in cavalry regiments had not suffered from these traumatic events and the seemingly unsatisfactory way in which the changes were being introduced. On parade and off, the world of the cavalryman had always been bounded by horses: most of his waking hours had been devoted to their care and that of their equipment. In war and peace the horse's welfare was, as it always had been, paramount. Now all this was to be swept away, and both officers and soldiers were finding it hard to come to terms with their future. But it would also be true that the inevitable was faced by most with a grim determination to master the new challenges. This attitude was summed up by the 4th's most eminent old comrade during a brief visit to the regimental Warrant Officers' and Sergeants' Mess in Aldershot: *'Whatever be the weapons which are given to the 4th Hussars'*, said Winston Churchill in those sonorous cadences which were all too soon to become familiar to the whole world, *'the regiment will play the same tune on them and will carry the same old traditions, whether it be the sabre and the wheel into line for the charge, whether it is as mounted infantry, as rifle-armed cavalry or, as you now are to be, as a mechanised unit.'* It was not to be long before his prediction came true – and not long either before, in the regiment's greatest hour of need, he became its Colonel.

CHAPTER FOUR

THE SECOND WORLD WAR

We herd sheep, we drive cattle, we lead people.
(General George S. Patton)

As the nations of Europe moved inexorably towards war, there was also unrest in the Middle East. The 8th were first into action with their new equipment, being deployed to Palestine in 1938 to keep the peace between warring factions of Jews and Arabs. The squadrons worked independently, patrolling, guarding the railway and the aerodrome at Gaza, escorting post-office employees as they repaired sabotaged telephone lines, and searching villages for arms and terrorists. These operations lasted a year, before the regiment, hearing the belligerent noises emanating from Germany, began to think that they would soon be home to prepare for yet another European war. It was not to be: the British government had discerned that war with Germany would almost certainly lead to war with the other fascist power, Italy, and there was a large Italian army in North Africa, where they had acquired colonies or protectorates in Libya, Eritrea and Somalia. Mussolini had also invaded and occupied Ethiopia in 1935, proclaiming an Italian African Empire. Accordingly a brigade-sized formation, named the Matruh Mobile Force, was created under the Cairo Cavalry Brigade Headquarters and deployed to Mersa Matruh on the Mediterranean coast halfway between Alexandria and the Libyan border. The Force was composed of the 7th, 8th and 11th Hussars, the 1st Royal Tank Regiment (1RTR) and the 3rd Regiment Royal Horse Artillery (3RHA). 1RTR was the only unit fully equipped with tanks (MkVIB), while the 11th Hussars, although the most experienced mechanized regiment in the British Army, were still having to make do with the Rolls-Royce armoured cars which had first appeared in the Great War. Later in 1938, the Matruh Mobile Force was joined by the 1st Battalion King's Royal Rifle Corps (KRRC) and became the forerunner of 7 Armoured Brigade, which was soon to grow into the 7th Armoured Division – 'The Desert Rats'.

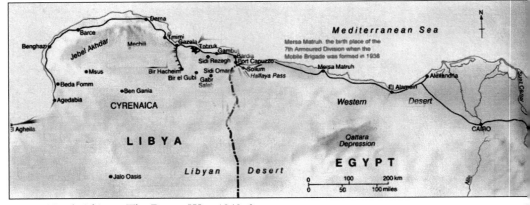

North Africa – The Desert War, 1940–3.

In June 1940 Italy declared war on Britain and France and 7 Armoured Brigade moved west across the Libyan border to engage its army. The tally of Italian prisoners of war was high – so high that there was little chance of counting them accurately. An imaginative officer of the 11th Hussars reported that he thought there was '*about an acre of officers and two and a half acres of other ranks*'. In October, the 3rd Hussars, having sailed round the Cape of Good Hope (it was now too dangerous for troopships to venture into the Mediterranean) arrived in Egypt, where they, too, were deployed to 7 Armoured Brigade, having attached one of their light squadrons to 2nd Royal Tank Regiment (in 4 Armoured Brigade) and received one of that regiment's heavier squadrons in return. For the next year or so the 3rd, 7th and 8th Hussars fought together in the newly formed 7th Armoured Division made up of the two brigades. The Division and the 4th Indian Division (later replaced by the 6th Australian Division) made up the Western Desert Force (WDF) under Lieutenant General Richard O'Connor which, during Operation Compass launched in December 1940, destroyed the Italian Tenth Army (more than four times its size), taking 140,000 prisoners and advancing to El Agheila deep into Cyrenaica – the eastern Libyan province. Of our regiments the 8th Hussars had a relatively quiet time and it was the 3rd who took the most casualties, losing three officers, seven men and thirteen of their tanks when A Squadron ran into a salt-marsh within point-blank range of the enemy. The regimental doctor, Captain Tom Somerville, displayed conspicuous bravery as he helped the injured and was awarded a DSO to add to the OBE, two MCs and the Croix de Guerre he had won in the Great War.

At the beginning of February, which saw the successful conclusion of Compass, the remnants of the 3rd and the 7th, who had already distinguished themselves in support of the Australian attack on Tobruk during which the Aussies credited the 7th with saving '*hundreds of lives*', now came

The 3rd Hussars at Tobruk, April 1941.

together in 4 Armoured Brigade at the battle for Beda Fomm, delivering the blow which saw the final humiliation of the Italians. Having taken El Agheila the WDF ran out of both serviceable tanks and political will – the Prime Minister being mindful of the urgent need to support the Greeks in their fight against the Italians in Albania and the threat of a German invasion of the Balkans. The 8th Hussars handed over what was left of their tanks to the 3rd and embarked on a period of training and re-equipping with the M5 Stuart (Honey) tanks which was to last until November 1941.

The reconstituted 3rd now found themselves joining 3 Armoured Brigade, a formation given the task of watching the frontier territory between Cyrenaica and Tripolitania (western Libya). By the spring of 1941 the regiment was in Tobruk, from where A and C squadrons were sent to Alexandria. Almost immediately, C Squadron, equipped with sixteen light tanks, sailed for Crete, where they were soon in action trying to repel a German air and seaborne invasion. After eleven days the squadron had lost all its tanks and most of its personnel, and when the remainder were evacuated on the last day of May, only eleven all-ranks were able to board the ship. The whole regiment came together briefly in Cyprus, until just before Christmas B Squadron was warned for 'service overseas'. In January, at a strength of 145 all-ranks, it sailed down the Suez Canal, bound, it was said, for Singapore. The 7th, too, had been broken up, B Squadron being detached to operate with one of the independent, all-arms mobile groups known as Jock Columns after their creator Lieutenant Colonel Jock Campbell of the Royal Horse Artillery. It was then ordered to support the KRRC in an attack on Fort Capuzzo, an Italian stronghold on the Libyan border. Up to that point the 7th had never met any Germans in battle, but in November, and now in 7 Armoured Brigade (commanded by a 3rd Hussar, Brigadier George Davy), they were involved in Operation Crusader, General Archibald Wavell's attempt to sweep the newly arrived Germans out of North Africa. The Afrika Korps – initially of two divisions – had been sent to Libya by Adolf Hitler to bolster the Italians, and when Compass put an end to the military effectiveness of their allies, the Germans, commanded by General Erwin Rommel, had moved east and were investing Tobruk. The 8th Hussars in 4 Armoured Brigade also took part in Crusader, which turned into one of the see-saw battles which had now become characteristic of the war in the desert. The 7th, at the fierce battles for the airfield at Sidi Rezegh were, by the last week in September after barely seven days, down to two tanks, the remnants of the regiment being then moved to Abbassia. The 8th, too, came off second best, losing twenty tanks in its first encounter with the enemy. On 20 November A Squadron was wiped out – its squadron leader killed. For twelve days the rest of the regiment, bolstered by reinforcements of both men and tanks, fought on, causing the commanding officer of 2 RHA to write:

> *I would like you to know how sorry we are at your heavy losses. I hope that the world will get to know that, far from being in vain, the 8th Hussars chiefly, together with the 3rd and 5th Royal Tank Regiments stood between the British Empire and perhaps defeat for eight days. They were simply magnificent.*

The 4th Queen's Own Hussars had a quiet start to the war, training in England until November 1940. Their journey to Egypt was leisurely, with a notable break for shore leave in Durban. The 1st Light Armoured Brigade, of which they were a part, assembled at a camp near Ismailia, known to its inhabitants – but emphatically not to the soldiers – as 'The City of Beauty and Enchantment', on the west bank of the Suez Canal. Equipped with the ubiquitous and largely useless Mark VIB, they prepared conscientiously for a desert war and looked forward with eager anticipation to their first contact with the enemy.

When this came it was not, however, in Egypt or Libya but in Greece. On 6 March 1941 the Brigade was deployed as the leading formation of an expeditionary force consisting of three British infantry divisions, the 2nd New Zealand Division and the 6th Australian Division sent to help the

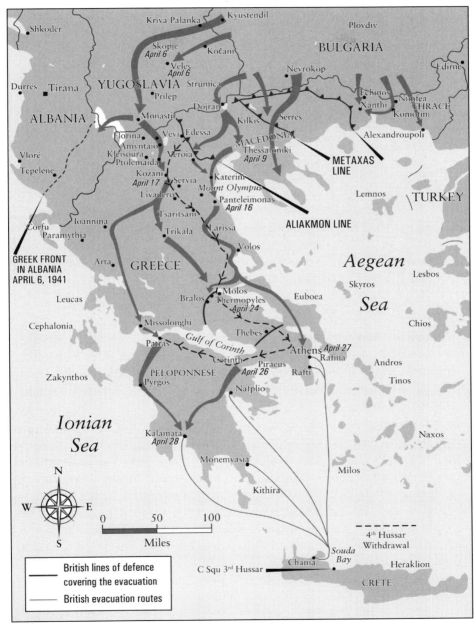

The 4th Hussars in Greece and C Squadron 3rd Hussars in Crete, 1941.

The answer to the Afrika Korps.

Greeks in case the Germans, sweeping south through the Balkans, invaded their country. It was not enough. In April, fifteen German divisions supported by 800 aircraft (the RAF could muster only 80) invaded Yugoslavia and Greece. The Allied forces were almost immediately forced to fight a series of delaying actions for which 1 Brigade invariably provided the bulk of the covering force. The 4th Hussars moved steadily southwards for fourteen days and nights, fighting all the way. When they reached Glyfada in the suburbs of Athens they had been reduced to ten tanks and seven scout cars. More fighting followed: the regiment – less one squadron sent 130 miles to Patras – was deployed over the Corinth Canal and into the Peloponnese. A series of intense but fragmented rearguard actions followed, and evacuation plans largely failed to materialize. Small parties took to the hills, or to the sea in small boats heading for either Crete or North Africa. Very few made it. Individual heroism was widespread, epitomized by the Commanding Officer, Lieutenant Colonel Edward Lillingston, who won a Distinguished Service Order. A further four Military Crosses, a Distinguished Conduct Medal and six Military Medals (MM) were also awarded, together with three battle honours. The 4th Hussars had landed in Egypt on 31 December 1940, fully equipped and manned. Within four months, 23 officers had either died or been taken prisoner and 350 soldiers had suffered similarly. By June, only 11 officers and 160 men had made it back to Egypt, and as far as equipment was concerned, the regiment could muster only two lorries, three motorcycles and eighty-five rifles. Morale was at rock bottom but was boosted by the announcement that Winston Churchill had been appointed the regiment's Honorary Colonel. Rebuilding began.

As 1941 turned into 1942, 7 Armoured Brigade, including the 7th Hussars now newly equipped with Honey tanks armed with a 2-pounder main armament and two .30 Browning machine guns, embarked for the Far East. They had no clear idea of their destination, but rumour control had settled on Malaya. When they reached Ceylon (now Sri Lanka) the news was gloomy: Singapore had fallen and the whole of Malaya was in Japanese hands. The Brigade, therefore, was to go to Burma to reinforce the Indian 17th Infantry Division, which had been pushed back from the Sittang River and was now abandoning Rangoon in the face of an overwhelming Japanese advance. The 7th landed at Rangoon on 21 February and were soon in action at Pegu, 50 miles to the north, destroying two and capturing a third enemy tank. From then on it was a steady but costly withdrawal. By May all of southern Burma was in enemy hands. When the remnants of 17th Division reached the Chindwin river, the 7th Hussars had lost ten of their tanks and had eleven men killed and thirty wounded. Lieutenant Michael Patteson, a troop leader, was captured. Refusing to talk to an interrogating Japanese officer who spoke perfect English, he was tied to a road block in an area being plastered by British 25-pounder guns. Grimly awaiting his end, he was surprised to find that a nearby explosion had severed his bonds without hurting him in any way. He ran off and was able to find the remains of his regiment, telling them that he had had a rather tiresome day. His squadron leader looked him up and down. '*I'd say you need a drink*', he said.

The hitherto friendly – or at worst neutral – Burmese, now seeing the way the wind was blowing, turned ugly, and it was dangerous to be unguarded: in one village a tank crew had been murdered while bartering for eggs. On 8 May the regiment fought its final battle of the campaign when, in support of the Gurkha Brigade, they dislodged an enemy position and secured the only small ferry still serviceable and able to cross the river. But this was far too small and rickety to carry vehicles, so the remaining tanks had to be rendered unusable– either by disabling the armaments or by dowsing them in petrol and setting fire to them. One, however – named 'The Curse of Scotland', presumably in remembrance of the 7th's history in that country – had managed to cross the Chindwin many miles upstream.

The Curse of Scotland, the only tank to survive the 7th Hussars' Burma campaign. Shown here, it has become the command tank of the Indian 7th Cavalry and led the victorious entry into Rangoon in 1945.

Astonishingly, it was to survive the war in the hands of the Indian 7th Light Cavalry Brigade and lead that brigade in its triumphal re-entry into Rangoon in May 1945.

Once across the river but now unhorsed, the regiment embarked on a 150-mile march to India, a slog which elicited from the soldiers a level of cursing which far outdid even that brought forth on their 2-mile march from Abbassia to church in Cairo in 1940! During their arduous retreat, the seemingly endless column of British, Indian, Gurkha, Burmese and Chinese soldiers plodded grimly on for seven days and nights before reaching the railway that took them to Imphal, and it says much for the endurance and morale of the 7th that only two men fell out, succumbing to cholera. But altogether three officers, and forty-three soldiers had been killed and a further fifty had been wounded in their three-month campaign. After a few welcome months of recuperation and refitting in India, the 7th embarked at Bombay for Iraq.

The 4th Queen's Own Hussars and the 8th King's Royal Irish Hussars had charged alongside each other at Balaklava, and now in the Western

Desert they were to be joined in an even closer relationship. The Alam Halfa ridge lay south-east of the village of El Alamein and it was there that the newly appointed commander of the British Eighth Army, Lieutenant General Bernard Montgomery, determined that the advance of Rommel's Afrika Korps should finally be halted in its attempt to take Alexandria and Cairo. The withdrawal from the Libyan border in the wake of the German victory at the Battle of Gazala in May and June had been a sorry affair. The 4th, now in 1 Armoured Brigade, had been in the thick of it and when they reached El Alamein at the end of June they were once again sadly depleted, down to 12 officers and 152 men with no tanks or wheeled transport. From this moment onwards, however, matters were to improve. The 8th, in 4 Armoured Brigade, had suffered similarly, having destroyed 30 of the 100 German tanks facing them. A Squadron had lost all its officers and Regimental Headquarters (RHQ) was overrun – but not before Lieutenant Colonel 'Smash' Kilkelly had himself destroyed an enemy tank at a range of 30yds. By the beginning of June the only fighting force available to the brigade commander was a composite squadron formed from the remnants of the 8th and 3RTR. For the battle of Alam Halfa, because they were at such a low strength, the 4th and 8th were joined together and equipped with Stuart tanks. There, on 31 August, the 4th/8th Hussars ambushed success-fully a German column and then, during the Battle of Alamein itself, the composite regiment took the lead in pursuing the Afrika Korps back into Libya. By Christmas both regiments had been relieved and shipped to Cyprus to reform and refit. There the 4th received a visit from their distin-guished Colonel, who came again to see them when the regiment returned to Egypt in June 1943. He was wearing his 4th Hussar uniform and noticed, having walked the whole length of the tanks and crews, that the men of his regiment were not wearing the ribbon of the Africa Star. Colonel Churchill demanded of his accompanying generals why this was the case. Within hours a convoy of seamstresses and yards of ribbon had been despatched from Cairo to make good this regrettable oversight. The 3rd The King's Own Hussars had been spared the retreat to El Alamein and had also been reinforced to form a new B Squadron to replace that about which nothing had been heard since it sailed for the Far East in January. The regiment was now in 9 Armoured Brigade, a part of General Bernard Freyberg's 2nd New Zealand Division. Under the command of the terrifyingly efficient fox-hunting fanatic, Lieutenant Colonel Sir Peter Farquhar, the regiment advanced from the Alamein positions, reaching the Miteiriya Ridge, from which they were invited to creep forward under cover of darkness to occupy the next feature. Finding themselves at first light in an unexpectedly deep depression they took heavy casualties, reducing their strength to two effective squadrons. After a period in reserve the regiment was switched to the north flank, where Montgomery personally gave Farquhar the task of 'opening a door' for the 1st Armoured Division. Farquhar murmured apologetically that this would mean suicide for his regiment. Montgomery replied that *'It has to be done with, if necessary, 100 per cent casualties.'* Farquhar, accepting that there was nothing more to be said, metaphorically turned to his right and saluted as he prepared for one of the proudest moments in his regiment's history. But he never forgot the army commander's words. *'My God'*, he said on his death-bed decades later, *'Monty really was a shit!'* The task given to the 3rd by Montgomery was, of course, achieved; the 'door' had been opened, the gap wide. General Freyberg drove up and climbed on to Farquhar's tank to say, *'Your regiment is magnificent'*, before disappearing in a cloud of dust which unfortunately attracted more enemy fire. The cost to the regiment had been grievously heavy: 21 officers and 98 soldiers had been killed, wounded or were missing, and out of the 51 tanks the commanding officer had led into battle, 47 had been destroyed. The remnants retired to the Nile Delta, where they received reinforcements of men and machines and cherished the black fern leaf sign of the New Zealand Division which General Freyberg asked them to paint on their tanks. It was there, too, that they heard what had happened to Major William-Powlett's B Squadron.

Like the 7th Hussars, B Squadron of the 3rd Hussars had set sail without any clear idea of its destination. Singapore was thought most likely, but the news from Malaya was so bad that Sumatra proved to be their unexpected landfall – an island of which few had even heard. Two days after the squadron landed in February 1942, Singapore surrendered. The Japanese had also invaded the Dutch East Indies, and after a stay of only a few days in Sumatra, B Squadron was ordered to Java, which proved to be the last Allied stronghold in South-East Asia. There it joined some 25,000 Dutch troops, three Australian infantry battalions, a battery of American gunners and assorted – but very few – aircraft. This little force was soon engaged with at least four enemy divisions, with the inevitable result. With their backs to the sea, and after they had enjoyed a last swim, William-Powlett explained the position to his men, making the point that escaping into the jungle would be hazardous in the extreme. Nevertheless, more than half the squadron, including the squadron leader and his second-in-command, set off to walk home. Nobody made it to freedom, and by the end of March the squadron was reunited, but this time in a Japanese prison camp. Three and a half years later, well over a third had died of starvation, sickness and ill-treatment or had drowned when a ship in which they were being transported to Japan was sunk by the Royal Navy. In August 1945 came the news, dropped from an aircraft, that the Japanese had surrendered and that they would be rescued as soon as possible.

Neither the 3rd nor the 7th Hussars took part in major operations in 1943 or during the first few months of 1944. Both spent that time re-equipping, training and receiving fresh drafts of recruits. The 3rd, still part of 9 Armoured Brigade along with the Royal Wiltshire Yeomanry and the Warwickshire Yeomanry with whom they had fought their final actions in North Africa, were sent to Aleppo in Syria in January and thence moved to Tripoli in Lebanon on the eastern seaboard of the Mediterranean. Colonel Farquhar was a hard taskmaster – the delights of the benign climate and a friendly population passed him by, so that where other regiments were inclined to relax he kept the 3rd working relentlessly at improving their gunnery, maintenance and wireless communication drills. This made him a less than popular commanding officer, but the regiment's reward was to come in Italy, when its casualties in action were almost negligible and its reputation for efficiency was second to none. The 7th, still in 7 Armoured Brigade with whom they had first gone into battle against the Germans, spent a year in Iraq and Syria before returning to a peaceful Egypt, where they were issued with American Sherman tanks, reputed to be the best Allied armoured fighting vehicle of the war.

In the wake of the invasion of Sicily, both regiments landed at Taranto on the west coast of the heel of mainland Italy in early May 1944, joining the pursuit of the German army northwards. By this time the Allies were in sight of Rome. On 25 May the 3rd were in action in support of the 78th Division and from then on for two months they were rarely out of battle, fighting their way to the Gothic Line, Field Marshal Kesselring's last major defensive position along the northern summits of the Apennine Mountains. For A Squadron the almost unremitting action was alleviated by a night or two in a castle in which resided not only (according to the squadron leader, Major Richard Heseltyne) an attractive and amenable *contessa* but a whole platoon of equally agreeable servant girls.

Not everyone in the regiment was engaged in the front line. Trooper Honeyball was a lorry driver in the administrative echelon and longed for

Italy, 1943–5.

some of the action his mates in the sabre squadrons boasted about but which had for so long been denied to him. One evening he was drinking with some Italian partisans, now also at war with the Germans, and they suggested that he might like to accompany them on a raid they were about to make on a house known to contain four of the enemy. Honeyball, fortified by many glasses of the local wine, enthusiastically agreed and a few hours later was safely back in the cab of his lorry, the proud possessor of four German officers' wristwatches. The next night, he thought he would make another raid, this time on his own and on a house he had been told also contained Germans. As he entered through a window he was spotted, shot in the leg and taken prisoner. His captors were not well disposed towards this irritating intruder: stripping him of his boots and all his clothes they locked him up for the night. As luck would have it, one of the regiment's tanks chose the house for target practice and blew a hole in it, through which Honeyball escaped, leaving behind two dead Germans. Legging it back to his own lines he was arrested for being improperly dressed and in the morning found himself before his commanding officer charged with losing his weapon, his kit and all his clothes. Trooper Honeyball was sad – not because of his punishment, which proved to be remarkably light, but because still in his trouser pocket, lost to him forever, had been four German watches. In August, Trooper Honeyball, who by now was relieved to be back within the safe confines of his truck, and the rest of the 3rd Hussars were withdrawn south to Lake Bracciano where they were joined by the 7th Hussars.

The 7th had fought with 7 Armoured Brigade until the fall of Rome in June, after which they were drafted to the 2nd Polish Corps under their formidable commander Lieutenant General Władyslaw Anders. With the Poles, the 7th advanced north for a month, ending with the capture of Ancona, a vital east coast port which would considerably shorten the Allies' supply line, and then joined in the pursuit of the enemy to the Gothic Line. In September the regiment said goodbye to their Polish friends, but not until General Anders had introduced the commanding officer, Lieutenant Colonel Francis Jayne, to King George VI on His Majesty's visit to Allied forces in Italy. General Anders in a later communication to the regiment in which he said, '*I once more thank you fervently for the magnificent work of your Regiment in the battles on the Adriatic Coast, true to the highest traditions of your Regiment and the British Army*', also granted the 7th Hussars permission to wear on their sleeves the Polish *Maid of Warsaw* badge – a tradition carried on by the Queen's Own Hussars and the Queen's Royal Hussars. When the regiment arrived at Lake Bracciano it found itself in 9 Armoured Brigade, together with the 3rd. Here the brigade's task was to train for an amphibious assault with both Valentine and Sherman duplex-drive (DD) tanks, fitted with propellers and a supposedly waterproof, all-enveloping canvas screen – which had the distinct disadvantage of rendering the 75mm main armament gun unusable. The training was both hilarious (the DDs were difficult to steer and looked like waterborne field lavatories) and tragic – both regiments lost crews drowned in the lake – but the DDs had nevertheless proved moderately successful in the Normandy landings earlier in the year. In Italy it was planned that they would lead an attack across the flooded marshes of the River Po once the Gothic Line defences had been overcome.

The 3rd Hussars were never to put this training to the test. Early in December 1944 they lost a high proportion of their manpower – those who had served for four and a half years in combat being repatriated to England. The regiment, having received a modicum of reinforcements, sailed from Taranto in January 1945 bound yet again for the Middle East. The 7th, having briefly been diverted to a dismounted role, were reunited with their DDs and then widely scattered in support of various units and formations of the Eighth Army. First across the River Po was A Squadron, and there then followed a headlong dash in true cavalry manner for Venice, A Squadron arriving in the van, closely followed by B, whose tanks were almost submerged under a cargo of happy Mahratta sepoys from the 4th Indian Infantry Division, relieved to be off their feet for a change. C Squadron made it with the New Zealanders to Trieste, and then came the welcome news that the battle for Italy was over. On 2 May Kesselring surrendered, and a few days later the scattered elements of the 7th came together once again in Mestre, the mainland town which serves as a gateway to Venice. Their war had ended and, as it turned out, they were never as the 7th Queen's Own Hussars to see active service again.

For the 4th Hussars, Italy was also the final theatre of the war. Having been visited by their distinguished Colonel in Egypt, they arrived in Italy in May 1944 and, as the armoured reconnaissance regiment of the 1st Armoured Division they staged south of Ancona (where Churchill again came to see them) before being launched into the Gothic Line battles in September. The German defences were in considerable depth and their positions were such that the taking of one ridge was followed inevitably by the appearance of another and then another. At Coriano, near the Adriatic coast, the regiment was heavily engaged in supporting an already depleted brigade of three Hampshire battalions and lost five officers and thirty-five soldiers killed in the first few days. Six weeks of debilitating fighting followed, and the Division was so reduced in both men and equipment that it was broken up, some units being sent to provide reinforcements for Normandy. The regiment also lost its outstanding commanding officer, Lieutenant Colonel Bobby Kidd, to a home posting. He had joined the 4th Hussars when it was impoverished and bewildered by the disaster in Greece. He restored its morale and had commanded it in every battle since that time. Fearless and innovative in action, universally respected and popular, he was cheered by all ranks as he set off for England. Shortly after his departure, two squadrons were deprived of their Sherman tanks and issued with armoured infantry carriers known as Kangaroos. To be reduced from an armoured fighting unit, highly trained and tested, to what the soldiers considered to be little short of bus drivers carrying others into battle, was a humiliation not lightly borne; and when the third squadron was similarly threatened, the new commanding officer, Lieutenant Colonel Tony Barne went to see the Army Commander to protest, hinting that if necessary he would report the matter to the Colonel of the Regiment. B Squadron retained its Shermans. As 1944 turned into 1945, the regiment also suffered from the same repatriation scheme as the 3rd and a consequent reduction in experienced officers and soldiers. Nevertheless, it distinguished itself in battles on the Rivers Senio and Po in April and May until finally, at the ceasefire, the scattered squadrons were reunited at Padua. Ten battle honours had been won, but at a cost in deaths alone of seventeen officers and 140 soldiers.

The 8th Hussars sailed home from Egypt in November 1943, having spent ten years, almost to the day, in North Africa. Their destination, together with the rest of 7thArmoured Division, was Norfolk where, as the division's armoured reconnaissance regiment, they were equipped with Cromwell tanks and began to train for the expected invasion of the European mainland.

In the early morning of 6 June 1944, from their final assembly area at Bognor Regis, they watched airborne troops fly over and, by 7.00pm on the 9th, they were all ashore in Normandy. No contrast could have been greater than that between the desert and the close, hedge-lined, *bocage* country in which they were now required to fight. Within four days, advancing at the head of the division, they had taken heavy casualties, including three officers killed. The next month, they lost three more, including Major Guy

The 8th Hussars cross the Seine, August 1944.

An 8th Hussar Cromwell tank passing Winston Churchill during a victory parade in Berlin, 21 July 1945.

Threlfall, who had been in every battle since 1940 and had had seven tanks shot from under him. Operations near Antwerp followed, and then the regiment was engaged in clearing Holland of Germans, fighting fierce engagements in October and November. At the end of March 1945 the 8th Hussars crossed the Rhine at Xanten in the Ruhr. The regiment now fought its way steadily east against a mixture of the veterans of the Hermann Goering Division and battalions of fanatical Nazi youths until, in April 1945, they reached the River Weser. The advance then quickened as the route to Hamburg appeared to be open. At Fallingbostel, which later was to play host to more than one generation of British cavalrymen, the reconnaissance troop liberated the 14,000 inmates of assorted Allied nationalities from the prisoner-of-war camp Stalag XIB. Finally, as the 8th Hussars occupied the villages of Wulmstorf, Daerstorf and Elstorf, overlooking the River Elbe and Hamburg, the war against Germany came finally to an end. Among the regimental tanks taking part in the victory parade in Berlin in July was 'Hurry On', which since landing in Normandy had covered 3,000 miles.

CHAPTER FIVE

THIRTEEN YEARS TO AMALGAMATION

There never was a good war, or a bad peace. (Benjamin Franklin)

For the 3rd The King's Own Hussars the signings of the various acts of surrender in Europe did not signal a return home. Instead, the regiment found itself keeping the peace in Syria and Lebanon in their new American Staghound armoured cars supplemented by a squadron of Sherman tanks. In the Lebanon they had little trouble: the Staghounds with their crew of five, screeching sirens, power-steering and a top speed of over 70mph enabled them to deploy quickly and effectively to scenes of prospective trouble. The victory over Japan, however, meant much to the regiment in that it signalled the release of the surviving officers and men of the old B Squadron who had been in Japanese captivity. The news they brought with them was appalling: of the 145 who had sailed from Egypt, 54 had not survived.

In Syria the regiment's primary task was to rescue the Vichy-French garrison, of whom the citizens of Damascus had taken a dim, indeed murderous, view. Departing French troops were escorted safely out of the country from other bases too, and it was only when that task was completed and the regiment was reunited at Adlun, a coastal town in south Lebanon, in the autumn of 1945, that they learned that they were to become the first airborne cavalry regiment and were to join the 6th Airborne Division, which had been deployed to Palestine to keep the peace between Jews and Arabs. Thirty officers and more than 300 soldiers became qualified parachutists and wore the red beret but were, alas, never called upon to jump into action. Instead, they became embroiled in an increasingly dirty ground war as the Jews struggled to establish a homeland in a country which had hitherto belonged mainly to Arabs. Extremist Zionist groupings such as Irgun and the Stern Gang also waged a guerrilla war against the British, whom they held responsible for preventing the entry into the country of shiploads of

3rd Hussars armoured car patrol, Haifa, 1948.

refugees from Europe. In Sarafand al-Amar, an Arab village south of Haifa where the 3rd was based, a Zionist raid succeeded in stealing arms and explosives from the camp, but the booty-laden lorry in which the terrorists had made their escape was pursued and captured by the regiment.

In Haifa, Tel Aviv, Ramla, Jerusalem and even in Nazareth, troops of the 3rd Hussars were heavily involved in anti-terrorist operations, imposing and enforcing curfews, searching for arms and explosives, tracking down illegal radio stations and setting up road blocks. In June 1947, B Squadron – singled out again – left the regiment, returning to England to join the 2nd Parachute Brigade based near Andover. Nine months later came the news that the airborne division was to be disbanded and the regiment was to revert to being a conventional tank regiment of the Royal Armoured Corps. But before the 3rd were able to leave Palestine a full-scale war had broken out between the Jewish settlers and the so-called Arab Liberation Army, formed first in Syria. Sometimes acting independently, 3rd Hussar troops were involved in protecting and rescuing civilians from both sides until in May, acting as rearguard for the remaining units in a general withdrawal aptly code-named Operation Scuttle, the 3rd left Palestine. Back in England they paused at Barnard Castle, where they were looked after by the

7th Hussars, and had some leave before, six weeks later, they left for Lübeck in Schleswig-Holstein, the most northerly province of Germany, where in 1948 B Squadron was waiting for them.

The first few years of peace were turbulent for the Army. Most of those who had served in the war and its immediate aftermath – both officers and soldiers – queued up impatiently to be discharged and resume their civilian occupations. Regiments lost around half their strength in a matter of months and the 3rd was no exception. Lübeck, however, was as good a station as any in which to do not a lot. It was only about 60 miles from Hamburg, in which city the regimental band played regularly to cheer up the badly war-scarred citizens and which was home to a booming red-light district whose economy benefited greatly from the eager visits of occupying troops. Lübeck itself, the former principal city of the medieval trading organization known as the Hanseatic League, had been fire-bombed by the Allies in 1942, causing immense damage to what had been a picturesque old city centre. Situated on the banks of the Traves River, it was now on the front line of the Cold War, the river forming part of the border between East and West Germany. The 3rd, a divisional reconnaissance regiment, mounted border patrols which at first were fairly relaxed affairs and composed practically the sum of their martial duties. By the end of the year came the news that their military designation was to change to armoured car regiment and then, only a few months later, to tank destroyer regiment – all without a change of equipment or any discernible change of role. In March 1949 the first draft of National Servicemen arrived, to be concentrated in A Squadron for a 16-week period of trade training (gunnery, driving or radio) before being dispersed to the other squadrons – an arrangement common to most armoured regiments. The easygoing nature of what tactical activity there was came to an abrupt end in April when a border patrol of B Squadron, engaged unwisely in taking photographs of the Soviet Zone, was seized by a Russian unit some 300 yards inside British territory. The news of this incident was lost in the much greater international furore ignited by the Soviet Military Government's road and rail blockade of Berlin, leading to the now historically famous 'airlift', but eight days later the men of B Squadron were released, happy to be free but nursing a grudge against all things Russian and particularly the potato soup which had formed their only sustenance whilst in captivity. Border patrolling suddenly assumed a more professional demeanour.

The 7th Hussars had arrived in the north of England by way of having spent a few months in north-east Italy before marching north and coming to rest in June 1946 at Soltau, an old German cavalry school between Hannover and Hamburg – the first time the regiment had been on German soil since they charged under the Marquess of Granby at Warburg in 1760. Here they found plenty of time to hone their gunnery skills at the nearby ranges at Munster Laager and joined the 4th Hussars, stationed less than two hours away at Lübeck with a small pack of hounds, in hunting roebuck and wild boar. There was little to do militarily and the soldiers had ample opportunity for all forms of sport. Regimental teams won both the 4 Armoured Brigade athletics tournament and, more importantly, the Cavalry Football Cup. In December 1947 they steamed into Harwich en route for Barnard Castle. Here – decimated by the loss of so many wartime officers and soldiers – their role was to train Yeomanry (TA) cavalry regiments who came to annual camp for about two weeks at a time. This task was, to say the least, often challenging. Officers of the Yeomanry, freed from the seriousness of war and the formal constraints circumscribing the activities of regular regiments, saw their periods of training as one long holiday, punctuated by formidably riotous after-dinner entertainment. The Northumberland Hussars (known to all as the Noodles) partied with such abandon that on one occasion their commanding officer had to be taken to hospital with a broken leg. Curiously, the 7th's commanding officer, Lieutenant Colonel Bill Rankin, also had a leg problem: he had lost one in the war and now sported a wooden substitute. As his second-in-command also had a wooden leg, it was their practice in a high wind to cling to each other for support. In 1947 came the splendid news that Her Majesty the Queen (later to become Queen Elizabeth, The Queen Mother) had been appointed Colonel-in-Chief of the regiment, and a year later the 7th moved to Lüneburg, another Hanseatic city but this time in Lower Saxony not far from Soltau, which had now become a major British training area.

In common with their comrades in our other regiments, the men of the 4th Queen's Own Hussars assumed that once the war was over they would all be going home. This proved to be far from the case, except for those conscripts that had been on active service longest. The regiment as a unit did not arrive in England for two and a half years after the enemy surrendered and even then they were more fortunate than some. By the end of May 1945 they were stationed in the Austrian province of Carinthia near the Yugoslav border, marshalling and caring for a sad polyglot mixture of refugees:

Hungarians, Cossacks, Italians, Russians and Yugoslavs, all fleeing for their lives from those who, for whatever reason, sought murderous revenge. And there were Germans there too, often hard-core Nazis who had found refuge in the mountainous border country awaiting the mirage of a resurgence of the Third Reich. Information on parties of this nature came flowing in to the regimental intelligence officer, and troops were sent off to hunt them down. Over thirty war criminals were apprehended in this way, one of whom, the notorious SS Gruppenführer Glovocnik, bit on a phial of prussic acid when he saw that there was no escape. From Austria the regiment moved to Trieste, where officers and men released from prisoner-of-war camps rejoined, their number including Captain George (Loopy) Kennard who was accompanied by four couple of foxhounds he had scrounged from hunts in England, all of whom escaped twice on the journey, once in Regent's Park and again in Rome, much to the astonishment of both the Italians and the occupying troops. Various moves followed, taking in temporary stops in Italy and Germany (Lübeck) until, in November 1947, the regiment, as had been the case in 1919, was sent to Colchester, where it was reduced to about half-strength. They were to enjoy but nine months of home life before being converted to armoured cars, warned for active service and supplemented by a draft of 400 regular soldiers. They were not to know it, but within three years their close comrades in the desert, the 8th King's Royal Irish Hussars, would also be embarking for war. The two campaigns for which the two regiments were bound, although very different in military character, had two things in common: they were both to be fought in the Far East and both were to be waged against communist attempts to overthrow a lawful government.

On 20 August 1948 the troopship *Dilwera* left Southampton bound for Singapore carrying 35 officers and 817 soldiers of the 4th Hussars led by Lieutenant Colonel George Kidston-Montgomerie, who had commanded four different cavalry regiments during the war and had been described by General Montgomery as being the finest of all armoured regimental commanders. The vast majority of the regiment had plenty of active service experience, although, of course, not in this theatre or in this role.

The enemy was the almost wholly ethnic Chinese Malayan Communist Party (MCP), who had already spent upwards of three years in the jungle engaged in a war against the Japanese invaders during which they were frequently allied with members of Force 136, the Far East branch of the British Special Operations Executive. After 1945 the MCP, led by the terrifyingly

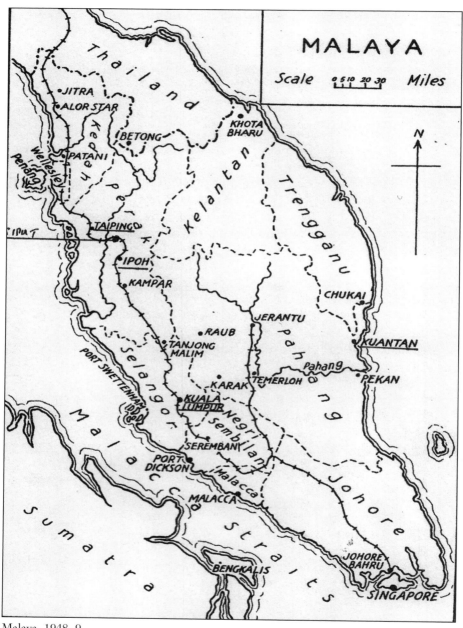

Malaya, 1948–9.

The 4th Hussars in Malaya, 1948–9. Inspecting a food lorry.

efficient and pitiless Chin Peng, who had been awarded the OBE by the British for outstanding leadership in the fight against the Japanese, turned its attention to ridding Malaya of its erstwhile allies and setting up a communist dictatorship, thus provoking the conflict which became known as the Malayan Emergency. After a short stay in a transit camp in Singapore

4th Hussars road patrol resting.

(occupied fourteen years later by a squadron of the Queen's Royal Irish Hussars, and later again by one from the Queen's Own Hussars), the 4th were deployed all over Malaya as the situation demanded – troops were often 100 miles from squadron headquarters and even further from RHQ, which was based towards the north of the country at Ipoh in Perak state. The regiment's primary role was to keep open the roads and major tracks for the free passage of both civilian and military traffic, and to that end squadrons stationed at Raub, Taiping, Kuala Lumpur and Kuantan commanded ever more widely dispersed troops.

As has often been the way when British forces have been deployed abroad for active service, there was not enough appropriate equipment for the regiment – certainly not for one as strong in manpower as the 4th Hussars. There were some reasonably well armed and protected Daimler armoured scout cars known as Dingos, but the bulk of the patrolling vehicles were the American General Motor Company's thinly protected armoured personnel carriers called simply GMCs. Troops were also often carried in open-backed 15cwt trucks. So it was that on 31 December 1948 – barely two months after its arrival in Malaya – 4th Troop, A Squadron, under the command of Lieutenant Michael Questier and accompanied by Second Lieutenant Jon Sutro, a young officer straight out of Sandhurst on his first assignment, set forth from Ipoh to patrol the 20 miles to Sungei Siput and from there to check out two smaller roads servicing rubber plantations. The troop was 19-strong and was carried in two GMCs and one 15cwt truck. Each vehicle mounted a Bren gun and each soldier carried hand grenades and was armed with either a rifle or Sten sub-machine gun. On one of the smaller roads they were ambushed by a force of over seventy communist terrorists (CT) who, it later transpired, had been in position for over two days hoping to engage a softer target – in the shape of infantry packed into 3-ton trucks. During the furious fire-fight that followed, Questier and six of his men, including Corporal Finch the acting troop sergeant, were killed and another nine wounded. On the death of the troop leader, Sutro took charge and skilfully extracted the remainder of the troop including the wounded. Six dead CTs were later found, together with copious amounts of blood from many more. For his conduct that day Sutro was awarded the Military Cross (MC) and Lance Corporal Smith the Distinguished Conduct Medal (DCM). In other actions during the tour four further DCMs and a Military Medal (MM) were awarded.

For the most part, life in Malaya was unexciting, consisting of routine patrolling and occasional mopping-up operations. VIPs had to be escorted, notably Sir Anthony Eden who came bearing warm messages from Churchill; families arrived and were housed; sports were played and there was swimming in the warm sea. A notable casualty occurred in January 1950 when Regimental Sergeant Major Read was killed in an accident. 'Busty' Read had served with the regiment for twenty-five years and had been its Regimental Sergeant Major for eight. Throughout the Second World War he had stood as a rock for the traditions and strength of the 4th Hussars; the regiment and horses were his life. In late 1949 the regiment was ordered to send a squadron to Hong Kong to bolster the military strength in the colony as its regular garrison became depleted by the need to send infantry battalions to the war in Korea. C Squadron, later to be replaced by A Squadron, went first and was stationed on the border with the now communist People's Republic of China where the massive flow of refugees which followed Mao Zedong's civil war victory threatened to overwhelm the colony's remaining security forces. The 4th Hussars left the Far East in the winter of 1951, arriving in England twelve days before Christmas, and were dispersed to Bhurtpore Barracks in Tidworth (RHQ and one squadron), Warminster (one squadron) and one squadron to Castlemartin in Pembrokeshire. Then it was time for some well-earned leave.

The year before the 4th arrived in Tidworth after this period of active service, another of our regiments had left the garrison – also for active service and also in the Far East. The 8th King's Royal Irish Hussars had finished the Second World War in Berlin and were then shifted to a series of successive locations in both Belgium and Germany before alighting at Lingen on the River Ems, north of Münster, from where one squadron was detached to become the first armoured demonstration squadron at the School of Infantry in Warminster, preceding that of the 4th Hussars. In 1948 the regiment was united again in a hutted, former RAF camp at Leicester East airfield where, like the 7th, their role was to train, mentor and otherwise mother a Territorial Army Brigade. The officers enjoyed in the Shires the best hunting they were ever likely to experience (causing not a little unhappiness among those in B Squadron who were stuck in Warminster), while a large number of soldiers made the best of their time by marrying Leicester girls and eventually settling in the area and founding one of the regiment's longest-standing troops of old comrades.

In the spring of 1950 came a move to Mooltan Barracks in Tidworth as a component of the strategic reserve, and it was there in June that they heard the news that the communist North Korean armed forces had crossed the frontier (the 38th Parallel) and invaded democratic South Korea. The United Nations acted with unaccustomed alacrity and, in the fortunate absence of the Soviet Union's delegation, the Security Council passed a unanimous resolution condemning North Korean aggression and called upon member nations to give all possible assistance to the South. On 30 June the first American troops arrived in the country, but by then the small South Korean army (ROK) had been pushed back within a tiny perimeter in the south-east of the country around the city of Pusan.

It would be fair to assume that few 8th Hussars had anything but the remotest idea of where Korea was or indeed what all the fuss was about, but they were soon to learn. They were about to find themselves in the first major war to be fought voluntarily by many nations allied together, not for personal or territorial advantage, but to put a stop to an act of aggression which threatened the only recently hard-won world peace. The regiment, as was generally the case in the Royal Armoured Corps, was short of fully-trained manpower, and there was also the problem that it would need a hefty reinforcement of officers to put it on a war footing. Manpower was provided by the call-up of reservists, many of them old friends who had fought in the Western Desert and in Europe. As for the officers, 8th Hussar reservists returned to the colours but they were not enough to fill all the active service posts, so a call went out to all cavalry and some other regiments. The result exceeded all expectations, and from the flood of volunteers eighteen were attached to the regiment, including two from the 3rd Hussars (one of whom was to die in a prisoner-of-war camp) and three from the 7th, one of whom, John Venner, was to win the Military Cross. One officer came from even further afield: Captain Mike Gorman of the Royal Australian Armoured Corps made his way from Singapore and was to serve with the regiment throughout the campaign. This scale of reinforcement was impressive, but another feature of the deployment was truly unique: the new Centurion tanks with their powerful 20-pounder main armament with which the regiment was to be equipped were still on the secret list – so secret that the commanding officer, Lieutenant Colonel Jumbo Phillips (torn away from his mastership of the Taunton Vale Foxhounds), was warned that none should be allowed to fall into enemy hands, and that should a situation arise where this became unavoidable the tank was to be stripped of its more

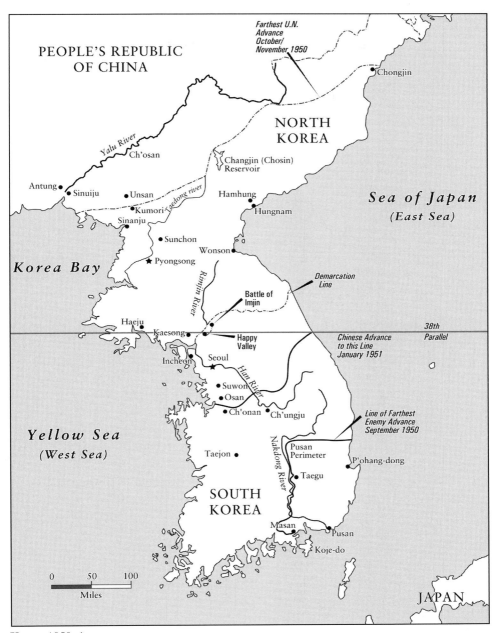

Korea, 1950–1.

sensitive equipment and then destroyed. This formerly unheard of stricture was to have serious tactical consequences.

On 12 October 1950 the regiment sailed from Southampton and a month later was disembarking at Pusan, where it learnt that it was to join 29 Infantry Brigade, one of two brigades provided to the United Nations by the United Kingdom. Its role was to provide armoured support to the brigade's three battalions of infantry, whose names were shortly to become known to the world as the embodiment of British valour: the Gloucestershire Regiment, the Royal Northumberland Fusiliers and the Royal Ulster Rifles. The news was not good. An initial advance by United Nations troops led by the Americans had thrown the North Koreans back across the 38th Parallel and, having taken P'yongyang, the North Korean capital, had reached the Yalu river, the frontier between Korea and China. However, this brought the Chinese into the war, and by the time the 8th Hussars were reunited with their tanks, a full-scale United Nations retreat was underway. First into action to try and stem this tide was A Squadron plus a troop of four tanks from RHQ, who reached P'yongyang by train after seven days of extreme cold and were then ordered further north to support the Ulster Rifles in an unavailing effort to halt the Chinese advance. By this time the rest of the regiment was also on a train heading north but were stopped near Seoul. Meanwhile, 29 Brigade was withdrawing south having left P'yongyang in flames, and it was during this move that one of the tanks became inextricably bogged, holding up the retreat until it could be blown up with the help of bombing by the US Air Force. While the regiment was re-assembling behind the Han River, south of Seoul, the Cromwell tanks of the reconnaissance troop commanded by Captain Donald Astley-Cooper and six more from Royal Artillery observation parties (OPs) had been ordered forward to support the Ulsters. In the battle that followed on 2 and 3 January 1951, the Ulster Rifles with Cooper Force, as it became known, fought a devastatingly costly counter-attack in an effort to restore lost ground in an area called, with black Irish humour, Happy Valley. In this action Astley-Cooper and Lieutenant Alexander were killed and Lieutenant Probyn of the 3rd Hussars taken prisoner; twenty other 8th Hussars were posted either killed or missing. The Ulsters lost over 200 of their number, but the delay on the Chinese advance imposed by Cooper Force and the equally valiant gunners was enough to avoid the probable annihilation of the battalion.

There now came a most curious decision by the British government: all Centurions were to be shipped out of Korea on security grounds. The regiment, less C Squadron, left their tanks on a quayside and were taken to Japan, where they learnt that the order they had just obeyed had been countermanded and they were to return to rejoin their tanks. This 'overcoats off, overcoats on' farce resulted in the bulk of the regiment being separated from their Centurions for five weeks, and no sub-unit of the regiment was able to be back in action until mid-February. Meanwhile, C Squadron had been split: half to support the Gloucesters and half to the Royal Northumberland Fusiliers as the UN slowly took the offensive again.

The 8th, now under the command of Lieutenant Colonel Sir William (Guy) Lowther, who had taken over from Phillips, began to suffer the worst of weather conditions: temperatures were dropping to −27°C, a new low, and the tanks were difficult to maintain – indeed, even touching metal with bare hands caused painful injuries. Overnight, tanks had to be parked on straw to prevent their tracks becoming frozen to the ground, engines had to be started every thirty minutes and each gear engaged in turn to prevent

C Squadron 8th Hussars and the Gloucesters move up before the attack on Hill 327, Korea, February 1951.

B Squadron 8th Hussars carrying men of the Royal Northumberland Fusiliers over the Imjin River, Korea, April 1951.

them freezing in place. A number of relatively small-scale actions followed as the Allied advance reached the Imjin River and patrolled beyond it, the Centurions often carrying whole platoons of infantry – at one stage the commanding officer counted fifty-one infantrymen clinging precariously to his own tank.

In the early morning of 22 April, as B Squadron was handing over its sector on high ground overlooking the Imjin River to C Squadron, the enemy counter-attack began. Immediately, the Ulsters, Gloucesters, Fusiliers and a Belgian battalion which had also performed heroically in earlier battles were engaged by successive waves of Chinese infantry, careless, it appeared, of the appalling casualties inflicted upon them. The Centurions, fighting in terrain for which they were never designed, nevertheless took extravagant toll of the enemy; troops were committed to tasks which entailed supreme sacrifice but which, when aggregated, saved the existence of a whole brigade. The Gloucesters became surrounded and elements of C Squadron, together with a Filipino battalion, tried unsuccessfully to clear the hills behind them. On the 25th the brigade withdrew, C Squadron's task being to impose enough delay to allow the infantry to reach the comparative safety of the main supply route south. Nothing further could be done, however, for the doomed Gloucesters, from whose positions only four officers and thirty men escaped. The last shot in the Battle of the Imjin, as it became known, was fired by Major Henry Huth, C Squadron's leader, who was awarded the Distinguished Service Order for his leadership, while three MCs, (including that to John Venner, who was later to command the Queen's Own Hussars), two MMs and two Mentions in Despatches went to members of the regiment.

The summer of 1951 passed relatively quietly in a new defensive area on the Kimpo peninsula on the Han River west of Seoul as the squadrons again deployed to support infantry formations while some individual officers trained as light aircraft observers – one of them, Lieutenant Randle Cooke, being shot down and taken prisoner. With autumn came incessant rain as the regiment, now under direct command of the 1st Commonwealth Division, probed forward in support of their battalions. Rumours that enemy tanks

C Squadron 8th Hussars Orders Group. Major Henry Huth, his gunner, two Belgian officers and Captain Hartwright, Korea, 1951.

had been sighted caused excitement amounting almost to a frenzy: at last, it was assumed, the Centurions would be able to engage armour. Amongst the tank commanders high excitement and wishful thinking abounded in equal measure: bushes, shadows and ox-carts were all identified as Soviet T34 tanks, until the rain-induced mists cleared and disappointment followed. Battle proper was joined again in September and early October as the Division attacked the key hill feature Kowang San with both A and B Squadrons in support of British battalions and 3rd Battalion The Royal Australian Regiment. In the next few weeks the regiment fought a number of battles east of the Imjin and north of the 38th Parallel, during which they were indeed to find armoured targets in the shape of personnel carriers and self-propelled guns, whose flashes as they fired were promptly engaged by the Centurions, bringing about a significant silence from the enemy. On 5 November Lieutenant Christopher Troughton, commanding 3rd Troop of B Squadron, reduced to himself and one other tank and under intense artillery, mortar and small-arms fire, broke up successive Chinese assaults while covering successfully the withdrawal of elements of the 1st Battalion The Royal Leicestershire Regiment, managing the while to pick up their casualties as well as wounded members of his own troop before withdrawing as darkness fell. For this action he was awarded the Military Cross; Troughton was, twenty years later, to command the Queen's Royal Irish Hussars.

Then thankfully it was all over. On 4 December Guy Lowther entered the officers' mess of 3rd Battalion The Royal Australian Regiment and drove a lance into the floor, declaring that the two regiments should henceforth be affiliated – and so they were from that moment on. Two days later, at midday, the flag at RHQ was lowered and that of the 5th Royal Inniskilling Dragoon Guards raised in its place. That evening, the 8th Hussars gathered together as one for virtually the first time since landing in Korea thirteen months before. Since the first broken Centurion had been destroyed, twenty-six others had been hit or otherwise disabled and every one had been recovered – sometimes after as long as five weeks, during which the Chinese had swarmed all over them but stolen nothing except the pin-ups! They had failed to identify the secret equipment which had so worried the Ministry of Defence. Left behind on the hills of Korea were the dead: four officers and thirteen soldiers in combat and Lieutenant Probyn who died in captivity; it was time for the rest to go home. Having enjoyed six weeks leave they reassembled in Lüneburg, one of many armoured regiments in Germany, but the only one that had been to war in the Centurion tank.

The year 1950 saw the 3rd Hussars still in Lübeck but awash with rumours. A move back to the United Kingdom was the odds-on favourite among those who gossiped in the officers' mess and the NAAFI, but this, for those who relished the thought of going home, proved to be over-optimistic. However, for those who had a taste for peacetime soldiering in Germany the news that the much discussed destination was to be Bielefeld in North-Rhine Westphalia (as of course was forecast accurately by the warrant officers' and sergeants' mess!) came as a relief. A half-squadron of tanks was, however, to be detached and sent to join the garrison in Berlin – the first British armour to be stationed there. Commanded by Captain Tim Fisher, this happy band of warriors became known as 'Fish Force' and was the forerunner of the many cavalry squadrons to be stationed in the city over the next forty years, a posting invariably seen as plum. Fish Force's journey to Berlin was by train, which involved passage through the Soviet Zone. Inevitably, it was halted at the Russian checkpoint and Fisher was questioned by a young officer who, the 3rd Hussar noted with interest, was holding the transit papers upside down. The conversation was conducted in German.

'I see', said the Russian, 'that you have come from Bielefeld.'

'Yes', said Fisher.

'Is that in England?'

'Mmm', the tactful Fisher mumbled.

'In that case, no further clearance is required.'

Back in prosaic Bielefeld at the foot of the Teutoburger Wald, the thickly forested ridge of hills which were the scene of the victory of an alliance of Germanic tribes over three legions of the Roman Empire in 9 BC, life was a round of exercises designed to determine and then practise the most effective way of countering a Soviet invasion, should that ever come about. One such manoeuvre brought under command a Norwegian bicycle company whose chief contribution to the newly-formed North Atlantic Treaty Organisation (NATO) alliance was to hold an uproarious party in a German pub at the conclusion of the exercise – a party in which the tank crewmen of the 3rd participated with enthusiasm. The arrival of the British military police coincided with smoke issuing forth from the doors and windows of the hostelry, and the red-caps, fully occupied with restoring law and some semblance of order, were surprised to find that, on returning to their vehicles, all their tyres had been let down.

Despite the busy training regime there was still ample time for sporting activity, with equestrianism still prominent, including an inter-squadron all-ranks mounted wrestling competition noted chiefly for the number of casualties seen by the regimental medical officer, and the outstanding performance of the polo team which won the British Army of the Rhine (BAOR) inter-regimental tournament in 1951, 1952 and 1953. A dismounted contingent of 3rd Hussars marched in the Queen's coronation procession in June 1953, and to further mark the occasion for the regiment it was announced that Her Royal Highness Princess Margaret, the newly crowned monarch's sister, had been appointed its Colonel-in-Chief.

The rather humdrum life of the 7th Hussars in Lüneburg, enlivened partially by a craze for regimental greyhound racing, followed a pattern (minus the Norwegian cyclists) which largely mirrored that of their sister regiment in Bielefeld. Two subalterns, Sam Scott and Ian Hart, thirsting for adventure, joined John Venner in volunteering for service with the 8th in Korea, and in their absence the regiment moved to Fallingbostel (known to generations of cavalry officers as 'EffingB') where they were to remain for three years engaged, like everybody else in BAOR, in an endless cycle of training against the day when the unthinkable might happen. As the result of an initiative by Colonel Bill Rankin, now the military attaché in Poland, the band went to play in Warsaw and were rewarded by being presented with personal copies of a rather less than riveting book, *The Industrial Progress and Six-Year Plan for Warsaw*, which the communist authorities no doubt presumed would become required reading for every musician. This, not surprisingly, turned out not to be the case, and the band was also disappointed to find that they were so closely policed that meeting any of the regiment's Polish friends from Italy proved almost impossible, although the *Maid of Warsaw* badge on their uniforms was widely admired.

In 1952 a young captain, Patrick Howard-Dobson, passed the entrance examination for the Army Staff College at Camberley – not then attempted by many cavalry officers – and later wrote for the regimental journal some words of advice for any 7th Hussar inclined to follow suit. They included the following:

> *You will meet here all sorts of conditions of men, including foreigners like the Americans. They are delightful and very clever but their terminology is*

sometimes confusing. When they say hunting they mean shooting, and when they say shooting they mean craps. So far I have said nothing about work. There is a certain amount to be done, but as a cavalryman you are not expected to do any of it. If you should come up against one of the Directing Staff who doesn't understand this, you can always get a gunner or sapper to do it for you.

It is clear that this young officer did not follow his own advice: he was in due time to become a four-star general, a member of the Army Board and Honorary Colonel of the Queen's Own Hussars. In 1953, when a small contingent marched in the coronation procession, came the exciting news that the regiment accompanied by its families was to undertake a three-year tour of Hong Kong, the first time that a complete armoured regiment was to be deployed to the colony, although the 4th Hussars and the 16th/5th Lancers had both provided squadrons there at various periods after the war.

In March 1952, a few months after the 4th Hussars returned to Tidworth and to their two squadron outstations at Warminster and Castlemartin, the Regimental Association – the old comrades and charitable arm of the regimental family – arranged a welcome-home dinner for them at the Royal Festival Hall at which 270 retired all-ranks and 250 of the serving regiment sat down. Such a large gathering had not been attempted before and despite its huge success has never been repeated – logistically and financially it has been found more practical to invite old comrades to visit the regiment *in situ*, whether it be in the United Kingdom or in Germany, occasions looked forward to by all our regiments. Just over a year later, another unique event followed when Captain Peter Adeley and seven soldiers provided a ceremonial full-dress mounted escort for the Colonel of the Regiment and Mrs Churchill as they rode in a carriage in the coronation procession. By then the regiment had left England for Hohne in Germany, a barracks adjacent to Lüneburg Heath and close to the site of the notorious Bergen-Belsen concentration camp. The accommodation and tank hangars were fairly typical of all those in BAOR, but the officers had landed a jewel of a mess in Schloss Bredebeck, a former manor house dating from the beginning of the twentieth century. Coronation year had also proved particularly memorable for the 8th Hussars as it marked the appointment of His Royal Highness The Prince Philip, Duke of Edinburgh as Colonel-in-Chief. Three of our four regiments now boasted a royal Colonel-in-Chief , while the 4th Hussars continued to bask in the glory of being headed, as Colonel, by the man who had become known as 'The Greatest Hussar of Them All'.

Royal visits now became red-letter days in regimental calendars, and although the Queen Mother had not yet had an opportunity to visit the 7th, Prince Philip was quickly off the mark, flying to Lüneburg in September to inspect his regiment. After drinks in the warrant officers' and sergeants' mess and lunch with the officers he rose to his feet. The regiment, he said, was fortunate, not so much that they now had a naval officer on their books as well as an airman (Air Chief Marshal Sir John Baldwin, a former 8th Hussar, was Honorary Colonel) but also, he added in a reference to his wife, his mother-in-law and his sister-in-law, who between them were Colonels-in-Chief of a number of cavalry regiments, because no officer would be required to dance with this Colonel-in-Chief. Princess Margaret's first visit to the 3rd took place at the regiment's new home at Iserlohn, south of Münster, the following July, but sadly her programme did not include an opportunity to dance. The year 1954 marked the centenary of the charge at Balaklava, an event commemorated by both the 4th and the 8th – the 4th having invited a large party of old comrades to join them – but the highlight of this special anniversary was the grand Light Brigade Ball at the Hyde Park Hotel in London in November, attended by the Queen, the Duke of Edinburgh and Queen Elizabeth, the Queen Mother. All five regiments that had charged at Balaklava were represented and the company amounted to over 650 – almost the same number that had set off down Tennyson's 'valley of death' a hundred years earlier – many of the men wearing the ceremonial full-dress of the Crimean period.

In 1955 the 4th Hussars were issued with five 63-ton Conqueror tanks armed with a 120mm main armament gun and featuring a revolutionary contra-rotating commander's cupola and range finder, the first to be issued to the Army. The Conqueror belied its weight and size by performing as well across country as the Centurion but remained in service for only slightly more than a decade, before both it and the Centurion were replaced by the Chieftain. The regiment's first Conqueror troop was commanded by its most diminutive troop leader, irresistibly reminding his fellow subalterns of a small pea perched on top of an extremely large pod. All four regiments were now settled into life in BAOR, with all ranks inevitably speculating where the Ministry of Defence might send them next – for this was the beginning of the system of roulement, whereby regiments and battalions of armour, artillery and infantry were regularly moved from station to station, often changing roles to add variety to their personal lives and a wider expertise to their military skills. The 3rd came close to being shaken out of this routine by being warned for active service – 'immediate movement' was how the military chain of command phrased it – in November 1956 during the so-called Suez Crisis, as British, French and Israeli troops invaded Egypt to try (unsuccessfully) to reverse the Egyptian takeover of the Suez Canal. After seventy-two hours of frantic preparation the regiment was disappointed to be stood down. The posting of the 7th Hussars to Hong Kong, however, had gone ahead as planned – an early example of what became known as arms plotting.

Curiously, the regiment travelled to the Far East in two troopships, the *Dilwera* and the *Cheshire*, the former sailing from Southampton and the latter from Liverpool in August 1954. The voyage was uneventful until Port Said, where a snook was noisily cocked at General Naguib, who had taken power as president of Egypt having deposed the British puppet King Farouk, by the regimental band on the *Dilwera* repeatedly playing Rule Britannia at top volume.

The voyage took four weeks, but there was some disappointment on arrival in Hong Kong because the barracks was not, as had been fondly imagined by some, close to the flesh-pots, but in Sek Kong in the New Territories, some 20 miles north of the city of Kowloon. The 7th were equipped with Centurions, the first British tanks to reach Hong Kong, and the camp was well built and spacious while, rather as in India before the war, each soldier's barrack-room had a (Chinese) servant to do the cleaning. The training areas were restricted by the paddy-fields on the low ground and the mountainous terrain which, although suiting the Royal Artillery regiments in the colony, were of limited use for tanks. Sport flourished, and there were ample opportunities to travel into Kowloon or take the Star Ferry from there to Victoria on Hong Kong Island. Great fun was to be had in the bars, night-clubs and hotels, and after one particularly inebriated and rowdy crossing of the harbour, a party of young officers on the way back to barracks raided the engine room of a ferry and subsequently behaved so boisterously in a walla-walla boat (water taxi) that they were arrested and spent the night in a far from salubrious jail. The court summons which followed was drafted inaccurately – a mistake spotted by a legally minded captain in the regiment – and the party got away with the charges, but did not escape the wrath of the commanding officer, who considered that, although they had been behaving badly badly as opposed to behaving badly well, their worst crime was to get caught. On another occasion a subaltern mistook a man in a white monkey jacket and black tie at the Royal Hong Kong Yacht Club for a waiter.

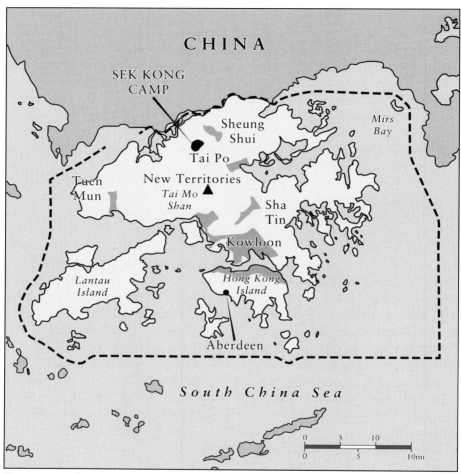

Hong Kong when a British Crown Colony.

Imperiously ordering a gin and tonic, he quickly discovered that he had been addressing His Excellency the Governor.

The one period of military excitement in the Colony occurred in 1956 during the celebrations on 10 October (the so called double-tenth anniversary of the revolution in China which resulted in the country becoming a republic in 1911) when there were violent clashes between communists and nationalists in Kowloon. As luck would have it, all three sabre squadrons were out on manoeuvres, so an 'aid to the civil power' party had to be quickly cobbled together from cooks, clerks, mechanics and storemen and despatched in a variety of wheeled vehicles to Kowloon where, in support of the police, order was restored without a shot being fired. A by-product of this operational turnout was the timely assistance of a Dingo crew to a Chinese woman in labour; before a hospital could be reached she had given birth in the commander's seat. The voyage home, beginning in June 1957, was a lengthy affair, as by that time the Suez Canal had been closed by General Naguib's successor and the troopship *Nevasa* had to sail round the Cape of Good Hope, thereby losing her captain a substantial bet, struck by the same band of unruly young officers involved in the ferry incident, that he would run out of Kümmel, despite the fact that he had doubled his stock of this favourite 7th Hussar drink. One officer who hitherto had contributed substantially to lowering the supplies had to be left behind in Colombo, the capital of Ceylon, when he was arrested for stealing the Soviet ambassador's flag from the latter's car parked outside the Mount Lavinia Hotel, having first got the driver drunk. After a period under civilian and then military arrest he was flown home by the Royal Air Force.

In 1957, as rumours of cuts in the military establishment became commonplace, regimental Colonels were informed that the following year would see the amalgamation of the 3rd and 7th Hussars and of the 4th and 8th. This was not welcomed by anyone serving in those regiments and received badly by their old comrades. The news hit the 3rd in March 1958 as they were preparing for another visit by Princess Margaret. The commanding officer, Lieutenant Colonel Derek Wormald, recognized that this was to be both the Colonel-in-Chief's (and his own) swansong. He summoned his adjutant.

'We must put on a superlative show. We will have a mounted parade.'

'But Colonel, we only have about thirty horses and most of those are polo ponies.'

'Not horses, you fool. Tanks.'

There was a pause, made pregnant by the obvious anxiety of the adjutant.

'But Colonel, we don't have any tanks on the road.'

It hardly needs saying that by the time of the visit this situation had changed radically and the parade was a splendidly faultless affair. The 3rd's prospective partners at Tidworth were also preparing for a visit from their Colonel-in-Chief as Lieutenant Colonel Tim Llewellen Palmer exchanged reassuring cables with Derek Wormald to say that the forthcoming marriage would be a happy one. At the 4th Hussars' old comrades Balaclava dinner in London Lieutenant Colonel Sir George (Loopy) Kennard urged everyone to accept the change: '*We have fought together at Balaklava and the Western Desert; if amalgamate we must then who could be better partners than our old friends the 8th?*' Lieutenant Colonel Henry Huth of the 8th promised that his regiment would take the greatest pains to make the amalgamation '*a rip-roaring success*'. Loopy Kennard was, despite his optimism, so worried about the effect of compulsory redundancy on some of his officers and most loyal non-commissioned officers that he placed an advertisement in *The Times* in which he personally guaranteed satisfaction to future employers. He finished by promising that should this not be forthcoming, '*three months pay will be returned in full*'. There was a remarkable response by way of job offers – and no salary compensation was ever demanded. And in that generous spirit the autumn of 1958 saw the passing into history of the 3rd The King's Own Hussars and the 4th Queen's Own Hussars after 273 years service to their country and its successive sovereigns. The 7th Queen's Own Hussars and the 8th King's Royal Irish Hussars, respectively five and eight years younger, could boast of equally distinguished service to the Crown, and the four regiments had fought, often alongside each other, in practically all the conflicts in which their country had been involved since 1685, and in so doing had between them won 165 battle honours.

CHAPTER SIX

THE PARENT REGIMENTS

If you haven't a smile for your parents, then neither will a god invite you to dinner nor a goddess to bed. (Virgil)

The amalgamation ceremony of the 3rd and 7th Hussars was a low key affair, partly because both regiments had enjoyed visits by their respective Colonels-in-Chief relatively recently. Queen Elizabeth, The Queen Mother, had gone to Candahar Barracks in Tidworth on 24 October 1957 and in her address to the assembled 7th Hussars she confidently predicted the future:

> *I feel certain that from the amalgamation will emerge one regiment, new in name but seasoned in character, embodying the great traditions of both.*

When at the conclusion of that day the regiment marched past Her Majesty and off parade it was for the last time, and there were few of those present who did not feel a profound sadness. There was, however, still a year's work in prospect. Exercises on Salisbury Plain, including handing over their tanks to be driven by visiting officers of the Joint Services Staff College, provided some entertainment, as a senior Malaysian policeman, a colonel of the US Marines, a Nigerian diplomat, a submariner and an RAF bomber pilot, among others, wrestled with the unfamiliar controls of the Centurion and the rough going of the training area. But it was sport which provided a fitting climax to the regiment's history: the football team won the United Kingdom division of the Cavalry Cup (they were beaten in the grand final by the 4th Hussars, who had won the competition in Germany), and the polo team won the inter-regimental tournament, a seventh victory in this event, more than any other non-amalgamated unit.

The 3rd spent their last summer in Germany preparing their equipment for handover to the Royal Scots Greys, before embarking by train and then boat from the Hook of Holland. The captain of the ferry, after displaying a certain reluctance, was persuaded to fly the regimental flag from the mast-head during the night crossing to Harwich. There, at disembarkation, they were met by their commanding officer and the commanding officer of the

Inspection of the 7th Hussars by HM Queen Elizabeth, the Queen Mother, Colonel-in-Chief, 24 October 1957. She is accompanied by the Commanding Officer, Lieutenant Colonel C.T. Llewellyn Palmer MC.

7th as the band played the regimental slow march. On 7 November, at a private ceremonial parade in Tidworth, the flags of both regiments were lowered for the last time. The significance of the moment was marked in the editorial of the first journal of the Queen's Own Hussars:

> *The ceremony was a moving one but its significance was only relative, as when the flag of the Queen's Own Hussars was broken it bore proudly the White Horse of Hanover of the 3rd Hussars and the cypher of the 7th which, only a few seconds before, had seemingly disappeared for ever. The true meaning of this event was simply that of uniting the past and showing the path for the future.*

The parade at which the 4th and 8th Hussars appeared for the last time, held at Hohne on 24 October – the eve of the 104th anniversary of the Charge of the Light Cavalry Brigade at Balaklava – was a more formal and public affair. In front of grandstands packed with families, old comrades, senior military officers and German guests, and on a parade square guarded at each corner by a Conqueror tank, the two regiments marched on to the music of the combined bands. The commanding officers, seconds-in-command and adjutants were mounted, and after a review by their respective Honorary Colonels and a final *Last Post*, the 4th and the 8th Hussars marched off parade for the final time to the melancholy strains of their slow marches. Then came the arrival of Prince Philip, already appointed Colonel-in-Chief of the new regiment and, to *The Entry of the Gladiators*, on marched rank after rank of the Queen's Royal Irish Hussars – the same men who had marched off but now wearing the new cap-badge. *Reveille* was sounded, the new flag was broken and the Irish Hussars for the first time advanced in review order and delivered a Royal Salute to His Royal Highness. To mark this historic occasion royal approval had been granted for the issue of a guidon – the light cavalry equivalent of the line infantry's colours – carrying, as directed by the Ministry of Defence, just forty of the new regiment's accumulated battle honours. The consecration service was conducted at the piled drums of the amalgamated band, after which the Colonel-in-Chief formally presented the guidon to the regiment, received by Squadron Sergeant Major Fred Rowan MM.

In his address, Prince Philip commended the way in which the regiments had prepared for amalgamation and drew attention to their common past:

From the word 'Go' both regiments set out to get to know one another: all ranks attended each other's sporting and social events and during this year's training period composite troops were formed and trained as one. The only

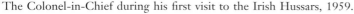

The Colonel-in-Chief during his first visit to the Irish Hussars, 1959.

drawback that I can see is that new members will have to learn twice as much history. They will find three items of special interest: the 4th and the 8th charged together at Balaklava and then in the last war they briefly became one at the Battle of Alam Halfa. And in 1895 the Sergeants Mess of the 8th gave their opposite numbers in the 4th Hussars a silver shield. Strange as it may seem, the badge below the inscription on this shield is, to all intents and purposes, that of the Queen's Royal Irish Hussars.

The Regiment, under its first commanding officer, Lieutenant Colonel George Butler DSO, MC (late of the 8th Hussars), then marched past its Colonel-in-Chief and off parade. It was not the end but a bright beginning.

A month after their own amalgamation ceremony the Queen's Own Hussars had a new commanding officer in the person of Lieutenant Colonel Hugh Davies MC, and it was he who was responsible for the parade on 20 March 1959 when the regiment received its guidon from Her Majesty the Colonel-in-Chief, who on this most auspicious occasion was accompanied by her daughter, Princess Margaret – an acknowledgement of the latter's popularity as Colonel-in-Chief of the 3rd. The day's programme was ambitious – not only was there a parade on foot and the guidon ceremony, but also a mounted review as Her Majesty drove past her regiment in their tanks. This was a great and nostalgic day for the old comrades, whose presence was greeted with particular pleasure by the Colonel-in-Chief as she went to talk to them on their own section of the parade ground. During her speech to the assembled company Queen Elizabeth drew attention to the history of guidons:

The guidon which I have presented to you marks the revival of a tradition which lapsed more than a hundred years ago for, since the Napoleonic wars, neither the 3rd nor the 7th have carried one. It is a symbol of chivalry and an emblem of loyalty; of loyalty to your Queen, to your country and to your regiment, and I know you will carry it with honour and with pride. I therefore entrust it into your safe-keeping, confident that you will guard it with courage and devotion, and that under it you will add lustre to the name of the regiment.

When their neighbours in Tidworth, the 10th Hussars, left for Germany that year, the Queen's Own Hussars became the only armoured regiment stationed in the United Kingdom, and as such, the military pressures, mainly in the form of teaching infantry formations the basics of infantry/tank co-operation, were great. Hardly a day went by when they were not manoeuvring in troops or squadrons on the vast expanses of Salisbury Plain, patiently tutoring their infantry friends, many of whom had never seen a tank. And there was also a summer's Territorial Army Camp to run at Tilshead (with the usual attendant high jinks) and annual firing at Castle-martin to be fitted in – the regiment's tanks travelling to Pembrokeshire by sea. But there was still time for fun and games: finishing as runners-up in both the Cavalry Cup football and in the Inter-Regimental polo tournament being the highlights. Equestrian sports still figured largely within the regi-ment: show-jumping, eventing, hunter-trials, point-to-points and steeple-chasing all saw Queen's Own Hussar teams or individuals taking part, while Regimental Sergeant Major Hinds led a modern pentathlon squad in the Army championships. Perhaps the outstanding equine success was Lieutenant Michael Meredith's win in the Grand Military Steeplechase at Sandown Park on his own *Cockshot* and in the presence of the Colonel-in-Chief. The regiment also learned to its delight that the City of Birmingham had adopted it as 'its regiment': recruiting henceforth would be concen-trated in the Midlands – particularly fitting as its affiliated Territorial Army unit was the Queen's Own Warwickshire and Worcestershire Yeomanry. Towards the end of that first full year of its existence the regiment learnt that it was to deploy a squadron to the Middle East in 1960.

In February, C Squadron, commanded by Major Robin Carnegie, and enhanced handsomely by an administrative element amounting in total to about a third of the regimental strength, embarked at Southampton on the troopship *Nevasa* for Aden, a British colony perched on the Arabian pen-insula at the southern end of the Red Sea.

C Squadron QOH unloading tanks in Aden, 1960.

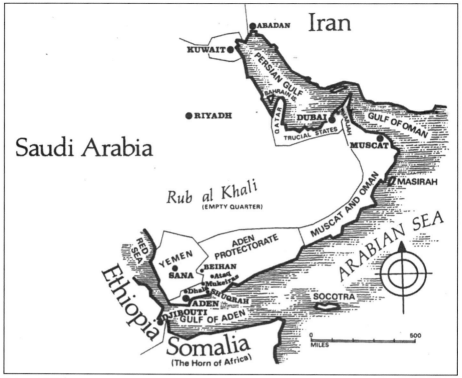

Aden, 1957.

Once Aden had been a coaling station, vital for British ships sailing to and from India, but since that country's independence the port's importance had much diminished, and the presence of troops was largely justified by the perceived need to discourage the virulent form of Arab nationalism preached by Egypt's president, Gamal Abdel Nasser, who four years earlier had taken control of the Suez Canal. The squadron's tanks had travelled separately, and once they were unloaded by landing craft – not without some difficulty ('*We never had this much trouble in the war*', said one veteran) – the squadron settled into a camp at Bir Fuqum, a barracks hastily renamed Falaise by an embarrassed Ministry of Defence official already anticipating political correctness. From there they trained, carried out amphibious exercises with the Royal Navy, provided an enemy force for units of 24 Infantry Brigade flown in from Kenya on a reinforcement exercise and, most importantly (and a blessed relief from the hot and humid climate of Aden itself), patrolled out and into the highlands of the tribal areas in the interior. A particularly popular destination was the village of Shuqra, reputedly the site of the oldest brothel in Arabia. Meanwhile, back on Salisbury Plain the rest of the regiment prepared for a move in the summer to Münster, where they were to join 6 Infantry Brigade.

The formation of the Queen's Royal Irish Hussars saw many old customs reaffirmed and others instituted. Notable among the former were the dark green brow-ribbon worn on the beret of all ranks and the 8th Hussar custom whereby the badge of rank for lance corporals was two stripes (as opposed to the one worn by the rest of the Army) while the two stripes of full corporals were surmounted by a harp. Other 8th Hussar customs adopted by the new regiment were the green and gold tent-hat of the officers and the practice of celebrating St Patrick's Day – attended that first year by Lord Wakehurst, the Governor of Northern Ireland. A further innovation, instigated by the Colonel-in-Chief, was the creation of an annual inter-squadron Duke of Edinburgh's Competition, encompassing a variety of military and sporting contests, to determine which would become the Duke of Edinburgh's Squadron for the following year and have the right to wear Prince Philip's cypher on the right sleeve of the No. 2 Dress uniform The regiment's role was that of an armoured regiment in 7 Armoured Brigade, and as such it once again joined the military round of manoeuvres and other training which made up the BAOR annual cycle. Football was, as always, the main sporting activity, while the officers were equally divided between the horse-men (fourteen races were won on German race courses) and the 'shooting swine' – the game book for 1959 recording, among the duck, wild boar, deer, hares and 100 brace of partridges, a German *forstmeister* (a sort of superior gamekeeper) who was, however, the entry made clear, only lightly winged.

In April 1960, the regiment, like the Queen's Own Hussars, also found itself providing a detached squadron, in this case to Castlemartin for six months to oversee the annual firing of TA regiments, including the North Irish Horse, to which the Irish Hussars were now formally affiliated. In the autumn the Colonel-in-Chief came to Hohne to see the remainder of the regiment in the field and startled everyone on the gunnery ranges by hitting the target every time. He also found time to visit Major Ken Bidie and the men of C (Duke of Edinburgh's Squadron) in Pembrokeshire. To complete a trio of visits that year, His Royal Highness attended the old comrades dinner in London at which Sir Winston Churchill (still the Colonel of the Regiment) was also present – the last time that he was able to attend a regimental occasion. As the year closed, the news broke that the Irish Hussars were to convert to an armoured reconnaissance role and prepare for a year's tour in Aden, followed by two years in the Far East.

For those who had served in the 3rd Hussars, Münster was familiar territory, as indeed was the seemingly immutable BAOR training cycle which
featured, as well as annual live-firing, individual, troop and squadron training early in the year and some sort of large formation exercise in the autumn
incorporating manoeuvres over extensive tracts of German farmland. The
Queen's Own Hussars became one again with the return of C Squadron
from Aden in February 1961 and later in the year were able to exercise at
Vogelsang, a Belgian Army training area within Germany which had very
different terrain from that at Soltau. The married quarters proved satisfactory, which was perhaps just as well since the children in regimental families
now outnumbered the soldiers. The regiment made an immediate impact
on the sporting scene, winning the German section of the Cavalry Cup and
the polo inter-regimental tournament. Both teams were beaten narrowly in
the grand finals in England. A more domestic sporting event took place in
November during the annual celebrations marking the anniversary of the
battle of El Alamein – a tradition now firmly entrenched in the new regimental calendar. A traditional feature of the day's activities, once the more
formal parades had taken place, was a football match between the officers'
and the sergeants' messes. Always played in fancy dress and a combative
spirit sometimes amounting to open warfare, the match nevertheless usually
saw some semblance of order and an approximate adherence to the rules.
Not this year: the appearance of a third team, made up of wives also wearing
a range of considerably more fetching fancy dress, threw the whole proceedings into chaos – a spectacle much enjoyed by families and junior ranks
alike.

In the summer of 1962 came a move to Hobart Barracks in Detmold, a
town they would come to know well over the years. The regiment – still in
an armoured (tank) role – now became part of 20 Armoured Brigade, one of
two brigades which went to make up the 4th Armoured Division. Hobart
Barracks was not well endowed with married quarters, so many families had
to live in German houses known as 'hirings' – often an inconvenience. By
this time a number of regimental occasions had become fixed so that new
traditions were established. In addition to El Alamein Day, the Lord Mayor
of Birmingham visited annually to cement relations between the city and the
regiment, and football matches were played, home and away, between
QOH and the Birmingham (later West Midlands) police. Perhaps the most
impressive and unusual enhancement of regimental life was the establishment of a museum within regimental lines thanks to the efforts of the long-

Trooper Bullock QOH on manoeuvres in Germany with the rest of his family, 1963.

serving Quartermaster, Major Blackshaw, known to everyone as 'Blackie'. This became an important port of call for all distinguished visitors – especially senior officers on tours of inspection who could, it was found, be happily diverted from delving into the furthest (and not always the most salubrious) corners of regimental life by a tour of the museum conducted by Blackie, its designated curator. Sport continued to play an important role in regimental life, and for non-sportsmen there was also the attractive alternative of adventurous training in sometimes quite challenging environments. One young officer, deciding in 1963 that the Baltic coast of north Germany would provide some interesting opportunities, chose a location by throwing a dart at a map. His aim was not good as the missile landed on the Danish island of Anholt, but gathering his party together, he set off by road and ferry. It was only after landing, when the soldiers found themselves surrounded by naked men and women, that he discovered that Anholt was a naturist reserve; never can an adventure training expedition have provided greater enjoyment. More routine celebrations followed that year when the regimental polo team distinguished itself by not only winning the inter-regimental in Germany, but going on to take the United Services trophy played in Tidworth between the winners in BAOR and the winner of the competition between regiments stationed in the United Kingdom.

In March 1961, the Irish Hussars trained as an armoured regiment for what was to prove the last time for nine years. In June the regiment staged at Tidworth before the deployment to the Middle East planned for the autumn, but within a month a party of over fifty flew to Aden to reinforce the regiment there who had been required to send a squadron to Kuwait to counter threats of an Iraqi invasion. However, the tension eased and Lieutenant Philip de Clermont and his men were returned to Tidworth. In Northern Ireland the bond between the regiment and the North Irish Horse was reinforced by the presentation by the latter of a number of silver-mounted blackthorns which were henceforth carried by the regimental sergeant major, the squadron sergeant majors and the provost sergeant. On Balaklava Day the regiment, under the command of Lieutenant Colonel Tim Pierson, sailed from Southampton on the troopship *Oxfordshire* to begin their new adventure.

The subsequent deployment saw one armoured car squadron responsible for internal security in Aden itself (where the married families lived), RHQ, Headquarter Squadron and one armoured car squadron in Little Aden in the appropriately named Balaklava Camp, responsible for giving support to the Aden Federal Army outposts on the Yemen border; the third squadron was over 1,000 miles away at Sharjah, a small emirate on the Persian Gulf, in support of the local but British-officered regiment, the Trucial Oman Scouts, where going out on patrol often meant trips of ten days covering 1,500 miles, mounted on occasion not in their armoured cars but on camels. From time to time the squadrons changed roles and it was all pretty exciting

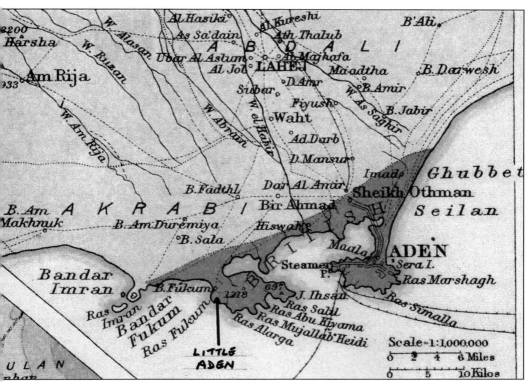

South Arabia, 1961.

stuff, being a completely new experience for most. Also new was the formation of 16 (QRIH) Flight Army Air Corps equipped with Auster and Beaver fixed-wing aircraft commanded by Captain Bryan Wright, the first such manifestation of the MOD's decision to give armoured reconnaissance regiments their own flight, manned and flown by Irish Hussars and maintained by a Royal Electrical and Mechanical Engineers (REME) detachment, also a part of the regiment.

The business of having a detached squadron is not popular with either commanding officers or regimental sergeant majors. RSM Hughie Burroughs, a Korean veteran and hugely admired by all ranks, did his considerable, but often frustrated, best to maintain standards in turnout and foot-drill. St Patrick's Day 1961 offered him a rare opportunity and he determined to produce as good a show as possible with the troops available to him. The drill at rehearsal fell far short of his requirements, causing him to inform the assembled ranks that they would stay there until either he was satisfied or there was a thunderstorm. In this he was on pretty safe ground – he knew that the rainfall in Aden in March averaged a negligible 2mm. No sooner had he delivered this threat, however, than the heavens opened and Balaklava camp was drenched in the heaviest downpour on record. The

Captain Bryan Wright, first commander of 16 Recce Flight QRIH, Aden, 1961.

regiment cheered as it ran for cover. Not on that parade or indeed in Aden at all – but left in England attached to a TA Headquarters at Shorncliffe, as a result of an inexplicable decision by 'higher authority' – was the band. Always noted for its wealth of sportsmen, it made the most of its temporary exile, distinguishing itself (with the addition of two officers from the Head-quarters) by winning the Army Hockey Cup – a quite astonishing sporting achievement.

In September 1962 the band rejoined the regiment by dint of being aboard the *Oxfordshire* when she called at Aden to pick everyone else up and carry them on to Malaya and Singapore. The bulk of the regiment was stationed at Ipoh, with a squadron detached at Nee Soon Camp in Singapore. This apparently settled state of affairs lasted only two months: in December there was an uprising in Brunei, a sultanate under British protection on the north-west coast of the island of Borneo, and unrest in Sarawak, a British Crown Colony since 1946, and also in north-west Borneo.

Two troops of Ferret scout-cars, followed by the rest of B Squadron from Singapore, were despatched by air and sea to Brunei together with two infantry battalions and a Royal Marine Commando, and in subsequent operations the rebellion was swiftly put down. In January the threat of an

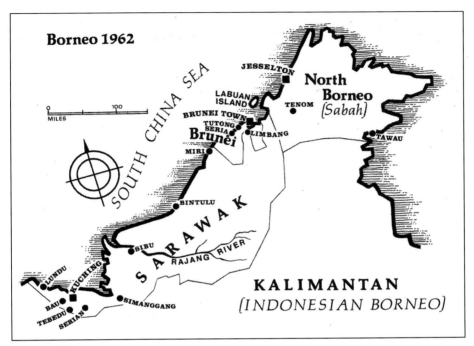

Borneo, 1962–7.

Indonesian intervention to support an expected clandestine Chinese communist uprising in Sarawak resulted in C Squadron motoring the 400 miles from Ipoh to Singapore in their Ferrets and six-wheeled Saladin armoured cars and embarking on a Landing-Ship Tank for the sea voyage to Kuching, Sarawak's seat of government. The squadron leader – a highly decorated and most warlike officer – warned his men that they should be prepared for an opposed landing, and C Squadron donned steel helmets and practised assiduously their Sterling sub-machine gun skills while in transit. In the event, the only discernible presence to meet them on the quayside was an ice cream seller. Also assured of a peaceful reception was a national newspaper who gathered together for a photograph in Singapore the five Patton brothers from Bushmills in Co. Antrim who were all serving in the regiment at the same time. That was a good enough story but not perhaps as newsworthy as the fact that one of the five had been arrested in Kenya while on exercise from Aden the previous year by yet another brother, the provost sergeant of the Royal Inniskilling Fusiliers.

The five Irish Hussar Patton brothers, Singapore, 1962.

C Squadron immediately deployed troops along Sarawak's sole main road to Serian and Simanggang, two of the principal villages, while the remainder were based at the Kuching police headquarters, where they were soon joined by a tactical headquarters commanded by Lieutenant Colonel John Strawson, the regiment's commanding officer designate, who was appointed Commander Kuching Force with elements of local police and military forces under command. Headquarters and living accommodation were in the police barracks until a purpose-built camp could be constructed near the airfield – a key installation guarded twenty-four hours a day against a half-expected Indonesian parachute drop. Troop tasks were rotated every three weeks and those based in Kuching began a programme of road and river patrols, the latter being delivered up the immense Rajang River by Royal Navy minesweepers, before taking to outboard-powered longboats to travel further and reassure the Iban people who inhabited the interior that they would not be forsaken. These patrols lasted around three weeks and were very popular with the soldiers (Iban women often went bare-breasted) – a good deal more popular than their foot equivalent, transported by helicopter deep into the jungle to patrol on their feet close to (and sometimes over) the Indonesian border.

In April 1963 came the first confirmed armed incursion as Indonesian troops attacked the border village of Tebedu. This was the signal for a Royal

Marine Commando and an infantry battalion to be flown into Kuching and for Lieutenant Colonel Strawson to hand over command to 3 Commando Brigade and move to Ipoh. The role of C Squadron now changed from all-purpose soldiering to patrolling the road and tracks in their vehicles, manning roadblocks and guarding the airfield. After six months the squadrons were rotated through Kuching, Ipoh and Singapore, while the Singapore squadron also provided troops in Brunei, Tenom in North Borneo (later Sabah) and in Miri, a town in Sarawak close to the Brunei border and the oilfields. This half-squadron was commanded by a captain in Brunei, 800 miles from RHQ and 400 miles from Squadron Headquarters, while

Irish Hussar Borneo Operations, 1963.

each troop was a healthily independent distance away from its own mini-headquarters.

Despite this wonderfully diverse soldiering there was still time for gunnery camps in Malaya and reconnaissance exercises on the east coast of that most beautiful of countries, as well as a taste of action during communal riots in Singapore and the repelling of a rather half-hearted Indonesian landing on the shores of Johore. There was also a welcome opportunity for sport: polo was played at Ipoh and Singapore, a swimming pool was built in the barracks at Ipoh, the football team won the Far East Command Cup and Bandsman Edwin (Joe) Joseph distinguished himself hugely by winning the first Malaysian decathlon championship, shortly after the formation of that country which initially comprised Malaya, Singapore, Sarawak and Sabah. A regimental tent-pegging team (a first for thirty years) performed enthusiastically (but, it has to be admitted, with little skill) in the national stadium in Kuala Lumpur to help celebrate Malaysia Day. All too soon this Far East adventure came to an end, and in September 1964 the regiment handed over the barracks at Ipoh to the Malaysian Rangers – the Irish Hussars being the last British regiment to occupy that historic outpost of Empire. Soldiers and families (now including the addition of fifteen Chinese wives) flew home *en route* to Wolfenbüttel in Lower Saxony, only 9 miles from the Inner German Border (IGB). Five polo ponies travelled by sea.

As the stay of the Queen's Own Hussars in Detmold drew to a close, the editor of the regimental journal of 1965 was in reflective mood as he considered the past five years and the general experience of British regiments in Germany since the end of a war now twenty years distant:

We have seen the Germans pass from the misery of defeat through the grinding poverty of occupation to the affluence of today; and with these changes have also come change in our own view of our old enemies. We have, perhaps, been slow to swing from conquerors to allies but the change has been made and one of the things to remember best about this year's manoeuvres was the ready friendliness and hospitality that we received in areas which have no reason to love the sight of tanks moving tactically across farmland. There are cynics who will ascribe this amiability to the generous damage compensation, or will point out that the nearer to the Inner German Border, the more friendly the population, but this is far from the whole truth. We like to think that there is something in the old story that the British soldier is the best of ambassadors and that there is a slowly growing understanding, if not affection, between ancient foes.

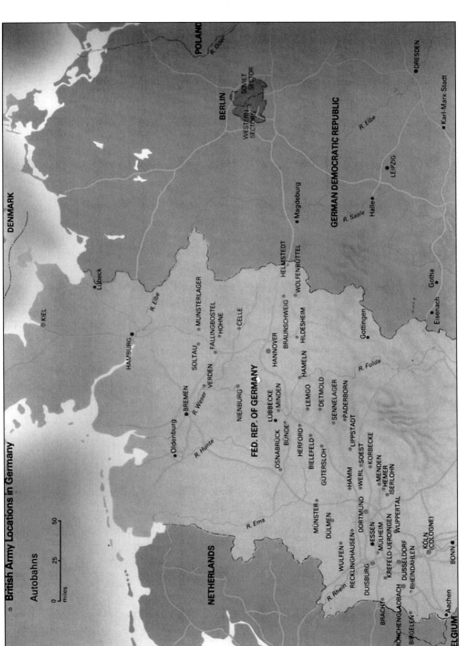

Stations of the British Army of the Rhine from 1945 to 2018.

Few dispassionate observers would disagree with his sentiments, and they probably represented fairly the views of many serving in Germany – those, that is, who were given to such philosophical musings. For most soldiers, though, there were more practical matters to consider: pay in the British Army of the Rhine was higher than that in England because of the additional local overseas allowance; married quarters were of a generally high standard and the cost of living measurably lower than that in the United Kingdom because of duty-free concessions. Drink, cigarettes and petrol were consequently cheaper, as was the capital cost of many items, including cars and domestic appliances. British Army garrisons such as Münster, Paderborn, Fallingbostel and Detmold, to name only a handful of the thirteen major centres and twice that number of smaller military installations, were largely self-sufficient communities and there was only sporadic mingling with the German population. Most servicemen spoke little or no German, although a remarkably high proportion of Germans – particularly of the professional classes – spoke good English.

It was, then, with decidedly mixed feelings leaning a little towards regret, that the soldiers of the Queen's Own Hussars learned that in 1965 they were to leave Detmold for Catterick Camp in North Yorkshire; but their misgivings were eased by the fact that Yorkshire was only a short journey from many of their family homes in the Midlands, and there was – as far as those who really did not want to leave Germany were concerned – the prospect of being part of A Squadron, which was to be detached and was bound for Berlin. The regiment also had to face the fact that not only was it to be split but – viewed by many as even worse – their role in England was to be that of the Royal Armoured Corps Training Regiment, responsible for turning those recruits joining cavalry and Royal Tank Regiments into trained soldiers ready to take their places as crewmen in armoured vehicles in peace and, if required, in war. For the officers, however, especially those of an equestrian or field-sports bent, there was a rich extramural scene to look forward to: there would be excellent hunting and shooting close by and fishing in Scotland not far away. The Queen's Own Hussars had had a successful final sporting year at Detmold, winning the BAOR hockey cup and the 4th Division rugby trophy. The footballers were looking forward to competing in the Cavalry Cup competition in England where there fewer opponents to overcome. Only the polo players were to find life difficult; little was played in Yorkshire and the regiment was keen to add to its triumphs in

Above: Prince Philip's visit to Operation Telic 8 in Iraq, 2006.

Below left : HRH The Princess Anne of Denmark.

Below right: Brigadier General Charles Seymour, First Colonel of the 3rd The King's Own Hussars.

Above left: Thomas Brown – Regaining the Standard at Dettingen.

Above right: George Daraugh – Hero of Dettingen.

Below: The Charge at Salamanca.

Iraq, 2004. Foot patrol in Basra.

Above: Preparing for the charge down the 'valley of death'. The regiment and old comrades' visit to Balaklava, 2004.

Below: The Balaklava Memorial.

Above and below: The Colonel–in–Chief in Basra, 2006.

Above: Foot patrol in Afghanistan, 2011–12.

Below: Warthogs about to cross the Helmand River, Afghanistan, 2011–12.

C (Churchill) Squadron at the London Olympics, 2012.

Above: The Regimental Association marches past. Cavalry Memorial Parade, Hyde Park, 2012.

Below: Remembrance Sunday, Birmingham, 2012.

Estonia, 2016.

Above: Members of the Germany-based Churchill Troop of the Regimental Association pictured in the Warrant Officers' and Sergeants' Mess, Athlone Barracks, 2016.

Below: Farewell luncheon for Major David Innes-Lumsden on his retirement after 17 years as regimental secretary, Cavalry and Guards Club, 2016.

Members of Gulf Troop of the Regimental Association, Coleraine, 2017. On and off parade.

the inter-regimental and United Services tournaments, now won from Detmold for two years running.

If the unchanging training cycle in Germany had proved a little tedious, the wearisome sausage machine involved in producing useful soldiers for armoured and armoured reconnaissance regiments left little scope for initiative. The three squadrons at Catterick (a D Squadron had been created) were supplemented by 90 civilian staff and 74 link instructors – officers and non-commissioned officers from other regiments. The challenge was initially to train annually around 1,500 recruits (all wearing a beret bearing the RAC mailed-fist badge, universally known as 'the wanking-spanner') in basic training – the first phase being known as General Military Training, which covered such subjects as drill, fitness, drill, weapon training, drill, education and drill. All this took some fourteen weeks, after which the recruit progressed to learn one of the three essential armoured skills of gunnery, radio and armoured fighting vehicle driving and maintenance (D&M), or the driving and maintenance of B Vehicles (Land Rovers, lorries and the like), before being tested and finally despatched to their regiments, proudly wearing their new cap-badges. There were, however, still opportunities for some adventurous training and, of course, sport. The Cavalry Cup eluded the football team when they lost in the final in London, but there were a myriad of other activities ranging from pistol-shooting to basketball to keep people busy. The polo team – backed by an impressive array of twenty-five ponies and no fewer than eleven soldier grooms – overcame their distance problems, sweeping the board and winning the United Services Cup in 1965 for a third consecutive time and capping that with a fourth the following year. On 24 June 1966 the Colonel-in-Chief came to Catterick – her first visit since the Guidon Parade some seven years earlier. This was a happy occasion enjoyed, too, by a strong party of old comrades and a small detachment from Berlin.

The officers and soldiers of A Squadron were much enjoying their independence in the divided city of Berlin: Smuts Barracks was comfortable and married quarters plentiful and of a high standard. The writer of the squadron's notes covering this period defined Berlin as '*a teutonic Hong Kong, being a tight-knit community whose incumbents wish to make sure that no newcomer rocks the boat*'. The squadron rocked no hallowed boats and, as the possessor of the only tanks in the British Zone, its troops were much in demand by the three infantry battalions of the Berlin Brigade for infantry/tank training, and to provide both spectacle and tone on ceremonial occasions. These

Visit of the Colonel-in-Chief to QOH, Catterick, 1966, with the drum-horse *Crusader*.

included the annual Berlin Tattoo, an opportunity for the Brits to show off in front of tens of thousands of Berliners in the Hitler-built Olympic Stadium – Berliners who, a few years earlier, had listened in bemusement to President John F. Kennedy describe himself as a doughnut during an ill-advised address in German. The 1965 Tattoo provided the artistically inclined troop leader, Lieutenant Michael Parker, with a first opportunity to display his theatrical talents to a wider public, and so impressed was the Berlin hierarchy that two years later, and now Captain Parker, he was temporarily seconded to run the Tattoo again – this time as its director. Some 700 bandsmen and 'The Biggest Union Jack in the World' were two of the features of this production, which (despite the fact that the helicopter towing the two-ton flag above the stadium dropped it) was the start of Parker's subsequently hugely successful career in creating national and international pageants on a heroic scale. In early 1967 A Squadron rejoined the regiment at Maresfield Camp in Sussex, where the Queen's Own Hussars, their stint in Catterick completed, began to convert to an armoured reconnaissance role prior to a move to Aden and Sharjah.

Northampton Barracks in Wolfenbüttel had housed a Wehrmacht anti-aircraft battalion before and during the Second World War, but its formidably grim appearance belied a higher standard of comfort than many others in Germany, and its isolation from larger British garrisons (and therefore from the prying eyes of senior officers) made it the most popular station in BAOR. Wolfenbüttel is a small town, north of the Harz Mountains (through which ran the Inner German Border), and only 8 miles from the much larger city of Brunswick, which provided good shops, restaurants and a much vaunted red-light area. The Irish Hussars arrived in October 1964, cold and shivering after three years in desert and jungle. Their role, as the armoured reconnaissance regiment of the 1st Armoured Division, was to patrol the border in times of peace and tension and, should war break out, to provide a screen as the division deployed into its battle positions. Its secondary role was to play host four times a year to a multinational force (British, American and French), whose task it was to confirm the rights of the three principal occupying nations to use unfettered the autobahn to Berlin. This exercise, formerly called Gay Cavalier, was renamed Happy Hussar by the regiment – but not as a nod towards political correctness; in 1964 'gay' still retained its original ('debonair') meaning. The regiment received a visit from its Colonel-in-Chief in the snow of December and then immediately took to the field as an entity for the first time in nearly four years. There was also a plethora of visits-cum-inspections by senior officers. One Brigadier was particularly interested in the Irishness of the regiment.

'How many of your men are from Ireland?' he asked a new troop leader.

The young officer didn't know precisely but hazarded a guess.

'All of them, Brigadier.'

'Humph', said the Brigadier, spotting Trooper George Pierre who had been born in the West Indies. Marching up to Pierre with a glint in his eye at having caught out the wretched cornet, he stopped.

'Where do you come from?' he demanded.

The trooper looked him steadfastly in the eye.

'Belfast, Sir', he said.

On 24 January 1965 the Colonel of the Regiment died. Sir Winston's association with the regiment had begun in 1895 when he joined the 4th Hussars and he had been, as Colonel of the 4th Hussars and Colonel of the Queen's Royal Irish Hussars, intensely interested in its affairs ever since. The regiment played a number of key roles in his state funeral. Fifteen subaltern officers kept vigil in Westminster Hall; eight field officers, led by Lieutenant Colonel Strawson, bore the Colonel's decorations and banners in

The Colonel's last journey. The body of Sir Winston Churchill is taken to Bladon by the Irish Hussar bearer party, 1965.

the funeral procession, positioned immediately in front of the gun carriage; Trumpet Major Basil King faultlessly blew Reveille at the conclusion of the service in St Paul's Cathedral, and finally a cloaked bearer party of twelve Warrant Officers and senior Non-Commissioned Officers led by Captain Barry de Morgan and Regimental Sergeant Major Bill Holberton, bore the coffin on to the train at Waterloo, travelled with it and finally laid it to rest in the little churchyard of St Martin's Bladon, close to Blenheim Palace, the place of Churchill's birth. The Earl Marshal, the Duke of Norfolk, was kind enough to describe the bearer party as *'the finest I have ever seen'*.

One of the joys of being an armoured reconnaissance regiment was the ability to roam freely over the German countryside instead of being confined to desperately limited training areas: Schleswig-Holstein for troop training, Hesse for squadron training and the Mosel Valley for a regimental exercise against an American 'enemy' was the programme for 1965 and typical of the years that followed. Such freedom was also enhanced by the Air Troop of four helicopters piloted by Irish Hussars who one year carried out their own specialized training in Denmark, attracting such close attention from the local girls that their stamina was sorely tested. The whole regiment motored to Sennelager in May for a stay of ten days with the 17th/21st Lancers in preparation for a Brigade-strength parade for Her Majesty the Queen during her visit to Germany, accompanied by the regiment's Colonel-in-Chief, who was quick to point out to the Queen that his regiment's performance was second to none! The regiment's time in Wolfenbüttel was also notable for several innovations: a war-dog troop was formed to help with barracks security; a pig farm was run by Corporal Vic Plows, the oldest soldier in the regiment, which helped enhance the rations and was a 'must see' institution for visiting VIPs, including President Lübke of West Germany and, of course, the Colonel-in-Chief; a rock group was formed by Cornet Patrick O'Neill, son of the Prime Minister of Northern Ireland, which proved a draw both in Germany and in Northern Ireland, where it was part of two highly successful recruiting tours; and, most importantly, there was the beginning of an exchange with the 8th Canadian Hussars (Princess Louise's) which saw the arrival of a captain from that regiment for a tour of two or three years, and the departure of an Irish Hussar officer of the same rank to join the 8th at Petawawa in Ontario – an arrangement which was to last for almost thirty years. This affiliation with the 8th was one of eight with allied regiments from Canada, Australia, Belgium, Germany and France.

The Queen's Royal Irish Hussars remained in Wolfenbüttel until 1968 under three different commanding officers. At sport the regiment had worked and played hard: the football team had reached the Cavalry Cup final twice without managing to overcome the final hurdle; the cricket team had reached the BAOR final and suffered a similar fate; the inter-regimental and captains' and subalterns' polo teams won a number of tournaments, the latter winning the final in 1967. The racing stable, formed in 1965 by

Captain the Hon. Terence O'Neill, Prime Minister of Northern Ireland, visits the Irish Hussars in Wölfenbuttel. His son, Cornet Patrick O'Neill, looks away.

Cornet Christopher Hanbury, produced five winners, and Captain Johnnie Powell won the Grand Military Steeplechase at Sandown Park. The new regimental sport of bobsleigh paid great dividends, with three young officers making the Army team. As the regiment prepared to leave Germany, it was with almost unanimous regret and a realization that as far as service in BAOR was concerned, they 'had never had it so good'. In February 1968 it moved to Perham Down, near Tidworth, en route to the Royal Armoured Corps (RAC) Centre at Bovington in Dorset. The six-month stay in Perham Down was devoted to training with the relatively new Chieftain tank – no one in the regiment had been on any tank for seven years, let alone this addition to the cavalry's armoury. The Chieftain, described at the time as 'the most formidable tank in the world', lived up to its reputation in terms of firepower (a 120mm main armament) and protection, but the reliability of its multi-fuel engine was always to be a problem. Nevertheless, the Irish Hussars took to their new equipment enthusiastically, exercising over the open expanses of Salisbury Plain and practising their gunnery at Castle-martin – all with excellent results.

The move to Bovington came in August, and the role of the RAC Centre Regiment was not just a challenge but a new venture for the Army, being the first time that this task had been undertaken by a regiment as opposed to a collection of officers and soldiers at extra-regimental duty. Just as the Queen's Own Hussars had found at Catterick, this required a radical re-organization. C Squadron became the Vehicle Squadron, responsible for providing and looking after all the nearly 200 vehicles of all description, from Chieftains to mini-vans and a road-sweeper, necessary to support the courses held at the Centre. A Squadron, based at Lulworth on the coast south of Bovington, was the Gunnery School Squadron, looking after all its own vehicles and equipment and the administration of the ranges. B Squadron, meanwhile, shrank to seven all-ranks and was responsible for the documentation across the whole Royal Armoured Corps, dealing with subjects ranging from absentees to employment. This left no little scope for the commanding officer, Lieutenant Colonel Kenneth Bidie, to exercise considerable flexibility in the deployment of both officers and soldiers: two strong independent troops were formed, one in Catterick attached to an infantry brigade and the other to the Armoured Trials and Development Unit in Bovington itself. Other troops travelled widely: two were attached to the 17th/21st Lancers in North Africa, and one went to Fort Hood in Texas to take on the Americans at tank gunnery where, in borrowed and unfamiliar equipment, they won the final competition – Trooper Samuel Coups destroying a US Army ceremonial steel helmet at 2,000 yards. The Colonel-in-Chief arrived in Dorset by royal train and provoked much press coverage as he drove a Chieftain and then fired on the ranges. Later that year, a regimental display was opened by Northern Ireland Prime Minister Terence O'Neill in Carrickfergus Castle in County Antrim as a part of an Irish Cavalry Museum in partnership with the 5th Royal Inniskilling Dragoon Guards and the North Irish Horse, and another notable occasion was the transfer of the Colonelcy from George Kidston-Montgomerie – for many years Churchill's deputy until succeeding in his own right – to General Sir John (Shan) Hackett, who had recently retired from the Army and was now Principal of King's College, London.

The rather mundane routine at Bovington and Lulworth was alleviated by adventurous training on Dartmoor and tactical exercises on Salisbury Plain. There was much time for sport, and in 1970 the football team, which had won all the local leagues and the Dorset League Cup, not only won the Cavalry Cup but were runners-up in the Army Cup. The much looked for-ward to shooting, fishing and hunting all had their enthusiastic adherents, and the polo team, keeping its ponies at Tidworth, made both the inter-regimental and captains' and subalterns' finals in 1969, being beaten in each case in extra time. This disappointment was made up for the following year, when the captains and subalterns team won the cup, beating in the final the Queen's Own Hussars. In June 1970 a regimental weekend was attended by over 200 old comrades and there were drinks parties, dances, a drum-head service and a past versus present cricket match. This whole-heartedly family occasion proved to be a fitting farewell to the regiment's many friends in Dorset, because that summer, too, came the news that in 1971 the Irish Hussars would move to Paderborn, once again to be part of the British Army of the Rhine.

For the Queen's Own Hussars the closing years of the sixties were rather more exciting. At the beginning of June 1967 the advance parties arrived in Aden and Sharjah – the latter being the destination of a detached B Squad-ron. Aden was a very different place from that experienced by C Squadron in 1960 and by the Irish Hussars a year later. Gone were the leisurely beach parties, the polo and evening strolls in the sunshine. The colony was now at war, both with the British and itself. Despite the fact that in 1964 the British government had promised independence for Aden within four years, rebel groups, fired up by President Gamal Abdel Nasser of Egypt, declared that they would not wait. Grenade attacks on British troops, civilians and government officials were frequent, and an aircraft was brought down, killing all on board. The internal security situation was complicated by the fact that there were two organizations which saw themselves as the government once the British had left: FLOSY (Front for the Liberation of South Yemen) and the NLF (National Liberation Front). They viciously fought each other as well as attacking the British, and there was also a fourth armed group, the South Arabian Federation Army (SAA), which represented the South Arabian Federation set up by the British in 1962 to include Aden and a number of other southern Yemeni states, and to which the British government intended to hand power. The SAA, despite constant exhortations by Cairo to rebel, remained loyal to this plan in the early stages, but the Arab-Israeli Six Day War in June 1967, and the accusations by Nasser that the British had sided with the Israelis, sparked a mutiny in the SAA and, more violently, within the Aden Armed Police, hitherto also loyal. The Queen's Own Hussars, commanded by Lieutenant Colonel Michael Hogge, could not have arrived at a more critical time.

C Squadron QOH on patrol in Crater, Aden, 1967.

RHQ and the administrative elements were based at Falaise Camp in Little Aden, the area of the colony which for over thirty years had been the home of the British Petroleum oil refinery which, in the past, had provided many facilities and comforts for the troops on whom the company largely depended for security. Close by was stationed the newly constituted Air Squadron of six Sioux helicopters, commanded by an Irish Hussar and with three QOH and two other pilots freshly off their flying course at Middle Wallop. A Squadron's area of responsibility was Crater, the ancient Arab district of Aden city where it was in support of – briefly – the Royal Northumberland Fusiliers and then the Argyll and Sutherland Highlanders. A full-scale mutiny by the Armed Police had resulted in them taking *de facto* control of Crater after a battle in which twenty-two British servicemen died, but in July the Argylls, led by the redoubtable Lieutenant Colonel 'Mad Mitch' Mitchell, reoccupied the area without any casualties. C Squadron's role was in support of the 1st Battalion The Parachute Regiment and the 1st Battalion The Lancashire Regiment as they attempted to keep order in the townships of Sheikh Othman and Mansoura on the northern boundary of Aden state. These settlements were the scenes of some of the fiercest fighting between FLOSY and the NLF, and during the twenty-four hours of 30/31 August there were over sixty incidents. In September a foot patrol of the Lancashires came under heavy fire and its members had to be rescued by a Saracen armoured personnel carrier, part of a troop commanded by Lieutenant Richard Vaughan-Griffiths of the regiment in an action which won him the Military Cross and two of his troop Mentions in Despatches.

Meanwhile, B Squadron's peaceful deployment in Sharjah largely mirrored that of the Irish Hussar squadrons six years earlier. The main enemy was boredom: one officer was heard to say that for the first three weeks he lay on his bed watching the fan go round and for the next three watching the ceiling going round. Exercises with the Trucial Oman Scouts, manoeuvres against the reconnaissance squadron of the neighbouring Abu Dhabi Defence Force – a private army owned by the ruler – and long treks across the desert (1,000 miles in one case) to coastal towns, showed the flag, and variety was provided when two troops and squadron headquarters were sent to Aden to cover the British withdrawal. By November it was all over: B Squadron was reunited in Sharjah and joined by an Air Troop of three helicopters, while the rest of the regiment embarked peacefully and travelled home to Maresfield by a variety of means: some were carried by the Royal Air Force and some went by sea on a direct route through the Suez Canal, while an intrepid band of volunteers sailed in a landing ship which was routed round the Cape of Good Hope. By the end of May 1968 the Sharjah warriors had also arrived in the United Kingdom and all ranks began to look forward to their next overseas deployment – this time to the Mediterranean and the Far East.

The regiment now embarked on a period of individual, troop and squadron training designed not only to ready them for their next move but also to help other units – infantry, Royal Marine and even Special Air Service – practise their own requirements. By October all this was over and the move to Hong Kong and Singapore began. A so-called advance headquarters – something of a misnomer, headed as it was by the commanding officer, Lieutenant Colonel Robin Carnegie, while main headquarters, back at Maresfield was led by the second-in-command – together with A Squadron were based at Selarang Barracks in the Changi district of Singapore, where they became part of 99 Gurkha Infantry Brigade. This was far from the most comfortable military installation on the island, and the married quarters

C Squadron QOH in Hong Kong, 1969.

were some 10 miles distant. The Borneo campaign (known as Confrontation), in which the Irish Hussars had been involved, was now over, and the squadron's role was difficult to define. It was equipped as an armoured reconnaissance unit, but training exercises ranged from jungle warfare (on foot), mounted patrolling of the roads and tracks of east coast Malaysia, amphibious landings in Penang and gunnery practice on Asahan ranges near the west coast, to internal security duties where, should they be called out, they would deploy in aid of the Singaporean civil police. All this was against a background of total British withdrawal from Malaysia and Singapore, a policy decision made in London and opposed bitterly by the Singapore government. None of it – except in the unlikely event of civil unrest in well ordered Singapore – made much sense and smacked rather of being cobbled together to 'keep the boys busy'.

C Squadron's destination was Sek Kong and it was familiar to all those who had served in Hong Kong a dozen years previously. There, as before, they joined 48 Gurkha Infantry Brigade, but this time the equipment was wheeled reconnaissance vehicles, the regiment's worth of tanks having been mothballed. The squadron's role was twofold: to be prepared to aid the civil power should there be periods of unrest between communist and nationalist Chinese factions and – as the regimental journal put it – chatting up the locals. This latter task was both interesting and productive, often involving parties of soldiers being landed on one of the many offshore islands to, for example, build generators for electricity or plants for water purification. Occasionally a troop would patrol on foot to remote villages accompanied by policemen and mules from the last Royal Army Service Corps pack-transport company, or spend a week perched in an observation post over-looking the Sham Chun River which marked the border with China, noting and reporting all vehicle movement – a task which all-ranks found absorb-ing. For both squadrons there was plenty of opportunity for sport, and both produced successful football, cricket and boxing teams relative to their size. Polo was played in Singapore, while at Sek Kong it was also played, but on the small (almost miniature) Borneo ponies which was a great deal of fun, enlivened for a period by the presence of Jimmy Edwards, a larger than life, handlebar-moustached British comedian made famous at that time by highly successful radio and television programmes.

Both A and C Squadrons generously made room for a succession of Irish Hussar young officers, eager to escape Bovington, and B Squadron, too, had an Irish Hussar subaltern when it deployed for six months in June 1969 to

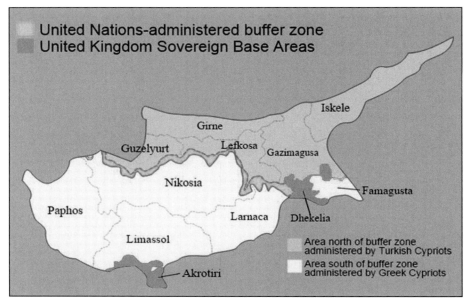

Cyprus, showing the British Sovereign Base Areas and the Green Line.

B Squadron QOH, Troodos Mountains, Cyprus, 1970.

Cyprus to join the United Nations force on the island. There, wearing the UN blue berets, it was based at Zyyi Camp on the coast east of Limassol as the reserve force to back up a bewildering array of army contingents from Sweden, Denmark, Ireland, Canada and Finland, and police detachments from Australia and Austria, all under command of a Finnish general. As the requirement to produce a stand-by force of two troops meant that they could not leave camp, squadron training as an entity proved almost impossible, but one notable exercise with a small cavalry squadron from Ireland proved great – if somewhat dangerous – fun, as the Irish Packard vehicles hurtled up and down the mountainous terrain. In December the squadron returned to Maresfield, each man proudly sporting a United Nations medal.

CHAPTER SEVEN

THE TROUBLES

I could wish that the English kept history in mind more and that the Irish kept it in mind less. (Elizabeth Bowen)

By the autumn of 1970 the Queen's Own Hussars had settled in Hohne, and the following year the officers signalled their arrival in this new station by holding a May Ball. Proceedings were enlivened by a pageant conceived and produced by the indefatigable Michael Parker which portrayed in words and music the Battle of Trafalgar. The lake outside the Bredebeck officers' mess was transformed: Royal Engineer assault boats disguised as men-o'-war under full sail, majestically patrolled the lake and the band performed on a floating platform. There were pyrotechnics galore, many of them triggered by frogmen, but suddenly and prematurely the sails caught fire and the resulting conflagrations melted the aluminium boats. Chaos reigned as the unfortunate crews leapt into the lake to save themselves, while the band bravely played on as rockets whizzed past their ears. The chief guest, the Commander of 1st (British) Corps, sighed as he turned to the commanding officer.

'I rather fear', he said, 'that I am the senior officer present.'

At the ensuing board of enquiry the proceedings were described (by Michael Parker) as hilarious. Shortly afterwards, he retired from the army to pursue a career on a wider stage which was to include the Queen's jubilees, the Royal Tournament, the Royal Fireworks and 'The Largest Children's Party in History'.

At Hohne the regiment found that there had been significant changes in both organization and equipment since Detmold five years before. The Chieftain tank and its 120mm main armament was now deployed throughout armoured regiments and was excellent in almost all respects apart from an exasperatingly unreliable engine, complex in construction and difficult to access. The advent of the Swingfire guided weapon system mounted on a tracked vehicle chassis had caused the formation of a Command and Support Squadron to supplement the three 15-tank sabre squadrons. Com-

Outline map of Northern Ireland.

mand and Support Squadrons (usefully shortened by the Queen's Own Hussars to Command Squadron) comprised a recce troop of tracked light vehicles armed with a 30mm cannon, the guided weapon (Swingfire) troop and a regimental headquarters led by the commanding officer in his tank, together with a number of specially converted armoured command vehicles. They would be expected to fight as an all-arms battlegroup so that, for example, the regiment might go to war with one or two sabre squadrons and one or more armoured infantry companies, the remaining squadrons being deployed with other battlegroups. Thus equipped and organized, the regiment looked forward to a relatively peaceful BAOR existence, training with these new formations and having their ordered life enhanced by many opportunities to excel at football, cricket, skiing, polo and any number of other sports and adventurous training expeditions. It therefore came as something of a shock when, towards the end of 1971, the commanding officer was warned that he, a small headquarters and one squadron would be deployed to Northern Ireland early the following year. The squadron would be equipped with Ferret Scout Cars (FSC) and Saracen armoured personnel carriers. Training would begin at once.

The decade had seen an escalation in the Troubles which were to beset Northern Ireland for over thirty years. For decades, dating from the partition of Ireland in the 1920s, gerrymandering and other forms of discrimination had been rife in the Province – usually, but not exclusively, with the Catholic minority as victims. Marches demanding civil rights had become popular among the nationalist population – a segment of Ulster society which was not only predominantly Roman Catholic but also demanded a speedy end to the Irish border and incorporation within a united Ireland. This had alarmed the predominantly Protestant loyalist majority who, egged on by extremists, began to attack Catholic areas. The security forces in the province led by the Royal Ulster Constabulary (RUC), but supplemented by Army units from the United Kingdom and BAOR, were seen at first to be welcome protectors of the minority, but this slowly changed in 1970 and was overturned violently, almost overnight, when a civil rights march in Londonderry in January 1972 which was confronted by British troops resulted in the deaths of fourteen demonstrators.

When he and his party arrived in Ulster, Lieutenant Colonel John Venner (he who, as a subaltern, had won a Military Cross with the 8th Hussars in Korea) was surprised to find that A Squadron would be deployed separately from his command, which would instead include elements of an infantry battalion, a Royal Horse Artillery regiment and the Royal Scots Dragoon Guards. A Squadron was based at Gosford Castle, an otherwise unoccupied and run-down listed building in Co. Armagh, close to the border with Co. Down. At that stage in the Troubles, the Army's main role in support of the RUC was to reassure peaceful inhabitants that they could call on help if needed. This A Squadron and John Venner's disparate command did with both efficiency and sensitivity, and all ranks returned to Hohne by early summer having sustained no casualties. That summer also saw a new experience for the soldiers of the Queen's Own Hussars when C Squadron was sent to the British Army Training Unit Suffield (BATUS) on the Albertan prairies of Canada, a new, 1,000-square-mile, all-arms, live-firing training area fully equipped with tanks and all the other armoured vehicles required by a visiting battlegroup, and in which live ammunition could be used almost without restriction on a series of six exercises known as Medicine Man held each year. The squadron was a part of a Green Howards battlegroup, which was only the second to be deployed to Suffield since the area was first leased from the Canadian government.

Two sides of the same coin. The Queen's Own Hussars in Belfast, 1973.

In 1973 John Venner was back in Northern Ireland and this time he was able to take his whole regiment, but dismounted and in an infantry role – the first time that a complete cavalry regiment had been unhorsed in this way for a tour in Ulster. After an intensive period of training at the infantry training area at Sennelager by the Northern Ireland Training and Advisory Team (NITAT), which included not only the transition to infantry but in the special skills (searches, roadblocks, anti-riot drills and so on) required in the Province, the regiment was deemed ready. The four-month tour was in south Belfast, a relatively quiet area of the city, but one which included a potentially explosive interface between Catholic and Protestant communities. The regiment's most testing experience was to be faced with a republican anti-internment march proceeding down the Suffolk Road which escalated into violence as the marchers veered off a previously agreed route and headed for a Protestant area. There were some gunshots and an almost continuous hail of rocks and other missiles, but A Squadron stood firm: the march was halted and there were only minor injuries. By October, after an eventful tour, the regiment was once again ensconced in Hohne, smugly (and deservedly) basking in the knowledge that it was the first unit to complete a tour of Northern Ireland without a single accidental or negligent discharge of a firearm. The following year, and now commanded by Lieutenant Colonel James Rucker (formerly of the 5th Royal Inniskilling Dragoon Guards), the regiment led a battlegroup to Suffield which included both B and C Squadrons, so that by the time they returned, the whole regiment had experienced both the challenges presented by active service in Northern Ireland and the thrills of live-fire manoeuvring on the Canadian prairie. In the autumn of 1974 the Queen's Own Hussars learnt that they were to become the RAC Centre Regiment at Bovington and Lulworth, with a detached squadron at the School of Infantry in Warminster.

The cathedral town of Paderborn in the German state of North-Rhine Westphalia was (and remains) a Catholic enclave in an otherwise predominantly Protestant region. When the Irish Hussars arrived in 1970 it had a large British garrison both in the town itself and in nearby Sennelager. The regiment's new home, Barker Barracks, had been built in the 1930s for Panzer regiments and was renamed after General Sir Evelyn Barker. Now it also housed an artillery regiment, but there was more than enough space for both; each had its own half of the installation and its own entrance and guard-room. The situation in Northern Ireland was having an alarming effect on recruitment: potential soldiers from the Province were now more likely to stay at home and protect their families and their future by joining the newly created Ulster Defence Regiment, which, although part-time, fielded seven infantry battalions, eventually to expand to eleven. Recruiting tours had to stop, or more accurately, were diverted to London and Sussex, which had been allotted to the regiment. Nevertheless, Irishmen from both sides of the border – and from across the religious divide – continued to trickle in. Again the Irishness of the regiment seemed to fascinate inspecting senior officers. One stopped to talk to Trooper Keith Deakin, newly arrived in B Squadron and on parade, standing by his bed.

'Where do you come from?' he asked.

'Yorkshire, Sir', said Deakin

'Why then did you join the Irish Hussars?'

'I was fookin' conned', said Deakin.

The brigadier hid his undoubted surprise well but was not prepared to leave it there.

'Are you happy?' he asked.

'Yes, Sir.'

'Then it was a good con.'

And at that the brigadier moved on. Regimental Sergeant Major Willie-John Stewart was not, however, moving anywhere; he lingered as the touring party left the room. Placing his blackthorn close to Deakin's nose, he spoke – his voice dropping to a hiss.

'I shall be after you, Deakin.'

In due time Keith Deakin, although spending the next few months dodging the RSM, himself became Regimental Sergeant Major – as, extraordinarily, did two other troopers serving in B Squadron at that time. By the beginning of 1972 the regiment was up to strength and, in common with the other Irish regiments – the Irish Guards, the Royal Irish Rangers and the 5th Royal Inniskilling Dragoon Guards – it was to spend more time at BATUS than was originally envisaged, because the rest of the Army was becoming increasingly engaged in Northern Ireland. Adventurous training now featured heavily in Canada, as parties climbed, trekked, skied and canoed in the nearby Rocky Mountains. Paderborn acted as a magnet for politicians and other dignitaries: Prime Minister Edward Heath, Secretary of State for Defence Lord Carrington and a Defence Junior Minister, Winston Churchill, all came to visit the regiment, the last named keen to view memorabilia of his grandfather, including the many acerbic comments

'Not that knob – that's the fire extinguisher!' Prime Minister Edward Heath learns to drive a Chieftain while visiting the Irish Hussars, Paderborn, 1971. Sergeant Major McLernon looks anxious.

in the officers' mess suggestions book penned by Lieutenant Churchill in the late 1890s.

The repetitive grind of BAOR soldiering was, as always, alleviated by almost annual visits from the Colonel-in-Chief, by sport, and by the music provided by the excellent band, which in 1976 was the only band in the Army to be awarded the coveted A Grading by the Royal Military School of Music. Three years earlier, the Irish Hussars emulated the Queen's Own Hussars by producing a notable spectacular in the form of a *Son et Lumière* commemorating the charge of the Light Cavalry Brigade at Balaklava, with music composed by Bandmaster Peter Smith and words by Major Robin Rhoderick-Jones, performed outdoors for the regiment and many invited guests. So successful was this foray into theatricals that it was repeated in a special programme produced world-wide by the British Forces Broadcasting Service. There were successes in sport, too: the football team won the

Cavalry Cup in 1975 and 1977, and the polo team were regular runners-up in the Inter-Regimental. Skiing was popular, and a team of four won the *Daily Telegraph*'s Exercise Parashot competition, consisting of parachute drops, navigation, patrol exercises, speed marching, ambush drills, first aid and shooting phases, against all-comers, including four teams from the Parachute Regiment. The subalterns found that there was a thriving social life to be found in the Westphalian countryside: parties could be found in more than one grand *Schloss* and young ladies could be pursued – sometimes with success. An unfortunate surprise confronted one young man when the girl he had danced with enthusiastically later led him to her bed. He could hardly believe his luck, until he discovered that 'she' was actually a 'he'. He compounded this horrifying revelation by incautiously relating the incident to a couple of his friends, who naturally passed it on with notable embellishments so that within twenty-four hours the whole regiment knew.

In 1975 the honorary colonelcy of the regiment passed from General Shan Hackett to Major General John Strawson, but not before the addition of a Pipes and Drums band, the brainchild of Lieutenant Colonel Brian O'Rorke and equipped largely through the generosity of Lord St Oswald who, as Rowland Winn, had served in the 8th Hussars. The Pipes and Drums were a valuable addition and often joined with the regimental band for concerts, parades and recordings. Prince Philip continued to visit regularly and on one such occasion a telephone call was received during dinner by the German police, warning them that a bomb had been placed in the officers' mess of the Queen's Royal Irish Hussars. The commanding officer suggested that they might therefore evacuate the building while it was searched. The Colonel-in-Chief demurred, but was eventually persuaded and, accompanied by a number of relieved officers and staff, allowed himself to be led out on to the lawn. That call was, of course, a hoax, but an unexpected telephone message in July 1974 proved, however, to be no such thing. Two aircraft, one containing the commanding officer, Lieutenant Colonel Brian Kenny, had left for BATUS training in Canada, shortly to be followed by others, when the regiment was warned that instead it was to deploy to Cyprus to help deal with the emergency caused by the Turkish invasion of the island. The aircraft were turned round, and the regiment spent a month converting to an armoured reconnaissance role, changing its organization to suit this unexpected assignment. B and C Squadrons, heavily reinforced, particularly from Command and Support Squadron, flew to Cyprus in September together with RHQ and an Administrative Squadron. RHQ, B Squadron and two companies of Coldstream Guards were based at, or near to, Paphos, which also contained a detachment of Australian Police, whose members were found to match even Irishmen in their prodigious consumption of canned beer. C Squadron was first stationed in Limassol under command of the Coldstreams but was later sent to Nicosia as the United Nations (UN) Force Reserve. All troops in Cyprus wore the UN blue beret, and for the next six months the regiment was given a well-earned opportunity (denied to it in Northern Ireland) to carry out peace-keeping operations. The workhorse was the troop: often independent and operating up to 30 miles away from its squadron headquarters, sometimes under temporary command of a company of infantry or Royal Marines or, in the case of the Force Reserve, working with Danish, Swedish and Austrian contingents. In January 1975 a small party from B Squadron attempting to enter the British Sovereign Base Area was set upon by a crowd of Greek Cypriots protesting at the release of some Turkish Cypriots from a refugee camp. In the ensuing fracas a Greek Cypriot was killed and a Land Rover and its crew captured – to be quickly released after a baton-wielding charge by Royal Air Force Police. The ensuing military Court of Inquiry and a civilian inquest praised the coolness and bravery of those involved. In March the regiment was reunited in Paderborn, and two months later the football team won the Cavalry Cup.

The Queen's Own Hussars' tour as the RAC Centre Regiment differed from that of the Irish Hussars in that one squadron was detached to the School of Infantry at Warminster. This meant that opportunities for officers and soldiers to be posted temporarily to more exciting stations were few. The highlight of the first year in Dorset was a visit from the Colonel-in-Chief, Her Majesty's first since 1966. A full programme in which wives and families and old comrades featured prominently led the Queen Mother to observe that she had been grateful to see so many facets of her regiment's life. In May 1976, the regiment's brief stay in the south-west of England came to an end and they returned again to Detmold to join 20 Armoured Brigade after an absence of eleven years. There they found that the powers that were had decreed that Command and Support Squadrons were to be abolished the next year, along with the recce and guided weapon troops. Instead, a fourth tank (sabre) squadron was to be formed. There was, however, very little time to retrain as an armoured regiment whatever its shape, for within a year, and after a period of NITAT, the regiment once again deployed for four months to Northern Ireland, this time to Co. Armagh with one squadron detached to Cookstown in Co. Tyrone. Despite the fact

that their area of responsibility included some 18 miles of border and a
number of illegal crossing points, there was little during the four-month
tour to exacerbate the nervous tension that all soldiers felt when sent to the
Province. There was one notable arms find in a disused farmhouse, gangs of
republican youths made a nuisance of themselves in Armagh city before they
were dispersed and a vehicle patrol from C Squadron was shot at inaccurately with three different weapons. Having taken no casualties, the regiment reassembled in Detmold in October.

The following year, and now sporting a fourth (D) tank squadron, the
regiment was able to enjoy the realistic armoured training that BATUS
had to offer and the unrivalled opportunities for adventurous training that
Canada and, in particular, the Rocky Mountains, provided. D Squadron had
enhanced its individual identity by calling itself the 'Black Pigs' after a large
stuffed creature which graced the squadron bar, a soubriquet which has
been applied to the squadron ever since – representations appearing from
time to time on the squadron flag and woven into camouflage patterns on its
tanks. At BATUS, RHQ with C and D Squadrons led a battlegroup while
A Squadron went a little later with the 1st Battalion The Duke of Wellington's Regiment. B Squadron enjoyed a fortnight in Berlin, manning the
tanks abandoned by the resident squadron who were required for a royal
occasion elsewhere. In November, and once again safely gathered together
in Detmold, the Colonel-in-Chief came for a day, Her Majesty's first visit
to Detmold. At the end of 1977 BAOR, in a rush of reorganizational zeal,
decided that armoured brigades were a thing of the past and were to be
replaced by flexible groupings called task forces. 20 Armoured Brigade
became Task Force Hotel but it remained under command of the erstwhile brigade commander, Brigadier Bernard Gordon-Lennox, a Grenadier
Guards martinet known to all (but certainly not in his presence) as 'Bernie
the Bolt'. The regiment marked this change in clandestine fashion at the
Hunter Trials it was organizing at Detmold by inserting a fictitious entry
into the programme which read, '*No. 9. Bernie the Bolt ridden by Herr T.F.
Hotel*'. Extraordinarily, this *lèse majesté* (and few were more *majestique* than
the Brigadier) went unnoticed at Task Force Headquarters and Lieutenant
Colonel Robin Greenwood was not, as he feared, marched off to the Tower.
Task Forces proved a short-lived experiment and by the end of the decade
brigades and battlegroups had been restored. Despite this busy period (the
regiment had begun to feel that there was no other), the football team
managed to win the BAOR section of the Cavalry Cup in 1977 and won the

whole competition in 1978 – an achievement to be repeated in 1979. Skiing, too, provided a triumph, the regimental team becoming BAOR champions and runners-up to the Army champions in 1978 – no mean feat when taking into account the advantages enjoyed by the much larger pools from which the Corps teams were able to call.

The final year of the seventies saw the Queen's Own Hussars once again in Ulster, this time organized as infantry in two very strong squadrons, A and B, heavily reinforced by the temporarily disbanded C and D Squadrons. A Squadron's area of responsibility included Twinbrook, a wholly republican housing estate in West Belfast, and neighbouring Lenadoon, which in the early years of the Troubles had had a politically and religiously mixed population but was now ethnically cleansed of loyalists. B Squadron was based in the purpose-built camp at Glasmullen with responsibility for the Andersonstown estate and its police station – the most attacked police station in the Province. Violence in Northern Ireland was now widespread, murders being an almost everyday occurrence. On 27 August eighteen British soldiers died in a Provisional IRA double ambush at Warrenpoint in Co. Down, and on the same day Earl Mountbatten of Burma was blown up when on his boat off Co. Sligo in the Republic. The Queen's Own Hussars were lucky enough to be rarely shot at: a patrol was a target at a Saturday market in Andersonstown but the only casualties were two women and a child. The regiment was, however, never less than busy: polling stations had to be guarded during the European elections; arms finds were made; two snipers were arrested – one having been shot and wounded; street barricades were dismantled (only to be rebuilt almost within minutes); and parades, one of them estimated as 3,000-strong, were policed successfully. Once again the regiment had led a charmed life – preserved without doubt by its professional approach to all the tasks assigned to it – and in October emerged from the four-month tour without any casualties but with two Mentions in Despatches, one of them to the commanding officer. From Detmold all ranks now embarked on some well-deserved leave.

For the Queen's Royal Irish Hussars the second half of the decade was particularly pleasurable for the number of times they were lucky enough to be able to welcome their Colonel-in-Chief. During his 1975 visit, Prince Philip also called on the *Burgermeister* and *Stadtdirektor* of Paderborn, and in 1976 his stay was even more notable for the fact that His Royal Highness spent two days with the regiment on manoeuvres, during which he ate lunch (out of mess-tins) with a squadron, attended another squadron's evening smoker, drank with the senior ranks in a marquee and dined with the officers in a village inn. The following day, from the turret of a Chieftain, he led a squadron across the start line of an attack phase of the exercise. In 1978 he came to Paderborn to celebrate his silver jubilee as Colonel-in-Chief. Again he stayed for two days, dining on one night with 400 soldiers in the regimental restaurant (over 100 more acted as waiters) during which he was presented with an inscribed carriage clock. The next day – an anniversary of the charge at Balaklava – he met 300 wives and children before taking a Trooping the Guidon Parade in the presence of over 1,000 spectators. It is impossible to exaggerate how much such visits were appreciated by the soldiers and families of the regiment.

Military activity followed the now familiar pattern of annual firing on the ranges at Bergen-Hohne and troop and squadron training in designated areas (usually Soltau), followed by formation exercises in the German countryside and frequent visits to BATUS, either as the lead battlegroup with two squadrons (as in 1978) or as individual squadrons attached to other battlegroups. In 1977, however, this well trodden path was diverted on 7 July by the 4th Armoured Division's mounted parade to celebrate the Queen's Silver Jubilee in the presence of Her Majesty.

Endless rehearsals involving 3,000 soldiers and 550 armoured vehicles in the black dust of the Sennelager ranges saw the commanding officer, Lieutenant Colonel Dick Webster, in his element as he fulfilled a secret ambition to drill the regiment in saluting and standing properly to attention in the turret of their tanks. His keen eye also noted that in the Division's line-up all the other commanding officers were dressed too far forward. The General disagreed – as did the other commanding officers. Dick Webster, in an unaccustomedly (and deceptively) mild tone, pointed out on the radio net (heard by everyone) that if the other commanding officers' vehicles remained where they were, Divisional Headquarters would run over them as the drive-past began. First there was silence; then total capitulation. Victory to the Irish Hussars! On the day all went well as the regiment, led by its immaculate commanding officer in his tank, was the first to drive past and salute Her Majesty and the regiment's Colonel-in Chief who had accompanied her. *The Times* reported the next day:

> *The 4th Armoured Division staged a brilliantly organized and faultless mixture of ceremony and armament, static and mobile. Soldiers among the spectators illustrated that there is no such thing as a British Army uniform.*

The Colonel-in-Chief meets drum-horse *Dettingen*, The Queen's Own Hussars, Detmold, 1978. The Commanding Officer, Lieutenant Colonel Robin Greenwood, looks on.

The Irish Hussars – the Queen's Silver Jubilee Parade, Sennelager, 1977. The Regiment is right of the line.

Outfits of almost every colour mingled with women onlookers who were wearing Ascot style hats and dresses. Officers in ceremonials patiently led small children by the hand; soldiers' wives pushed babies in prams ... Not a soldier fainted, not a spark-plug failed. This was the reward for months of rehearsals and meticulous planning.

Busy as the Irish Hussars were, sport was not neglected. The far too frequent near misses in the Cavalry Cup football were mirrored in polo, where the regimental team seemed rooted as losing finalists in the inter-regimental tournament but in 1978 the captains and subalterns won their cup. The athletics team won the brigade and divisional meets and was the only regimental (as opposed to corps) team to reach the BAOR finals, finishing fourth. The most notable individual achievement was that of the boxer Lance Corporal Holdsworth, who for two years in succession won both the Army and Combined Services lightweight championship. Adventurous training both in groups and individually was also very much to the fore. Parties had travelled to Spain, Morocco, Israel and Egypt and had driven overland to India, crossing Iran, Afghanistan and Pakistan – a journey rendered impossible to repeat by events at the end of the decade.

It is sometimes ruefully said by officers of the regiment that the advent of a new commanding officer heralds a costly change in either dress or accoutrements, the most obvious (and expensive) example being the intro-duction by Lieutenant Colonel John Strawson on the return of the regiment from Malaysia and Singapore in 1964, of the leather cavalry crossbelt in place of the Sam Browne. Dick Webster did not confine his contribution in this respect to the officers. It was his initiative which introduced the green beret for all ranks – a move enthusiastically backed by both the Colonel of the Regiment (the now Major General John Strawson) and the Colonel-in-Chief, and which has endured in the Queen's Royal Hussars. In 1978, the Irish Hussars were warned that the following year they were to leave Paderborn and move to Bhurtpore Barracks in Tidworth – to be, as had been the case with the Queen's Own Hussars twenty years earlier, the sole armoured regiment stationed in the United Kingdom.

CHAPTER EIGHT

ON TO THE TERCENTENARIES

There I could marvel my birthday away, but the weather turned around. (Dylan Thomas)

The opening three years of the 1980s saw the Queen's Own Hussars still at Detmold but enjoying – at least on paper – a more peaceful period than the previous five. They had no Northern Ireland tours to contend with and although they led a battlegroup to BATUS in both 1980 and 1982 and provided a squadron with another battlegroup in 1981, they were able to achieve the sort of continuity often denied to them in the late 1970s in regimental tactical training, in gunnery and on the sports field. Disappointingly, however, neither the football nor the polo teams which had previously excelled produced the hoped-for results. The former suffered from the departure of a number of relatively ageing stars and the latter from a shortage of both players and the necessary finances. A notable triumph, however, was the winning of the divisional swimming gala. Adventurous training, especially that available in Canada after the tactical training on the plains of Alberta was over, provided tremendous scope for expeditions of which the regiment took full advantage. In 1980, for example, over 100 young officers and soldiers trekked, climbed, skied and otherwise frolicked in the Rocky Mountains, while others ventured further, into the United States.

A significant birthday of the Colonel-in-Chief – as old as the century – was celebrated at the London Royal Tournament in 1980 by the armed forces in general and the regiment in particular. A guidon party led by the Regimental Sergeant Major and accompanied by *Dettingen* – the drum-horse presented by Her Majesty in 1975 – were proudly on parade. The possession of a drum-horse, long after cavalry bands became dismounted, was a tradition of the 3rd Hussars and carried on after amalgamation when, in 1958, Her Royal Highness Princess Margaret gave the new regiment *Crusader*, *Dettingen*'s immediate predecessor. Until amalgamation, the

The Queen's Own Hussars Battlegroup, BATUS, Canada, 1982.

3rd Hussars battle honours had been carried on the silver kettledrums (first captured from the French at Dettingen by the 3rd Hussars) and shabraque (saddle-cloth) with which successive drum-horses were accoutred – in effect, a substitute for a guidon – and always appeared on important parades. *Dettingen* was ridden by a groom in full ceremonial dress, including the silver collar presented to the regiment in 1772 by the wife of the then commanding officer. In 1982 came the news that in their twenty-fifth year the Queen's Own Hussars were to move from Detmold once again to assume the role they last relinquished in 1967 – that of the Royal Armoured Corps training regiment in Catterick – while at the same time providing the armoured squadron in Berlin.

In striking contrast to the routine of BAOR enjoyed by the Queen's Own Hussars, life in the Irish Hussars in the three years from 1979 to 1982 was nothing if not varied. First came the move from Paderborn and the various rounds of farewells to its leading citizens and to the military hierarchy under whom the regiment had served (mostly) happily for nearly ten years. They also relinquished the sponsorship of the school for the blind in the city and were relieved when 3rd Royal Tank Regiment, their successors in Barker Barracks, agreed to take on this hugely worthwhile responsibility.

Bhurtpore Barracks in Tidworth, one of many strung along the garrison's Great Trunk Road, had not much changed since it was built, in common with its equally evocative neighbours (Aliwal, Assaye, Candahar, Delhi, Jellalabad, Lucknow and Mooltan) in the early years of the century. The accommodation had been modernized, tank hangars added and relatively new offices built, but the layout still owed much to similar garrisons all over India before independence. Bhurtpore housed RHQ, two Chieftain tank squadrons (A and B) and D Squadron, which was organized into six armoured reconnaissance troops equipped with the Scimitar tracked vehicle. By the end of their first year in the United Kingdom, troops of D Squadron, assigned to the Army Command Europe Mobile Force, had served in five different countries. Across the 30-mile width of Salisbury Plain to Warminster went C Squadron, fulfilling the role (well known to squadrons of both QOH and QRIH) of Demonstration Squadron to the School of Infantry. The two Tidworth tank squadrons also became well travelled, taking it in turn to be deployed to Cyprus for six months to join the United Nations force on the so-called Green Line – the buffer zone which separated Greek Cyprus from its Turkish neighbour to the north.

All had gone according to plan and the training programmes were all running smoothly until, on 7 November, late in the afternoon, the commanding officer's telephone rang to say that the Garrison Commander, a brigadier, wished to see him. This was odd – he was not the regiment's operational commander and he was due to come to an officers' mess guest night that evening. What could be concerning him so urgently? Lieutenant Colonel Robin Rhoderick-Jones was soon to find out. Within weeks he and four other commanding officers of regiments in the United Kingdom were to be taken away and sent to Rhodesia (the old Southern Rhodesia, later to become Zimbabwe) as part of a Commonwealth Monitoring Force (CMF) set up by the British government to monitor a cease-fire between the warring factions in that country, oversee the assembly areas in which guerrillas (armed) would gather, and supervise the forthcoming elections designed to form a government which would take forward an independent Zimbabwe.

Rhoderick-Jones had some questions: how many Irish Hussars could he take with him (answer, twenty-five)? How long would this operation take (nobody knew)? In the event, the 1,200-strong CMF gathered in Salisbury (later Harare) just before Christmas. Rhoderick-Jones' area of responsibility was the Rhodesian Joint Operational Command area known to the Rhodesian Security Force's (RSF) 2nd Brigade as 'JOC Hurricane' – effectively,

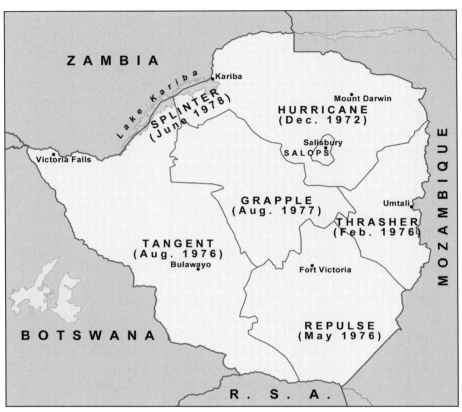

Rhodesia/Zimbabwe before Independence, 1980–1.

that part of Rhodesia north of Salisbury and stretching from Kariba near the
Zambian border in the west to the Mozambique border in the east. It was
the largest of five JOCs and, in terms of incidents, the nastiest – and the
place where the 14-year-old civil war had kicked off. His team was 350-
strong, half of them Australian, the rest British and New Zealanders. Five
sub-JOCS (four Australian and one provided by New Zealand) monitored
the activities of the RSF, while six Assembly Places (APs) had to be organized and manned – four of them to receive Robert Mugabe's ZANLA
(Zimbabwe African National Liberation Army, racially Mashona) fighters,
and two to look after Joshua Nkomo's ZIPRA (Zimbabwe Peoples Revolutionary Army, racially Ndebele) guerrillas. Each AP was manned by around
50 CMF soldiers and towards the end of this phase would hold up to

5,000 armed and sometimes ill-disciplined men and women. There were no text books, no manuals, no precedents, no blue-prints. All sides hated each other; the tightrope was narrow. Fearful odds indeed, should a breakdown in trust occur. But apart from sporadic incidents dealt with by the monitors with tact and good humour, all went well. There were no serious casualties.

The much heralded elections took place in March. The British government and its Governor in Salisbury were strongly briefed by Foreign Office officials flown in for the period that an alliance of Nkomo and the interim prime minister, Bishop Abel Muzorewa, would win enough seats to form a government. The CMF soldiers on the ground knew differently. All predicted a Mugabe landslide. And so it proved. By April 1980 all the Irish Hussars were back in Tidworth, having experienced an operation which was the first of its kind and which has never been – and almost certainly never will be – repeated.

The Colonel-in-Chief came to Tidworth in June, his visit coinciding with an old comrades weekend. Informality was the keynote – there was no parade – and, as the sun shone, His Royal Highness was able to meet the old and bold and the wives and children as well as the officers and soldiers. Among the guests was Colonel Sir Guy Lowther, who was commanding the 8th Hussars when Prince Philip first became Colonel-in-Chief. Notable, too, was the fact that because the county boundary between Hampshire and Wiltshire runs through Tidworth, two Lords Lieutenant were present. Also that month, the Band and Pipes and Drums took part in a Beating the Retreat ceremony on Horse Guards conducted by the massed bands of Irish regiments.

'The great thing about the Irish', mused Her Majesty the Queen Mother as she watched the ceremony from a window high above the parade in the company of the commanding officer, 'is that they have all the best tunes.' Praise indeed from Scotland's most distinguished lady. That summer, too, saw a dinner in the officers' mess for all past colonels and commanding officers of the regiment and its predecessors. Only three out of a possible seventeen were unable to be there.

September 1980 saw the advent of Exercise Crusader, during which some 30,000 regular and reserve soldiers stationed in the United Kingdom embarked with their equipment to reinforce the British Army of the Rhine in manoeuvres designed to rehearse what would be necessary should Western Europe be invaded. This exercise – the largest of its kind since the end of the Second World War – saw the Irish Hussars (less D Squadron

The Irish Hussars deploying by road, sea and rail – Exercise Crusader, the largest military crossing of the Channel since 1944.

who were engaged in practising home defence duties) drive their tanks from Warminster and Tidworth to Southampton docks before embarking for the sea voyage to northern Germany. That all the Chieftains arrived at their destination without a major breakdown was in itself something of a maintenance triumph – tanks had not motored this journey since the 8th Hussars did so in their Centurions in 1951. Their progress was watched by a large contingent of the British media, many of them anxious to report some sort

Exercise Crusader.

of newsworthy disaster. Instead, they were treated to the warming spectacle of a huge turnout of members of the regimental wives' club (led by the wife of the commanding officer), who had set up a champagne breakfast bar in a lay-by on the Winchester bypass. This incident received wide press coverage and provoked not a little outrage from those at the very top of the military hierarchy, who pompously considered the wives' conduct and the evident enjoyment of the soldiers to be 'unacceptably frivolous'. Once reinforcement was complete, the manoeuvres in Germany included a number of other NATO nations and again attracted media attention. The Canadian Broadcasting Corporation made a feature-length film of the conduct of the exercise during which the Irish Hussars were given great prominence. At the conclusion of three weeks of excitement the regiment returned to its more humdrum duties on Salisbury Plain.

The Colonel-in-Chief made two further visits when in March 1981 and 1982 he presented the shamrock. For the first of these he piloted himself to Tidworth in a helicopter of the Queen's Flight. This time there was a

The Thin White Line. Irish Hussars, Duke of Edinburgh's Squadron, Cyprus, 1981.

full dismounted parade finishing with a march-past at which Prince Philip took the salute. He then embarked – not without some evident trepidation as to the steadiness of the combination – in a pony and trap for his journey to open the recently refurbished corporals' mess, staying for lunch before flying away in the afternoon. The year was a somewhat disappointing one for sport – with the notable exception of winning the Captains' and Subalterns' polo cup. This was, however, to change dramatically in 1982: the football team won three major trophies including the Cavalry Cup, and the polo teams won six tournaments in a row including the Captains' and Subalterns' (for the third time in three years), the Inter-Regimental and the United Services, as well as providing half the Army team against the Royal Navy in the annual Rundle Cup. This was the first time that the Irish Hussars had achieved the hat-trick of military polo – an achievement attained several times by their old rivals the Queen's Own Hussars. There was, however, no polo ground at Münster, to where the regiment, under Lieutenant Colonel Richard Barron, moved in late summer. One would have to be constructed.

The year 1982 saw Falklands War, and although neither the Irish Hussars nor the Queen's Own Hussars played a part in that conflict, the County Class destroyer, HMS *Antrim* did. Landing special forces in Falkland Sound, giving them accurate and sustained covering fire while herself coming under continual air attack, including being hit by a bomb which luckily did not explode, and finally playing a major role in the re-taking of South Georgia, *Antrim*, affiliated to the Irish Hussars (as was the frigate HMS *Londonderry* and, later, the Landing Platform Dock HMS *Fearless*) performed with distinction. Naval affiliations were also close to the heart of the Queen's Own Hussars, notably the connection with the frigate HMS *Naiad* and the destroyer HMS *Birmingham*, both of which during their service often received parties of soldiers from the regiment eager to experience life on board ship. Both regiments also had close ties with armoured regiments from the Commonwealth and with their NATO allies. Perhaps the closest was that of the Irish Hussars with the 8th Canadian Hussars (Princess Louise's), which was cemented in an arrangement lasting for three decades whereby officers were exchanged for a two- or three-year tour. The Royal Canadian Hussars, three Australian regiments (including the infantry 3rd Royal Australian Regiment) and armoured regiments from Belgium, Germany and France were also affiliated, while close ties with the North Irish Horse arose out of the twinning of Territorial Army cavalry regiments with those of the regular Army. The Queen's Own Hussars' affiliations were with three Commonwealth units, one each from Canada, Australia and New Zealand, but perhaps their most sentimental attachment was to the 2nd Polish Corps, alongside which the 7th Hussars fought in Italy and whose *Maid of Warsaw* badge had been worn ever since, the tradition being carried on by the Queen's Royal Hussars. The Territorial Army units with which the QOH were most closely associated over the years began with the Warwickshire Yeomanry and the Worcestershire Yeomanry, which later amalgamated to become the Queen's Own Warwickshire and Worcestershire Yeomanry and was eventually absorbed into the Queen's Own Mercian Yeomanry.

The twenty-fifth or Silver Jubilee Year of the Queen's Own Hussars and the Queen's Royal Irish Hussars in 1983 went unmarked by any high-profile celebrations in either regiment. The Queen's Own Hussars cut anniversary cakes in both Catterick and Berlin and presented a silver rose-bowl to the Colonel-in Chief, while the Irish Hussars, split between the Canadian prairies and Münster, produced a special edition of *The Crossbelts* journal. Both regiments had very much in mind that within two years they would be remembering that they had reached their 300th birthday. The year was, however, momentous for the Irish Hussars in that they were about to embark for the first time on training for a role in Northern Ireland in providing the Prison Guard Force (PGF) for the notorious Maze prison on the outskirts of Lisburn which held violent paramilitaries from both sides of the political and religious divides, and the Crumlin Road Jail in Belfast which had held the prominent Sinn Feiner, Martin McGuinness, who was in due course to became a senior minister in the government of Northern Ireland. One hundred and forty-four officers and soldiers were deployed in November and they found that the Maze (formerly Long Kesh) was every bit as dispiriting as the most gloomy forecasts had suggested. Policed by over 1,000 warders, the inmates were all lifers, faced, often in their early twenties, with the prospect of never being released. The Guard Force worked on a fifteen-day cycle, manning sentry towers and gates, providing a stand-by force and doing a spell at Crumlin Road. There were also patrols with a battalion of the Ulster Defence Regiment and with the Royal Highland Fusiliers. Most importantly, more than half of the force were able to visit their homes – some for the first time in ten years; a small step in the regiment's fervent wish to being able to re-establish its historic links. All went well, and in February 1984 they were back in Münster, where the well-ordered cycle of BAOR and BATUS training was resumed. Recce and guided weapons troops had been reinstated, and most of the regiment went to Canada. The sporting summer was noted for the fact that the polo players again swept the board, winning all three major tournaments, including the United Services Cup played at Windsor.

The tour of the Queen's Own Hussars in Catterick and Berlin was very much a repeat of that of the mid-1960s, enlivened by the enthusiasm of the commanding officer, Lieutenant Colonel Jeremy Phipps, for escape and evasion exercises (acquired, it was assumed by the regiment, as a result of his tours with the Special Air Service) and the welcome deployment of a strong reconnaissance troop to Belize in Central America. D Squadron in Berlin, having welcomed visitors which included the Secretary of State for Defence and the Chief of the General Staff, distinguished itself with another Michael Parker production of the Berlin Tattoo, this time featuring the coronation of King George IV – apparently for no better reason than a perceived resemblance between that monarch and the D Squadron Leader, Major Malcolm Watson.

In 1985 Lieutenant Colonel David Jenkins of the Queen's Own Hussars had only just taken over command, and although plans for the tercentenary were well in hand, he was conscious that this, in contrast to the absence of any celebrations in 1885, was to be a high-profile event which simply had to be a success in every sense. The arrangements were complicated, made so by the need to gather in his Berlin squadron, organize the presentation of a new guidon, receive the Freedom of the City of Birmingham, and finally to take forward the process of moving his regiment from Catterick to Hohne almost immediately the celebrations were over. As was confidently (if secretly) predicted, all went well – indeed, supremely well – with one exception: the weather. From the moment the Colonel-in-Chief arrived on Tuesday, 14 May at nearby Darlington railway station to name one of British Rail's finest and newest locomotives 'The Queen's Own Hussars', the rain came down, and came down and came down. Her Majesty, accompanied by her daughter, Princess Margaret (the Senior Old Comrade), bravely carried on. In front of a packed, if damp, crowd of families, friends and old comrades, she received the Royal Salute, presented the new guidon, took the salute as the regiment marched past and made her speech.

Under cover of her transparent umbrella she met members of the Regimental Association and watched them also march past. Having had a few words with *Dettingen*, she ate lunch, after which she toured a display illustrating what her regiment was up to, and met the families. At tea-time she left, confident (in words taken from her address) that *'whatsoever is demanded of you, you will perform with the energy and efficiency for which you are renowned'*.

The next day was devoted to old comrades and families, with displays showing some of the history of the regiment. There were other entertainments, too, and in improved weather a barbecue lunch for everybody. There was then a day's break while the centre of operations moved to Birmingham. On Friday, 17 May, the old guidon was laid up in Birmingham Cathedral, the regiment received the Freedom of the City and, led by two mounted soldiers in full dress and the phlegmatic *Dettingen*, marched through it with bayonets fixed, the new guidon flying and drums beating. There was then a civic luncheon which finally sealed the close connection between city and regiment. In June the Queen's Own Hussars returned to Hohne, the garrison they had left eleven years previously.

The tercentenary celebrations of the Queen's Royal Irish Hussars took place in Münster a week later. Lieutenant Colonel Stephen Daniell had been in command for some time, and as the ceremonial part of the weekend was to take place on the nearby Dorbaum training area he was especially anxious about the weather. He had a word in this regard with the regimental padre and the padre did whatever padres do in these circumstances. Whatever it was, it worked, and the events took place in hot sunshine. The programme involved a mounted parade, the presentation of a new guidon, lunch for all the regiment, families and old comrades, a regimental revue, dances in the officers' and warrant officers' and sergeants' messes, and finally a church service, followed by barbecues. The old comrades began to arrive by air, train and road during Friday, 24 May and moved into accommodation provided by families, neighbouring regiments and hotels, before gathering for buffet suppers in both messes. On Saturday at 11.00 o'clock the Colonel-in-Chief arrived, inspected his regiment from a Land Rover flanked by a full-dress mounted escort of four. The old guidon was trooped, carried in a white Ferret scout car and driven off parade for the last time to be eventually laid up in Windsor Castle. The new guidon was then presented by Prince Philip and consecrated during a short drum-head service. Finally, the regiment drove past its Colonel-in-Chief, Chieftain guns traversing and dipping as the tanks rumbled past the saluting base. After lunch for the 2,400 participants and spectators, Prince Philip mingled with the families and old comrades. In the evening, at a local cinema, came the revue, traditionally an occasion when old scores are hilariously settled, and then, after drinks in the sergeants' mess for the Colonel-in-Chief, there was dinner and dancing until, in some cases, dawn. On Sunday came the church service conducted by the Chaplain General, then barbecue lunches, after which Prince Philip departed having spent two nights with his regiment. His presence and that of so many old comrades had contributed much to the family feeling fostered by the regiment since its formation twenty-seven years earlier. Like David Jenkins, Stephen Daniell and his whole regiment could now rest easy in the knowledge of a job well done and hugely appreciated by all who were present.

CHAPTER NINE

THE GULF WAR AND AMALGAMATION AGAIN

War settles nothing. (Agatha Christie)

The Queen's Own Hussars spent the last eight years of their existence quartered in Hohne. There they found much improved soldiers' accommodation and enough married quarters for all. The word was that their stay there was likely to be a lengthy one: the frequent changes of station and role for regiments of the Royal Armoured Corps were, it was forecast, about to be things of the past. Money was tight and regiments should be prepared to serve longer in one place. Another forecast change was the advent of simulation gunnery to enhance, and even partly replace, some aspects of the annual live firing on ranges in Germany and the United Kingdom which had so long been a familiar part of the training programme but was, of course, very expensive. To this end, simulation exercises (SIMEX) were being initiated in BAOR, and in 1986 the regiment was involved in trying out the new equipment. Otherwise little in the annual cycle had changed. In 1987 the regiment provided the Prison Guard Force in Northern Ireland, based on A Squadron but heavily reinforced to a strength of 160 all ranks by D Squadron. The following year, a regimental battlegroup, which included for the first time a Canadian infantry company, went to BATUS, while back in Europe the regiment won both the Cavalry Cup and the Royal Armoured Corps' hockey competition for the Jubilee Cup. The much loved drum horse *Dettingen* retired but was swiftly replaced by the Colonel-in-Chief with an equally handsome fellow, who after much deliberation (some of it quite passionate) was named *Peninsula* – a nod towards the fact that both the 3rd and 7th Hussars had served in that ultimately successful campaign.

In 1989 came the greatest innovation seen by the regiment since it was first mechanized, with the introduction of the Challenger tank to replace the ever creakier Chieftain. Not all fifty-seven of the designated establishment arrived at the same time, so that the mixture of old and new provided considerable training difficulties as crewmen learned the complexities of their new charges – and in particular the sophisticated fire-control systems – without forgetting their old drills. To enable the regiment to wrestle with unfamiliar equipment it enjoyed a relatively peaceful twelve months, but the following year saw two squadrons going to Canada with an infantry-led battlegroup and having again to come to grips with the Chieftains with which BATUS was still equipped. The best of the footballers were clearly not included in this deployment, for the regiment again won the Cavalry Cup against a backdrop of monumental convulsions in Europe, as the Berlin Wall came down and erstwhile component nations of the Soviet Union made their declarations of independence, while those countries under communist governments, free of the menace of Soviet interference, made moves towards democracy. The Cold War, if not over, was thawing rapidly and throwing up the question of whether the whole edifice of the British Army of the Rhine would also fade away. The more pressing news for the regiment, however, was the announcement that at the end of the year most of it was to deploy to Cyprus.

The Irish Hussars had spent the best part of the two years following Tercentenary still at Münster, and in 1986 the first Challenger tanks began to arrive. The two squadrons going to BATUS as a part of the 1st Battalion Queen's Lancashire Regiment battlegroup had not yet started to convert, and it was also in Chieftains that the regiment deployed for a major Northern Army Group exercise in Germany. A welcome addition to the music scene was the now fully fledged Pipes and Drums, twelve-strong and much in demand for both military and civilian functions, often in concert with the band, with whom they also made recordings. Its members were all crewmen – there being no official establishment for musicians other than those in the band – and it said much for their enthusiasm and the forbearance of often hard-pressed squadron leaders that they were able to find the time to rehearse properly and undertake engagements, often being away for days at a time. In 1987 the Colonel-in-Chief came to Münster, this time to see not only the regiment but the Grenadier Guards, who were also stationed in York Barracks. A further notable event was the arrival of the 8th Canadian Hussars at Lahr, a small garrison town some 30 miles southwest of Strasbourg, further cementing that regiment's close relationship with the Irish Hussars – a total of thirteen Canadian officers were to serve in the Irish Hussars over the years, with a similar number reciprocating. Lord

until, at last, on 25 February, the Brigade, led by the Irish Hussars (minus C Squadron attached to the Staffords battlegroup) crossed the start line – H-Hour being signalled by the commanding officer on his hunting horn. By 28 February they had reached the Basra Road, and at just after 0900 hours on that day 'Cease Fire' was ordered – Iraqi troops had been comprehensively thrown out of Kuwait. By St Patrick's Day all were safely back in Fallingbostel, having suffered no casualties other than an accidental injury to a soldier and a 'blue-on-blue' attack perpetrated by an American tank; neither incident was life-threatening. Two months later, the Colonel-in-Chief came to meet his regiment, hear the war stories and talk to the families who had waited so anxiously for nearly five months. Awards for gallantry and distinguished service followed: an OBE for the commanding officer, a Military Cross for Major Toby Maddison (D Squadron Leader), a Military Medal for Sergeant Nicholas Scott, three Mentions in Despatches, one British Empire Medal and fifteen official commendations from senior military commanders. The regiment gained many plaudits from the chain of command and from members of the world press who spent time with them, but perhaps the most meaningful was that written by the young captain of the 17th/21st Lancers who led his regiments' soldiers in joining the Irish Hussars for the campaign:

> On behalf of all 17th/21st Lancers who served with the Irish Hussars I would like to thank you for being so welcoming, professional and accommodating. Although it was frustrating for us not to have been serving with our own regiment in the Gulf, we could think of no better regiment we would rather have joined and served alongside. Like many of our forebears and brother officers we have established a close and strong friendship with your regiment and we will not forget the time we spent together.*

The historic events of 1990 were not confined to the Gulf. Europe also saw cataclysmic changes, most notably the opening of the Inner German Border, which followed the fall of the Soviet Empire, and the disintegration of the Warsaw Pact. Such events were unparalleled, but in the midst of them the Queen's Own Hussars quietly got on with the job and, in November, deployed to Cyprus. The regiment had already sent two squadrons to

---

* A detailed diary of the preparations for and the execution of the regiment's part in this war is set out in *The Crossbelts* (1991), pp. 352–401, the regimental journal of the Queen's Royal Irish Hussars, Vol. 6, No. 5.

BATUS with 1st Battalion Scots Guards, won the Cavalry Cup and done their considerable bit in helping to prepare regiments for the Gulf War, when training for their new role began. This involved the formation of two purpose-built squadrons; one from the combined strength of A and D Squadrons, was re-lettered G, while H Squadron was born out of B and C. G Squadron deployed as the Cyprus Emergency Reinforcement Regiment (CERR) responsible for the security of the Sovereign Base Areas (SBA) of Akrotiri (which included an RAF Station) in the south and Dhekelia in the east of the island. H Squadron joined the United Nations Forces in Cyprus (UNFICYP) contingent, patrolling and observing the Green Line and buffer zone. H Squadron shared this role with a Royal Tank Regiment squadron, but when that left in March 1991, G Squadron handed over SBA security to an infantry battalion, joined the rest of the regiment and donned blue berets. The tour was trouble-free, and despite the sun, sea and sand, most were happy when the six months were completed and the regiment was able in June to rejoin its families in Hohne.

On 23 July 1991 Lieutenant Colonel Charles Carter, commanding the Queen's Own Hussars, and Lieutenant Colonel Arthur Denaro of the Irish Hussars, called their men together and announced to all ranks that in 1993 their regiments were to amalgamate. Their respective Honorary Colonels, Brigadier James Rucker and General Sir Brian Kenny, wrote in their regimental journals of their sadness but emphasised their determination to make the amalgamation work. All four officers, while bitterly regretting this Ministry of Defence decision, made it clear that they welcomed with open arms the choice of partner. Prince Philip wrote to his regiment of his regret, concluding on a note of optimism:

> Over the last thirty-five years the Queen's Royal Irish Hussars have established an enviable reputation for loyal and dedicated service to the Queen and to their fellow countrymen. I am confident that this will be carried forward into the new regiment.

Having broken the bad news, both commanding officers came to the end of their tenures and it became the lot of Lieutenant Colonel Michael Bromley-Gardner of the Queen's Own Hussars and Lieutenant Colonel Andrew Bellamy of the Irish Hussars to prepare the way for amalgamation. A small committee was set up, chaired jointly by Brian Kenny and James Rucker and composed of a sprinkling of the old and bold, which included Major

General Richard Barron, late of the Irish Hussars, who was to become the first Honorary Colonel of the new regiment. The committee was charged with coming to an agreement on a variety of topics which included a new name and title, regimental cap and collar badges, various items of dress and accoutrements, commemorative customs and music. The name was settled quickly: Queen's Royal Hussars (The Queen's Own and Royal Irish) – the bracket containing a proper acknowledgement of the parent regiments. Badges and privileges were also subjects of early agreement. Figuring prominently are the Angel Harp of Armagh, the White Horse of Hannover and the circlet and motto of the Order of the Garter – the last being a legacy of the 3rd Hussars. The *Maid of Warsaw* was to be worn on the left sleeve of the khaki No. 2 Dress, and the New Zealand fern leaf was to be carried on all vehicles. Lance corporals would wear two stripes and the regimental motto would be *Mente et Manu* (by mind and hand, sometimes paraphrased as 'might and main'). The green beret would be worn by all ranks, and officers would retain the green and gold tent hat and would be encouraged to buy the distinctive green suit worn with black tie at dinner in the mess. In all, a fine and fair amalgam of the most distinctive visible features of both regiments.

The most serious problem facing both commanding officers was the matter of redundancies. The amalgamation and others like it across the Army had been brought about because of a perceived need by the Ministry of Defence to make economies – often dressed up as a reduction in the Army made possible by the ending of the Cold War. It had been announced that a proportion of the required redundancies in both regiments – amounting to a total of around 150 – would be voluntary, and for these the terms would be, if not generous, at least satisfactory. But there would also be forced redundancy: the discharging or transfer of soldiers who did not wish to go. And with all these weighty matters to be considered, amid a climate of no little uncertainty, life would have to go on as usual.

The Queen's Own Hussars were able to complete 1991 in routine BAOR duties, but the following year once again saw the regiment forced to split. In June, B Squadron, heavily reinforced by soldiers from A Squadron, went again to Cyprus to assume the role of SBA security, while four months later the Black Pigs, at a strength of 150 thanks to drafts from a thoroughly depleted C Squadron, went to Northern Ireland to man the Prison Guard Force. Although getting sporting teams together in these two years was sometimes difficult, there were some notable triumphs: in 1991 the hitherto unheralded fishing team won the BAOR Team Angling Competition, and the next year the regiment won both the BAOR Golf Championship and the polo Inter-Regimental – a competition won by the Irish Hussars the previous year, when they had also won the United Services Cup.

After the return from the Gulf and participation in the national 'welcome home' parade organized by the government in London, the Queen's Royal Irish Hussars also had little time for reflection. The Pipes and Drums appeared at the Royal Tournament, the officers gave a ball at the Dorchester hotel, and there was a great deal of activity forecast for 1992 for which to plan, all of which helped to concentrate minds on the present and push thoughts of amalgamation into the background. In June, the Colonel-in-Chief invited the serving regiment and the old comrades to a reception at St James's Palace during which the band beat retreat, a ceremonial prelude to the deployment in July of a regimental battlegroup to BATUS where, unusually if not uniquely, there were no infantry companies available, forcing them to produce their own – a situation which caused a great deal of initial glee among those who temporarily became 'grunts', followed by a quick realization that they were better off in their tanks.

Balaklava weekend saw the Irish Hussars troop the guidon for the last time in front of an appreciative audience in Fallingbostel of over 250 old comrades as well as regimental families and friends. In December the regiment deployed to Cyprus and, as was always necessary in this role, had to reorganize along the same lines as G and H Squadrons of the Queen's Own Hussars two years earlier. The opportunity was taken to demonstrate a pre-amalgamation unity by naming the squadrons imaginatively: the administrative element (Headquarter Squadron) became Alamein Squadron, while the two sabre squadrons, each around 150-strong, became Balaklava (commanded by a Queen's Own Hussar in the person of Major Nick Smith) and Dettingen, thereby encompassing the three battles which were to be commemorated annually by the Queen's Royal Hussars. On their return from Cyprus in June 1993 the regiment now embarked on a series of 'lasts': last all-ranks dance, last wives' club dinner, last sergeants' mess dinner, last officers' mess party, last drumhead service and, above all, the last visit of the Colonel-in-Chief in July. Soldiers, vehicles and property of the Queen's Own Hussars began the move from Hohne to Fallingbostel.

The ineffable sadness and sense of loss was felt every bit as deeply by the Queen's Own Hussars as D Squadron returned from Ulster and the regiment was gathered together for the final time. Their run-down, their redundancies and their myriad 'last' events were accentuated by the fact that they were also to lose the home they had occupied for eight years. It was all very hard to bear, and in store there was another morale-shattering blow to be borne by the new regiment. In April the Ministry of Defence announced its decision that regimental bands were to disappear. Another dearly held tradition was to be lost.

CHAPTER TEN

THE QUEEN'S ROYAL HUSSARS – THE FIRST FIVE YEARS

The old order changeth, yielding place to new. (Alfred, Lord Tennyson)

The last of the thirteen commanding officers of the Queen's Royal Irish Hussars was also the first of the Queen's Royal Hussars, and it was he who led the new regiment on its first parade, advancing in review order to report to the Colonel of the Regiment, Major General Richard Barron, also late of the Irish Hussars. Events on 1 September 1993 had begun with two fifty-strong guards furnished by officers and soldiers of the old regiments marching on to the parade ground with their guidons. The Queen's Own Hussars contingent was commanded by Lieutenant Colonel Michael Bromley-Gardner, the last of sixteen commanding officers, while the Irish Hussars were commanded by the regiment's second-in-command, Major Mark O'Reilly. Each guidon party was commanded by the regimental sergeant majors, Warrant Officers Class 1 Paul Foster and Billy Parkinson.

The guards were inspected by their own Honorary Colonels, Brigadier James Rucker and General Sir Brian Kenny. Both talked to every man before joining forces to inspect the combined Band, Pipes and Drums, led by *Peninsula* and *Winston*, after which the guidons were trooped through the ranks of the respective guards before being laid to rest on the piled drums as the two guards marched off parade in slow time. The proceedings so far had been witnessed by four guards of the Queen's Royal Hussars, who now came into their own under command of Lieutenant Colonel Andrew Bellamy, advancing in review order for thirty-five symbolic paces – one for each year of the existence of the Queen's Own and the Queen's Royal Irish Hussars – before crashing to a halt. Having been dedicated to the service of the new regiment, the guidons were trooped through the ranks, after which the Queen's Royal Hussars (The Queen's Own and Royal Irish), marched to their original positions and again advanced in review order to present arms to the first Honorary Colonel of the new regiment. General Barron then read to the assembled troops, families and other spectators, messages from both Her Majesty Queen Elizabeth, The Queen Mother, now Colonel-in-Chief of the Queen's Royal Hussars, and from the Deputy Colonel-in-Chief, His Royal Highness The Prince Philip, Duke of Edinburgh:

> *Clarence House*
> *On the formation of The Queen's Royal Hussars (The Queen's Own and Royal Irish) I send all ranks my warmest greetings. I am confident that the reputations for loyalty and courage which The Queen's Own Hussars and The Queen's Royal Irish Hussars have earned in their past history will be inherited and fully sustained in the future, and I trust that the new regiment will not only uphold but will enhance the noble traditions which are your heritage. I am indeed proud to be your Colonel-in-Chief and I can assure you that the interests of the regiment will always be close to my heart.*
> *Elizabeth R*
>
> *Balmoral*
> *Amalgamations are always sad occasions. Inevitably this amalgamation will be regretted by all ranks, and particularly by the old comrades, but both regiments have been through it before and the outcomes proved to be highly successful. I have no doubt that the Queen's Royal Hussars (The Queen's Own and Royal Irish) will be equally successful and will maintain all the special qualities of its famous parents and grandparents.*
> *Philip, Deputy Colonel-in-Chief*

The regiment, after one and a half hours on a parade which was at first heart-breaking and then radiated optimism, marched off the square to join families and guests – 1,000 in all – for lunch. Andrew Bellamy and those concerned with the faultless organization could well feel proud that they had given their regiment a fine start.

Each new squadron was composed identically, half the manpower and half the equipment being provided by each of the parent regiments. Similarly, each Challenger tank crew of four had two members from each regiment, and the shared accommodation for single soldiers was arranged similarly. It remained to be seen how successful this imposed reorganization would be as the regiment began for the first time to train as an entity. The remainder of the year was relatively quiet as troops and squadrons bedded in – a period of squadron training proving that things were working well as thoughts turned to a projected deployment of a regimental battlegroup to BATUS in the summer of 1994. On its formation the Queen's Royal Hussars served as a part of BAOR, but the government defence review of 1991, known as *Options for Change*, had decided that, as the Warsaw Pact had disintegrated, there was no military imperative to maintain a force of 55,000 in Germany; the numbers were to be cut by just over half and re-designated British Forces Germany (BFG). Among the Army-wide casualties of this decision were military bands.

The regiment was far from happy at the prospect of losing its band, a valued feature of life for over 200 years: accompanying the regiment wherever it was posted, providing the trumpet calls which regulated daily routine in peace and transmitted orders in war, and providing music, not just for the regiment but for the community in which it lived – a priceless contribution to winning and retaining the hearts and minds of that community clearly underestimated by the Ministry of Defence. Until mechanization in the 1930s, cavalry bands were mounted; thereafter, musicians were trained in first aid and stretcher-bearing, being in combat an essential part of the regiment's medical facilities. All this expertise was now to be lost through a decision described by General Richard Barron in a foreword to

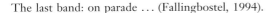

The last band: on parade ... (Fallingbostel, 1994).

The last band: …and off (Fallingbostel, 1994).

The Crossbelts, the first Queen's Royal Hussar journal, as '*disgraceful, illustrating a fundamental lack of understanding of the role of the band in a regiment such as ours*'. In April 1994, in Fallingbostel, the band gave its last performance under Bandmaster David Cresswell (who was soon to be commissioned as a Director of Music), before its musicians dispersed to a variety of central bands, among which was one to be called the Band of the Hussars and Light Dragoons designed to serve all three remaining hussar regiments – an arrangement which was not to last for more than a few years before falling to further cuts in military music. The regiment would now be largely dependent on the Pipes and Drums to add regular musical colour, a valuable and much appreciated adornment not available to most cavalry regiments. Also a wrench was the departure of *Winston*. The regiment was not authorized to hold two drum horses and he, as the junior partner, was despatched amidst great regret from all ranks to a settled life in the Royal Paddocks at Hampton Court. *Peninsula*, happily, was to remain on strength as the official regimental mascot – one of only two drum-horses serving in the line cavalry, the other being with the Royal Scots Dragoon Guards.

Two aspects of Queen's Royal Hussar life were in some ways enhanced by the amalgamation: the Regimental Association grew in scope and membership and the number of Territorial Army affiliations and allied regiments was, if anything, strengthened. The Association's formal structure was based at Home Headquarters at Regent's Park Barracks in London, presided over by the Regimental Secretary (always a retired officer), Major Bob Smith, assisted by a very small team of civil servants and ably supported by Mrs Inge Smith, Bob's wife, who for years had been personal assistant to generations of Irish Hussar commanding officers. The first chairman of the QRH Association was Brigadier Robin Greenwood, late of the Queen's Own Hussars, who presided over a network of eleven troops, each with their own distinctive banner, distributed over England, Ireland and Germany – those in Germany being formed by retired soldiers who had married German girls and settled locally. Each troop held at least one gathering a year, and in addition there was an annual dinner in London (attended in 1994 by over 300 members) which took place on the eve of the Cavalry Memorial Parade in May, as well as a dinner in Birmingham on the evening before that city's Remembrance parade – which in 1993 also attracted over 300 and was followed by participation in the parade in the city centre the next day.

Territorial affiliations embraced both the North Irish Horse, now reduced to an independent reconnaissance squadron, and A (Warwickshire and Worcestershire) Squadron of the Royal Mercian and Lancastrian Yeomanry. Neither was to retain those designations for long as the reserve Army underwent many changes, but happily they were to remain identifiable in their new organizations. Allied regiments numbered twelve: three Canadian, four Australian, three from post-apartheid South Africa, one from New Zealand and one from Belgium. For the moment, the tradition of having an 8th Canadian Hussar officer (always a captain) on strength while a Queen's Royal Hussar officer reciprocated, remained in place – despite threats to the contrary by cost-cutting minions of 'higher authority'. Two further affiliations were also important: the regiment sponsored army cadet troops in both Northern Ireland and Worcestershire, and these keen young men were able to visit the regiment on official trips and wore the cap-badge. The affiliated warship in 1993 was still HMS *Birmingham*.

In 1994 the regiment's major engagement after taking a battlegroup to BATUS in July was forecast to be the deployment of a Prison Guard Force towards the end of the year. The Canadian trip was of great significance, being an opportunity for the Queen's Royal Hussars to demonstrate that they were combat-ready and fit to take their place in the BFG order of battle. The Commanding Officer took RHQ, A and D Squadrons and a company of the Devon and Dorset mechanized infantry battalion across the Atlantic and proceeded to demonstrate to the entire satisfaction of the Commander of the 1st Armoured Division that they were indeed ready, the general declaring himself delighted by the regiment's performance on the final test exercise. Having completed his tour of command and negotiated with commendable aplomb the last tricky twelve months, Andrew Bellamy handed over command to Lieutenant Colonel Nigel Beer – but not before he was able with much satisfaction to witness victory in the Cavalry Cup and the inter-regimental polo tournament, and watch the alpine ski team come third in the Army competition, the highest placed of all regimental teams.

The new commanding officer faced a period of considerable uncertainty: training for the PGF deployment to Northern Ireland by a considerably enhanced (160-strong) A Squadron was cancelled almost as soon as it began – the early fruit of an IRA ceasefire; a projected second visit to BATUS in the winter of 1994 was also called off after training had started, and there were two unsettling rumours, one speculating that the expected move of the regiment to Catterick in 1995 would be postponed, if not cancelled, and the other that the regiment would be sent to Bosnia-Herzegovina to take part in a United Nations operation attendant upon the civil war which had broken out in that part of the former Yugoslavia. Amidst all this confusion, relevant training was difficult to plan, but it soon became apparent that a regimental battlegroup would after all go to Canada, but not until April 1995, and that the move to Catterick would indeed take place in the summer; the position regarding Bosnia remained uncertain. As the future became clearer, the Lord Mayor of Birmingham, Sir Richard Knowles, arrived for a visit in March, and on St Patrick's Day Lady Knowles, Enniskillen born and bred, presented the shamrock. The deployment to BATUS broke new ground as the regiment became guinea pigs for new concepts involving laser-based tactical engagement simulation against an uncontrolled enemy – the most realistic approach to combat training that most tank crews had ever experienced. It did, however, deprive the football team of some key players, resulting in the loss of the Cavalry Cup in the final. The rugby team, however, excelled itself, only losing in the Army Cup to the eventual winners, while the alpine skiers became Army champions, triumphantly seeing off the much fancied Corps teams.

The regiment's role in Catterick bore no resemblance to that carried out in the past by both the parent regiments. Basic training for Royal Armoured Corps recruits, together with those for the Royal Artillery, Royal Engineers

The Cavalry Tradition. The QRH contingent at a meet of the Bedale Hunt.

and seven other Corps, had now been moved to Winchester, after which trade training took place at the Armour Centre at Bovington. The barracks in Yorkshire had been modernized, and a new tank park which did justice to the complex equipment had been built to accommodate the regiment, which was now to provide the heavy armour for 19 Mechanised Brigade. Some things in Yorkshire had, however, not changed: the beauty of the countryside, the friendliness of the locals, the sporting opportunities – and the weather! Almost immediately after arrival Nigel Beer found himself swopping his tent hat for a United Nations beret and flying to Bosnia.

The war in Bosnia-Herzegovina (henceforth in this account abbreviated to Bosnia) was part of the violent break-up of Yugoslavia which saw, in 1991, the secession of Croatia and Slovenia from the old communist federation. In early 1992 the multi-ethnic population of Bosnia (44 per cent Muslim Bosniaks, 33 per cent Orthodox Serbs and 17 per cent Catholic Croats) voted in a referendum for independence. The Serbs in the country, backed by the neighbouring Serbian government to the east, rejected the results of the vote, mobilizing their forces to secure Serb territory within

Bosnia and Herzegovina, 1995–6.

Bosnia, including the ethnic cleansing of Bosniak and Croat towns and villages in eastern Bosnia. Croatia, with a long border on the north and west of Bosnia, also aimed at securing parts of the country as Croatian. The war was bitter, featuring the indiscriminate shelling of towns and villages, widespread ethnic cleansing and systematic killings and mass rape, mainly perpetrated by Serbs, but also to a lesser extent by Croat and Bosnian forces – the Serb massacre of Muslims at Srebrenica being the most notorious in scale. A United Nations Protection Force (UNPROFOR) had been deployed to, first, Croatia and then Bosnia since 1992 to support the delivery of humanitarian aid and 'police safe areas', and it was under its auspices that Beer conducted his reconnaissance. By the time a peace treaty was signed in December 1995, plans were afoot that the United Nations should withdraw and be replaced by IFOR, a NATO-led Implementation Force to monitor – and if necessary enforce – the terms of that treaty. It was as a component of IFOR that the Queen's Royal Hussars would be deployed – and with them would go their tanks.

For this task the regiment was to be composed of its headquarters, Recce Troop (Scimitar tracked combat vehicles), support echelons and two sabre squadrons. Live-firing training was intensified at both Castlemartin and the Warcop Ranges in Cumbria, concentrating on techniques appropriate to the Bosnian topography. The commanding officer had decided that B Squadron would undertake the whole six-month tour but that A and C Squadrons would rotate at the halfway point. D Squadron would provide a formed troop for each of the other squadrons, thereby ensuring that almost all members of the regiment would have a taste of whatever the deployment had to offer. Entry to Bosnia for both vehicles (by sea) and men (by air) would be through Split, a Croatian port on the Adriatic. On 10 January 1996, vehicles and crews were reunited and were taken by transporters into Bosnia. The QRH battlegroup, made up of A Squadron, a company of the Royal Canadian Regiment and a company of the 2nd Battalion Light Infantry, came under command of 2 (Canadian) Multi-National Brigade, much to the delight (or perhaps apprehension!) of Captain John Malevich, the regiment's 8th Canadian Hussar exchange officer who was second-in-command of A Squadron. B Squadron was detached to 4 (UK) Armoured Brigade and then divided, each half coming under command of an infantry battalion.

The first problem was to find suitable accommodation within the regiment's allotted area in the north-west of the country. Initially, RHQ and A Squadron were co-located at Bosanski Petrovac, where there were garages and workshops. It was, however, deemed desirable that A Squadron should be left to get on with the job and that RHQ should move away. Regimental Sergeant Major Tom Hamilton found a small industrial complex a few kilometres away in a small town called Kljuc. The lavatories were blocked and the place was littered with long dead animals and other detritus, but Hamilton nevertheless advised the commanding officer that he would have it cleaned up in a few days. During this extremely unpleasant work one of the lavatories backfired, covering an unfortunate soldier with excrement, and a dead cow, while being cut up with a chainsaw into manageable pieces for burning, exploded, throwing its stomach contents over the operator as its gases exploded. Regimental Sergeant Majors are not generally known for being prone to helpless laughter, but Hamilton took several minutes to recover from the paroxysms of mirth which engulfed him.

The IFOR mission involved the keeping apart of the former belligerents by patrolling, the manning of roadblocks and high-visibility deterrence of unlawful military manoeuvres by Serb, Croat or Bosnian forces. The topography – mountainous, forested, with narrow tracks often bordered by vertical precipices – was hardly suitable for the movement of tanks, and young drivers more accustomed to the flat plains of Germany and Yorkshire often found their task daunting. Nevertheless, employing a mixture of cavalry elan and careful route selection, the Challengers of the regiment proved the infantry sceptics ('You'll never get those tanks up there') wrong – just as the 8th Hussars had done with their Centurions in Korea. The value of having tanks on hand was highlighted by an incident in March when troops of A Squadron were deployed to block the route of a Bosnian armoured column bound for the town of Kulen Vakuf, near the border with Croatia, to chase out elements of Croat military which occupied the west of the town. On seeing, first, the Scimitars of Recce Troop, the Bosnian general halted his force and explored forward in his staff car. Sighting the Challengers, he ordered a precipitate withdrawal.

The second half of the six-month tour was largely devoted to overseeing the safe return of the civilian population to their devastated towns and villages. When B Squadron first arrived at Mrkonjic Grad, a town with a pre-war population of 27,000, only six people remained; by the end of the tour it had become busy again as families returned home. C Squadron arrived at the end of March, having had a pretty torrid time in Yorkshire trying to fulfil a regiment's worth of commitments, and took over an area of 1,200km^2. They managed, without casualties, one serious incident at the end of April by keeping a party of Serbs, who wanted to visit graves, apart from an angry crowd of Muslims, who had been unable to visit the graves of their compatriots in Serbian territory. The squadron was also deployed to the troublesome Kulen Vakuf when, contrary to the ceasefire agreement, Bosnian Croat forces refused to move back into their barracks. The arrival of the Challengers clearly visible on the hills around the town was enough to persuade the rebels to move out. So far not a round had been fired by either a tank or recce vehicle, so with the twin aim of gunnery practice for the crews and a firepower demonstration to illustrate IFOR's armoured

Bosnia, 1996. B Squadron's Challengers en route to Kulen Vakuf.

capability to the various military factions, a range was set up near Glamoč, another little town which had suffered terribly in the civil war. Recce Troop, B and C Squadrons all fired there in May and June in front of audiences mightily impressed by both the accuracy and the destruction of targets.

Every bit as important as the military operations undertaken by the regiment were those described generically in NATO jargon as G5, that is civil affairs: working and liaising with local civilians, providing help and advice and, until an international police task force arrived, dealing with police matters. The battlegroup's G5 officer was Major Keith Deakin – the same man who had carefully explained to a surprised brigadier visiting the Irish Hussars twenty years earlier that 'he had been fookin' conned' into joining the regiment but who was now commanding Headquarters Squadron. Deakin, with advice from the Canadian headquarters and help from two New Zealand liaison officers, concentrated on three population centres within the battlegroup's orbit – Kljuc, Bosanski Petrovac and Sanski. All had been predominantly Muslim before the war, and the ethnically cleansed citizens who had been forced to leave were now trickling back. The key people with whom Deakin and his men had to work were local heads of government and public utilities, together with senior policemen and heads of schools. Infrastructure in these towns had collapsed, the houses vandalized, the streets full of rubbish and dead animals, the buildings without heat or light. QRH vehicles, borrowed military engineer equipment and heavy transport were all used to improve matters to such an extent that the initially suspicious locals were persuaded that peace was better than war. Streets were cleared, rubbish burnt and trees chopped down to provide fuel. Deakin and his senior ranks spent hours listening to refugees' problems and then seeking out the appropriate authority who could best help – often the United Nations High Commission for Refugees. Some cash became available from the British Overseas Development Fund and was used where necessary. In this way, after months of patient work, not only were the streets cleared but over thirty schools, colleges, small businesses, medical centres and local utilities were either working again or had funds with which to restart.

As the six months came to an end, a C Squadron Land Rover drove over an anti-personnel mine which luckily damaged only a wheel, causing no casualties – a gentle foretaste of what was to lie ahead in even more violent countries. But there was one potentially more serious incident when a fire broke out in a five-storey building in Kljuc. This was spotted by chance by a party of soldiers returning from a night out. The local fire brigade were at the scene but seemed uncertain how to begin a rescue. The second-in-command, Andrew Ledger, arrived (dressed in shirt, baggy blue shorts and loafers) and took charge, but by that time Lance Corporal Sean Begley had commandeered a vehicle with a jib-arm and bucket and was, with the help of one or two others, engaged in rescuing people from the second floor, watched by a party of apparently helpless firemen and locals. By the end of June the regiment was back in Catterick, joined shortly by their tanks. It had been a successful tour, exemplified formally by the award to the regiment of a Canadian Forces Unit Commendation, the first to a non-Canadian unit, a Queen's Commendation for Valuable Service (QCVS) to the commanding officer and seven other commendations (including one to Begley) awarded by the joint operational and multi-national divisional commanders to soldiers ranging in rank from Trooper to Warrant Officer. The Canadian citation read:

The Queen's Royal Hussars Battlegroup made a critical contribution to the IFOR mission in the 2 Canadian Multinational Brigade area of operations during the period January to June 1996. The battlegroup achieved outstanding success in all dimensions of this challenging operation, enhancing the overall effectiveness, image and credibility through its successful implementation of both military and related civil tasks. The professionalism and resolve displayed by all ranks of the Queen's Royal Hussars Battlegroup were of the highest standard.

After being reunited with their families and having enjoyed a spot of leave, there was but little time for the squadrons to draw breath, especially for A and the newly reformed Black Pigs. They began a period of intensive but very brief training prior to deploying to BATUS in September as part of the King's Own Royal Border Regiment battlegroup, while a month later a regimental battlegroup with the other two squadrons and recce troop was also BATUS-bound under the command of Lieutenant Colonel Nick Smith, who had taken over from Nigel Beer. None of the four squadrons or Regimental Headquarters had had the benefit of the usual pre-BATUS training packages and it was much to the regiment's credit that the Chief of the General Staff expressed himself impressed with their performance.

As 1996 drew to a close, planning was already in hand for a major event due to take place in June the following year. The Queen's Royal Hussars had no guidon; instead, for nearly four years, it had continued to cherish and, when appropriate, parade the guidons of both its parent regiments. On Friday, 13 June 1997 this unique state of affairs was to come to an end with the presentation of a new guidon by Queen Elizabeth. Nick Smith set up a small team within the regiment to plan for this event, while at Home Headquarters in Regent's Park Barracks the new Regimental Secretary, Major Chris Owen, began the task of collating the plans made by Association troops and individuals intent on gathering at Catterick – the first time that the Association had had the opportunity to visit the regiment, an earlier old comrades' weekend having been cancelled because of the Bosnia deployment. It soon became apparent that around 1,000 of them intended to join in the weekend's events – testing Chris Owen's newly acquired computer skills to the limit.

Preparation for the great day took over regimental life: the diary of events for 1997 shows the period from 2 to 11 June as 'Regimental Drill Parades', incorporating at the behest of the Commanding Officer some complicated movements which were strangely absent from the RSM's drill manuals. It was much to the credit of Tom Hamilton that he met this considerable challenge so successfully. Then came the dress rehearsal, at which Captain Charlie Duff, dressed as the Pink Panther, played the part of the Colonel-in-Chief, a sight so arresting that although it threatened solemnity it undoubtedly eliminated inattention. The preliminary parades had all taken place in brilliant sunshine, but it rained on the dress rehearsal and the forecast for the day itself was not good. In the event, however, the weather turned out to be a great deal better than that endured by the Queen's Own Hussars at their tercentenary parade. The old comrades began to assemble on the Thursday, as did the representatives from most of the affiliated regiments who attended receptions in the officers' and sergeants' messes that evening. The next morning saw the arrival of Her Majesty, the Colonel-in-Chief, entering her fiftieth year in that capacity, accompanied by her deputy, Prince Philip. The old guidons were trooped through the ranks and marched off to the strains of Auld Lang Syne and not a few bursting hearts and flowing tears from the old comrades. They were eventually to be laid up in the warrant officers' and sergeants' mess. The new guidon, resplendent with the regulation (now forty-four) accumulated battle honours, was dedicated on the piled drums, and Queen Elizabeth delivered her clearly heartfelt congratulatory words. After lunch for nearly 2,000, Her Majesty (remarkably, now aged ninety-six) went walkabout among the families and old comrades, while Prince Philip viewed a number of stands illustrating life in the regiment and was introduced to Challenger 2, the next generation of tank which the regiment was due to receive in 1999.

The royal party left late in the afternoon, and in the evening, as the sun set, the Band of the Hussars and Light Dragoons, together with the regiment's Pipes and Drums, beat retreat; this stirring occasion was followed by supper parties given by the messes and individual squadrons. The weekend concluded after some rousing singing at a church service the following day and a barbecue lunch for everyone, at which Trooper Ramsay was presented with a brand-new Rover motorcar won in the draw – a fortuitous piece of timing as he had written off his old car during the previous week. As everyone went home, the officers and men of the regiment could reflect that not only did they now possess their own guidon but that they had given all their guests a most happy few days and a spiritual uplift which would live long in the memory.

There was now only a scant three months until the regiment deployed on its feet to Northern Ireland. There was much specialist training to fit in: re-familiarization with rifles and other small arms; urban Northern Ireland

Northern Ireland 1997–8. Rural patrolling.

training at the Cinque Ports Training Area at Lydd and Hythe in Kent; and rural Northern Ireland training on the training area at Thetford in Norfolk. A Squadron was put into suspended animation – its officers and soldiers transferred to reinforce the others for the six months of the tour. The role was that of the so-called Drumadd Roulement Battalion, roulement being a term used by the Army to describe short tours by major units, while Drumadd Barracks in Armagh had once been the home of HQ 3 Infantry Brigade, under whose command the regiment came. Although this HQ had moved to Mahon Barracks in Portadown, Nick Smith and a small regimental headquarters were in Drumadd where, curiously, there was no proper role for him: the three operational squadrons, B based in Bessbrook Mill, near Newry, being under command of the King's Own Scottish Borderers, C at Keady and Middletown close to the border with the Republic under command of the Home Service 8th Battalion of the Royal Irish Regiment, while D, although in Drumadd, was the brigade reserve force. This gave Nick Smith and Tom Hamilton freedom to roam (and in the commanding officer's case, an occasional day's hunting) and to join in some of the lengthy and demanding patrols, during one of which the RSM was startled to be told by a Lance Corporal pointing at a building, 'That's my house!' By the end of April 1998 the regiment had completed its tour and enjoyed some three weeks leave.

While they were away, the Colonel of the Regiment invited Queen Elizabeth to lunch with the trustees in the Cavalry Club to mark her fiftieth anniversary as Colonel-in-Chief. This notable event took place in November, and Richard Barron widened the scope to include five former colonels of the Queen's Own Hussars and the Irish Hussars, so that Generals Howard-Dobson, Carnegie, Kenny and Strawson and Brigadier Rucker were able to join what was to be a very happy gathering – so happy, indeed, that two of the trustees who had booked seats back to the West Country at 4.00 o'clock found themselves still seated at the table as their train left Waterloo, the Colonel-in-Chief showing no sign of wishing to bring proceedings to a close. Planning at Catterick now focussed on the move to Germany, due to take place in July and August, and the re-forming of A Squadron was put on hold until commitments for the following year became clear. In the event, it was to be another four years before it was resurrected, while Athlone Barracks in Sennelager was to become the regiment's home for upwards of two decades.

CHAPTER ELEVEN

ATHLONE BARRACKS – NEW HOME, NEW TANKS, NEW ADVENTURES

What's the good of a home if you are never in it? (George Grossmith)

Athlone Barracks was first occupied in 1945 by the Canadian Army and named after Major General the (first) Earl of Athlone who had been Governor-General of Canada throughout the Second World War. The impressively multi-named earl (Alexander Augustus Frederick William George Cambridge) had been born Prince Alexander of Teck, his family changing its name to Cambridge in 1917, and was well connected, being both a cousin and brother-in-law to King George V. As Prince Alexander he had joined the 7th Hussars and in 1896 was fighting in southern Africa against the rebel Matabele and Mashona people. In the Great War he had commanded the 2nd Life Guards, later becoming a Brigadier General and the head of the British Mission to the Belgian Army. In 1917 he was ennobled (he turned down a marquessate as being too Germanic) and in 1924 became Honorary Colonel of the 7th, a position he held for twenty-two years. The Queen's Royal Hussars could hardly have occupied a more appropriately named barracks.

The first year in Germany as an armoured regiment in 20 Armoured Brigade had as its main focus the conversion of tank crewmen to the mysteries of Challenger 2. The tank and its simulated training aids were a major leap in technology from anything the regiment had experienced. Complicated training problems were, however, constantly being interrupted by the need to provide young officers and soldiers to reinforce the commitment of other regiments to the messy operations in the Balkans – there was now a need to deploy units not only to Bosnia but also to Kosovo, and on occasions upwards of fifty men were away at any one time. There were few new tanks available on site, and some training courses had to take

Prince Alexander of Teck, Earl of Athlone, 7th Hussars, after whom Athlone Barracks, Sennelager is named.

place at Bovington. Manpower turbulence was the order of the day, and in the circumstances it was decided that A Squadron should remain in suspended animation while the other three provided troop and squadron support to infantry battalions as they prepared to deploy to the Balkans. There were, however, advantages in this new station, principally the respite from the two operational tours launched from Catterick – a relative stability which was welcomed by the families. This was also a time of many hierarchical changes: Richard Barron, who as Honorary Colonel had set the new regiment the highest of standards, retired and handed over to Major General David Jenkins (late of the Queen's Own Hussars); the commanding officer was now Lieutenant Colonel Chris Vernon and the RSM was WO I Mark Butler who, like Tom Hamilton, was to be commissioned into the regiment and would hand over to WO I Ken Sparkes at the end of 1999. At Home Headquarters in London, Chris Owen had retired and Major David Innes-Lumsden had sportingly agreed to fill the gap for a year until another regimental secretary could be found. He was still in post seventeen years later and for most of this time was supported by the same assistant secretary, Major Timmy Timmons.

The appointment of Honorary Colonel, more usually called Colonel of the Regiment, is an important one and requires a great deal of administrative support provided by the regimental secretary, with whom he works closely. The Colonel has three major functions, the first being his chairmanship of the regimental trustees, in which post he is ultimately responsible for the prudent management of the regiment's wealth. Next is his role in the selection of the regiment's commanding officer, a process in which the view of the Colonel is important but not overriding, the final choice being ultimately in the hands of the Military Secretary at the Ministry of Defence, who is in a position to judge the military merits of each candidate. This was not always the case: there was a time when, for example, the likes of General Pat Howard-Dobson of the Queen's Own Hussars and Major General John Strawson of the Irish Hussars had absolute discretion as to who would command 'their regiments' next. Thirdly, and most importantly for the future well-being of the regiment, comes the interviewing and subsequent selection of young potential officers. Young men, at the Royal Military Academy, Sandhurst or while still at school or university, who wish to join the Queen's Royal Hussars, are interviewed by the Colonel and usually sent to the regiment for a few days to determine whether they would fit in happily. If the signs are positive, then the Colonel is in a position to accept the would-be entrant, the final decision being his as long as it fits in with the quotas imposed from time to time by the Ministry. In order to keep in touch with regimental affairs, the Colonel receives regular bulletins from the incumbent commanding officer and makes frequent visits, sometimes low-key but often more formally, for example to present campaign medals, accompany the Colonel-in-Chief or as the senior member of the Regimental Association (of which he is president) on their occasional trips to the regiment. One such occasion took place in June 1999 when 150 members of the Association went to Sennelager for a long weekend, led by their new chairman, Lieutenant Colonel Kenneth Bidie, and were, as usual, royally entertained, proceedings beginning in a splendid newly-furnished corporals' mess. The sun shone and the old comrades saw the regiment at work and play ('It's all changed since my day'), inspected a command and operations centre in the field ('We never had anything like this'), made a huge fuss of *Peninsula*, who was paraded in all his finery ('Awe'), and ate and drank in the finest traditions of England and Ireland while being entertained, it seemed almost endlessly, by the Dragoons Band and the regimental Pipes and Drums. A leisurely Sunday began with a not-too-early church service, and the mass departure of all the guests on Monday morning was accompanied by a genuine and unanimous appreciation of the planning and effort made by all ranks to ensure a happy and informative time for their predecessors. Two royal occasions followed, the first being a visit by Prince Philip in October, when he took a keen, and it need hardly be said, knowledgeable interest in the intricacies of Challenger 2 and was so taken by the newly acquired tartan trews of the Pipes and Drums that a bolt of the cloth was despatched to Buckingham Palace forthwith. In November, the Colonel-in-Chief gave a reception for the Association in St James's Palace, at which Her Majesty was able to meet an impressively large gathering of members and their wives. During all these and similar events the Colonel of the Regiment is the key figure.

The Queen Mother dominated the news in the year 2000, during which the country celebrated her one hundredth birthday. On 19 July, on Horse Guards, Major Michael Parker, now the unchallenged doyen of nationwide spectacular events, produced a truly British occasion. As well as the military splendour, over 300 charities and organizations with which Queen Elizabeth was involved – from the Sussex Winkle Club ('Oh yes, I'm a Winkle, I must remember to wear my badge', she said) to the Victoria Cross and George Cross Association – were actively present. Three mounted officers represented the Colonel-in-Chief's cavalry regiments, Captain Simon Maggs of the regiment being flanked by a Queen's Dragoon Guard and a 9th/12th Lancer. The guidon was marched past the saluting dais in company with the colours, standards and guidons of Queen Elizabeth's regiments from all over the Commonwealth, and the Pipes and Drums were among the thousands of military musicians and choristers. Parker, who had also masterminded the celebrations attendant on Her Majesty's eightieth and ninetieth birthdays, was knighted after this triumphal apotheosis of his career.

The regiment, still of three tank squadrons, was now conversant with Challenger 2 and in May and June went as a battlegroup to BATUS, Chris Vernon having under his command Recce Troop with its Scimitar tracked, light combat vehicles (CVR(T)), C and D Squadrons and two companies of infantry. Unusually, B Squadron also crossed the Atlantic to play the part of OPFOR, the term used to denote the enemy during the exercises at Suffield, and were equipped for the purpose with a variety of CVR(T) vehicles visually disguised as tanks. Later that year, a regimental battlegroup deployed again, this time to Poland, which had now become a major armoured training area for NATO, replacing the far more limited Soltau which had been handed back to the Germans and was being turned into a wildlife reserve. In D Squadron one of the troops on this exercise was led by His Royal Highness, Crown Prince Hamzah of Jordan who, having completed courses at the Royal Military Academy, Sandhurst and Bovington, was attached to the regiment for six months. He clearly enjoyed himself:

> *The troop I was working with was welcoming and full of energy and enthusiasm ... It was a wonderful experience but I could not have done it without the support and guidance of Sergeant Christie and Corporal Robertson. I am grateful to have served with such a fine regiment.*

B Squadron, meanwhile, having been reunited with their Challengers, prepared for active service in the Balkans.

Until the late 1980s when, in common with other parts of communist Eastern Europe, it began to break up, the Federal Republic of Yugoslavia was made up of six socialist republics: Bosnia and Herzegovina, Macedonia, Montenegro, Croatia, Slovenia and Serbia. Within Serbia were two largely autonomous provinces, one of which, about the size of Yorkshire, was Kosovo (the other being Vojvodina) which had a common border with Albania, a country which in the early 1990s was itself beginning to overthrow its communist government. At the beginning of the twentieth century Kosovo's demographic make-up was almost equally divided between ethnic

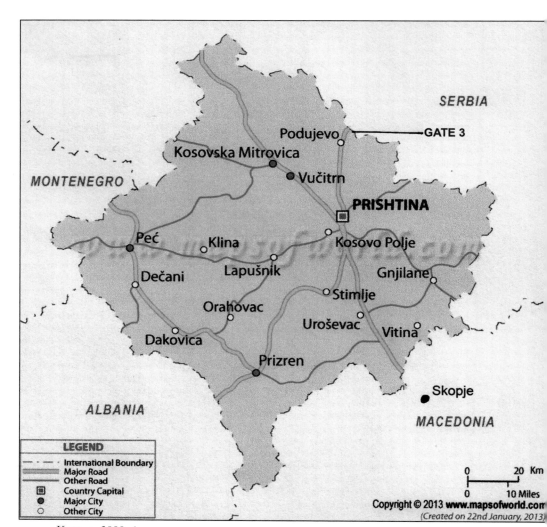

Kosovo, 2000–1.

Serbs and Albanians, but by 1990 the Serb proportion had declined to less than 10 per cent, and the overwhelmingly Albanian population, resenting Serb dominance, was in a state of revolt. During the next decade a rebel group calling itself the Kosovo Liberation Army (KLA), equipped with arms smuggled from Albania and large quantities captured from police and army barracks, became a major force, triggering a reaction which saw Serb paramilitaries and regular forces begin a campaign of retribution, targeting KLA activists and sympathisers and killing around 2,000. In 1999 NATO intervened by setting up the Kosovo Force (KFOR) of international peace-keepers with a mandate to deter hostility against Kosovo by the Serb military, demilitarize the KLA, establish a secure environment and support an international humanitarian aid effort. By the year 2000 KFOR had deployed in Kosovo five brigade-sized formations from, respectively, the United Kingdom, the United States, France, Germany and Italy, under command of the NATO Allied Rapid Reaction Force. B Squadron, part of a 1st Battalion Princess of Wales's Royal Regiment (1PWRR) battlegroup under command of 3 Commando Brigade Royal Marines, travelled by sea to Greece and then by rail and road to set up their base in Podujevo, a town 20 miles north of the capital Pristina and the scene of a notorious massacre of fourteen Albanian women and children by the Serb military in 1999.

B Squadron's mission was to help maintain the peace and security of their operational area by the manning of observation posts on the border with Serbia and frequent patrols by tank, foot, Land Rover and, in the case of the specially formed Alamein Platoon, within a PWRR company, occasionally mounted on horses. Weapons were confiscated, blood feuds defused and visitors escorted and protected. The final two months of the tour, January and February 2001, were by far the most eventful. In January a group of Kosovo-Albanian terrorists crossed into Serbia to try and claim disputed land, and dismounted troops of the squadron were despatched to cut off their supply routes, young troop leaders being surprised to find themselves poised for a platoon attack – a military manoeuvre they thought they had left behind at Sandhurst. Despite the seriousness of the military activities, there was time for a variety of recreational activities: the Squadron Quartermaster Sergeant (SQMS) set up a thriving trading company; 1st Troop confiscated its Troop Leader's red trousers and flew them from every available flagpole; 2nd Troop tirelessly patrolled the American PX stores (equivalent of NAAFI but more exotic); 3rd Troop, tired of having its Troop Leader mistaken for a local tramp, instituted a batman service; and the Troop Leader and Troop Sergeant of 4th Troop, at their evening poker school, earned enough cash to pay for their expected leave on return to Germany. In February they all returned, without casualties, to Athlone Barracks to be met by the commanding officer – now Lieutenant Colonel David Swann – the orderly officer and a piper.

The planning for the deployment of a complete Queen's Royal Hussar battlegroup to Kosovo in October was beset with uncertainty. At first it appeared that C Squadron and the Black Pigs would be in their Challengers, but this was changed within a scant two months of the departure date by a decision that the battlegroup would be one of dismounted infantry, necessitating some hurried specialized training. There was also a complication over their role, caused by the Czech and Slovak governments' commitment to increase their KFOR contribution from a reconnaissance company to a full-blown battlegroup. This change materially altered QRH's area of operations midway through the six-month tour but had a positive spin-off in that some personnel would be able to return to Sennelager early. In the event, David Swann had under his command not only his two squadrons but a company of infantry from the 1st Battalion The Highlanders and elements of a Royal Artillery battery. RHQ, D Squadron and the administrative elements of the battlegroup were based at Waterloo Lines, a former airfield about 3 miles south of Podujevo, while C Squadron was located in the town's police station. To begin with, the area of operations within Kosovo was much the same as that of 1PWRR previously, but the New Year saw C Squadron hand over large parts of its area to the Czech/Slovak battle-group. This highlighted some differences in soldierly conduct. At Gate 3, a major crossing-point into Serbia, a Czech sergeant was mystified to be told by a trooper from the regiment that he should not smoke while manning the barriers and that if cold he should wear gloves rather than put his hands in his pockets. The Black Pigs also experienced a variety of different military cultures. As the quick reaction force, their remit was wide-ranging, working at one stage under Norwegian command with a Swedish platoon in a Finnish area. All was well, except perhaps for the Finnish habit of conduct-ing conferences in a sauna while in a very un-British state of undress. It was a horrendous winter, with the harshest blizzards to hit the Balkans for twenty years – weather which provided SQMS Andy Milton with an oppor-tunity to make a satisfactory amount of money to buy comforts for D Squadron soldiers by trading in the padded jackets which he found he could get at a price far lower than in Germany. Unfortunately, his main supplier was in Macedonia, involving a hairy drive over the mountains, a journey which his driver, Lance Corporal Finbar Findlay (a talented piper), found increasingly uncongenial. Findlay was also disenchanted by an un-fortunate shunt to his vehicle in Skopje, Macedonia's capital city, which was only resolved after an acrimonious exchange of views and a carton of 200 duty-free cigarettes. After another incident, this time in Pristina, where Milton was trying to procure costumes for the regimental padre's nativity play and two anxious-to-please seamstresses were mistaken for an altogether different sort of working girl, Findlay became convinced that he was very much safer in the Pipes and Drums. By the middle of April, the battlegroup had returned to Germany, a successful tour marked by the award of a QCVS to the commanding officer and to the quartermaster, and ten commendations of various degrees. Manpower having improved considerably, David Swann was now able to reform A Squadron – a long cherished ambition. He was not, however, to have his four sabre squadrons gathered around him for long – before the end of the year B Squadron was again to deploy to Kosovo, and there were other unexpected excitements in store.

Swann also had another problem, one which turned the traditionally ordered peacetime life of an armoured regiment on its head. This was the introduction of a concept known as Whole Fleet Management (WFM), whereby regiments would no longer hold a full establishment of its A (fighting) and B (support) vehicles; instead, the bulk of them would be stored and maintained in central locations to be known as Theatre Fleet Support Units (TSFU) – one in Germany at Mönchengladbach and one in the United Kingdom. Training organizations such as BATUS, the Armour Centre at Bovington and the School of Infantry would not be affected. The theory was that keeping a full complement of vehicles (particularly tanks) in regimental lines was wasteful in terms of time spent in maintenance, and that soldiers could be better employed. At the TSFU the vehicles would be kept in a controlled environment and would therefore, in a perfect world, be ready in tip-top condition should they be required for operations or urgent training. But the envisaged perfect world did not exist, largely because the manpower and equipment allotted to the TSFUs were inadequate. It was found that Challenger needed to be operated on a regular basis if it was not to encounter a wide range of problems, among them fuel contamination. The number of tanks to be left with regiments became a matter for furious debate, Swann and other commanding officers arguing for at least two squadrons worth, while the MOD wanted there to be only one. For a few years it seemed that the commanding officers had won; thirty tanks were initially left in regimental lines. But by 2005 around a third of that number had been taken away, although those remaining in Athlone Barracks could be supplemented on demand if more were needed temporarily. The regiment was to find that when it was away on operations, practically all its tanks went into storage.

On 30 March 2002 the Colonel-in-Chief died. She had lived for the whole of the twentieth century and had seen six monarchs, to four of whom she had been closely related as, successively, daughter-in-law, sister-in-law, wife and mother. Her husband, King George VI, had appointed her Colonel-in-Chief

The last journey of Her Majesty Queen Elizabeth, the Queen Mother, first Colonel-in-Chief of The Queen's Royal Hussars (The Queen's Own and Royal Irish). The Colonel of the Regiment, Major General David Jenkins, is wearing his crossbelt.

of the 7th Hussars in 1947, and her colonelcy had been carried forward seamlessly to the Queen's Own Hussars and then to the Queen's Royal Hussars. All eight current Honorary Colonels of her regiments, plus the Captain of HMS *Ark Royal* and the Commandant of the RAF's Central Flying School, were by virtue of their appointments in possession of a file containing details of her funeral, in which it was made clear that, as the senior representatives of military organizations with which she had a personal connection, they were to be pall-bearers. This involved escorting the gun-carriage carrying Her Majesty's coffin from the Chapel Royal at St James' Palace to Westminster Hall, where she was to lie in state, and then, four days later, providing the escort from Westminster Hall to Westminster Abbey for the funeral service itself. The Army pall-bearers were to wear No. 1 Dress uniform – sometimes called Blues – and carry swords. This posed, for General David Jenkins, two immediate worries: after a number of years as under-treasurer of Gray's Inn (one of the four Inns of Court) and the many formal luncheons and dinners that went with this appointment, he found that his Blues required some discreet adjustment; and what about the drill movements which his funeral duties would certainly require? He had never been fond of drill, even at Sandhurst, and he was years out of practice. In the event, all was well: his Blues were massaged to fit; his sword and its accoutrements were found and assembled; and the drill rehearsals were conducted by an immaculate Foot Guards sergeant major who knew all about that sort of thing and was not at all abashed by the combined seniority of those he was licking into shape. For the funeral on 9 April the crowds lining the route were huge; the pall-bearers slow-marched immaculately in step and then had front seats in the Abbey; a small contingent from the serving regiment marched in the parade. It was a fitting and faultless ceremony for a much-loved Queen and, as a side benefit, the regiment now had a Colonel who knew a thing or two about drill.* Prince Philip became Colonel-in-Chief, resuming the appointment he first took up with the 8th Hussars in 1953.

His Royal Highness's first visit in that capacity was in August, at a weekend in which the Regimental Association was also welcomed in the usual generous manner. Sadly, Ken Bidie had died, and the chairmanship had passed to Brigadier Robin Rhoderick-Jones, who led 150 members as they were entertained by a formal parade, during which the Colonel-in-Chief presented Golden Jubilee medals to mark Her Majesty's half-century on the throne, and afterwards viewed a number of stands illustrating regimental life. Splendid dinners were given in the various messes, and Prince Philip was also able to lunch with the old comrades as well as inspecting the newly arrived *Winston*, returning as the official drum-horse after the retirement of *Peninsula* because of ill health. After the Colonel-in-Chief's departure a most moving Beating of Retreat and Sunset ceremony was performed for the regiment, its families and the members of the Association by the Band of the Lancers and the regimental Pipes and Drums. The organization of the weekend was something of a last hurrah for David Swann as he prepared to hand over what seemed to be a well-ordered forecast of events to his successor. In the event, well-ordered it was not to be.

The British Fire Brigades Union, having balloted its members, voted to strike over their unmet demand for a 39 per cent (39 per cent!) pay rise. The strike began in November 2002, at which stage the regiment, as part of the Army-wide Operation Fresco, deployed two large squadrons to carry

* As related by David Jenkins!

out fire-fighting duties in Manchester and Liverpool, utilizing a variety of equipment including the infamous Green Goddesses, not seen in service since the last such industrial dispute in the early 1980s. D Squadron alone was able to carry out normal armoured training. As Christmas approached it was warned for service in Iraq (Operation Telic 3) in the wake of the second Gulf War, which had seen the comprehensive invasion of Iraq and the toppling of the regime of the dictator Saddam Hussein. For the regiment Op Fresco was a messy affair: as settlement of the strike veered between agreement and further industrial action, the fire-fighting squadrons were stood down and then stood to again. The Black Pigs now also became involved as their warning order for Iraq was rescinded, and they too were despatched on fire-fighting duties, this time in Kent. When Lieutenant Colonel Andrew Cuthbert took over command in mid-November, Athlone Barracks was three-quarters empty of its soldiery, and it was with much relief all round that the regiment's commitment to fire-fighting came to an end in early 2003 and training exercises in preparation for BATUS were begun. They were much needed: service in Kosovo and then during Fresco meant that armoured skills had not been recently practised and were, to say the least of it, rusty.

In late April a QRH battlegroup, with B and C Squadrons and two armoured infantry companies, went to Canada, where the fine weather which had at first welcomed this 1,000-strong force turned nasty; so cold did it become on the prairie in early May that two feet of snow fell, resulting in half a dozen cases of hypothermia and even one of trench foot – not an affliction normally suffered by cavalry soldiers. The regiment's battlegroup was followed by one based on the Royal Regiment of Wales, which included A and D Squadrons. Shortly after the return from BATUS the fiftieth anniversary of the Colonel-in-Chief's appointment to the 8th Hussars was celebrated at St James's Palace, where over 300 members of the Association were present and David Jenkins, on the regiment's behalf, presented His Royal Highness with a carriage-driving whip.

The regiment was now fully back in the armoured swing. They were not, however, to be allowed to lead this traditional life for long. No sooner were they all together in Sennelager than they were warned that in October they would join the rest of 20 Armoured Brigade in Basra, Iraq, and that this would entail the deployment of one squadron of tanks, while the rest of the regiment would be mounted in a variety of wheeled vehicles. Small-arms training now became a priority, and yet again the unfortunate A Squadron was put into suspended animation as its officers and soldiers were required to increase the strengths of B and C to infantry company levels.

In the early autumn the General Officer Commanding the 3rd Armoured Division addressed the officers and senior ranks on the developing situation in south-east Iraq. The regiment was to take over an area of operations which included north Basra and Maysan, a province north of the city about the size of Northern Ireland. The general summed up the task facing the regiment in a very few words.

'It will be', he said, 'as difficult as difficult gets.'

The battlegroup deployed at the end of September with, under command, C Squadron and Recce Troop, merged and equipped with Land Rovers and tracked reconnaissance vehicles, D Squadron in a light infantry role but also with fourteen rarely to be used Challenger tanks, a company from 1st Battalion The Light Infantry and two companies from 1st Battalion The Royal Scots. B Squadron was deployed in Maysan as part of the Light Infantry battlegroup, while Major Robert Bell, erstwhile frustrated leader of A Squadron, found himself commanding a company from the Royal Regiment of Wales. RSM John Nutt had been commissioned and was replaced by Euan Johnston. The regiment's mission was to provide security in the North Basra area of operations; this included about a third of Basra city and large expanses of semi-urban and rural districts including the Shatt al Arab waterway. Here the main threat came from Former Regime Extremists (FRE), their favourite weapon being the Improvised Explosive Device (IED), well known to those who had served in Northern Ireland. The term FRE was something of a catch-all invented by the British and it included, for example, gangs formed under Saddam Hussein and other groups trained in Iran. All were Shia, none were Sunni and none wanted the return of a Ba'athist regime. Search-and-arrest operations for suspected terrorists took up much of the time, interspersed with riot control, anti-looting operations and monitoring the distribution of food provided by the World Food Programme to upwards of 2 million Iraqis. The Black Pigs were able to deploy two tanks to help quell a violent inter-tribal squabble, while B Squadron with the Light Infantry in the wilds of Maysan patrolled widely from their base at Abu Naji, searching for weapons and terrorists; one troop was reduced to helpless laughter as they watched a group of surprised looters emerge from a hole with a sunken cache of copper cable and flee, completely naked, into the desert night. In January serious rioting broke out in Al Amarah, Maysan's first city, the squadron displaying a high degree of

Iraq.

professionalism in facing this down, one alert soldier shooting dead an Iraqi he spotted in the act of throwing a grenade. This excitement was followed by a four-day desert operation aimed at interdicting gun-running and supposedly gathering information on a fundamentalist Al-Qaeda (Salafist jihadist) cell operating in the area – a wild-goose chase, in that any Salafists in Maysan, being Sunni, would long ago have been killed by the Shia population.

The last few weeks of the six-month tour saw a startling change of role as the brigade commander chose the battlegroup to train and establish an effective Iraqi police service, border police and criminal justice system in Basra and Maysan, an essential step in normalizing the process of mentoring the Iraqis until they could become self-reliant. The reality was that this operation, although difficult, was only half the problem; just as important was convincing the citizens that their new police and justice bodies were not, as had been the norm, cowardly and corrupt, but credible and capable. The QRH battlegroup's composition now changed: the two infantry companies were shed, a squadron of 9th/12th Lancers was added and in February B Squadron returned to the fold. From December to April, teams of Security Sector Reform troops, made up of regimental personnel, created training facilities for the 20,000-strong police force, screened and tested them and conducted joint security operations. Typically, a troop would be responsible for mentoring three or four police stations and, with little or no knowledge of how to train police, would rely on their military skills to convert an Iraqi policeman from an idle, incompetent and often corrupt individual into something several times more reliable and effective, while Royal Military Police detachments were attached to teach technical policing. To a hugely disappointing extent the measurable success of the regiment's work in this field was negated by an uprising fermented by Muqtada al-Sadr, a fundamentalist Shia cleric. Attacks on coalition troops reached a so far unprecedented level, delivered not only by small-arms fire but also by grenade launchers and machine guns. A team from C Squadron teaching radio procedures to policemen was surrounded by a mob and had to be extracted by armoured vehicles, and a B Squadron troop leader was made aware that his vehicle was under attack when a bullet hole suddenly appeared in his map. A Land Rover patrol, also from B Squadron, was ambushed, but the driver of the lead vehicle, although severely wounded, managed to drive out of the contact zone. Lance Corporal Christopher (Barney) Balmforth, the commander of the three-man crew, dismounted and, with covering fire from follow-up Land Rovers attacked the enemy position on his own. The Iraqi ambush team – later identified as five rogue policemen – disengaged, but not before Balmforth's accurate fire had severely wounded four, all of whom later died of their wounds. For this action he was awarded the Military Cross. The Balmforth family had a history in Iraq operations: Barney's uncle, also Lance Corporal Balmforth, had been one of those wounded in a blue-on-blue incident inflicted by an American tank on an Irish Hussar vehicle in the first Gulf War. In the last four weeks of Op Telic 3 it was claimed that there were more British casualties and more assailants killed than in any comparable period – the regiment counting itself lucky that it incurred no fatalities. The increase in insurgent activity did not, however, prevent the regiment gathering together at the Shatt al Arab hotel to commemorate St Patrick's Day with its attendant celebrations, which included an Ulster Fry breakfast, the traditional bed race and presentation of the shamrock to all ranks, as well as to a rather bemused Iraqi chief of police and a party of Czech military. At the close of April the regiment returned to Germany, the men of B Squadron wearing sweatshirts on which was emblazoned:

> B Squadron, The Queen's Royal Hussars
> Putting the **Fun** Back into **Fun**damentalism

Practically the first action once gathered together after post-deployment leave was again to re-form the dispersed personnel of A Squadron. The officers and men of the squadron had felt a strong sense of being part of a low point in its history and were elated to be once again under the leadership of Major 'Dinger' Bell, whose black Range Rover, sometimes used as an alternative squadron headquarters, had become a familiar and emblematic sight around Athlone barracks. A Squadron's reward for having suffered its indignities with a marked stoicism was to be warned that in October they would deploy in a dismounted role to Cyprus as part of a United Nations battlegroup led by 26 Regiment Royal Artillery and tasked to keep the peace in the buffer zone between the Turks in the north and the Greeks in the south.

In July Major General David Jenkins paid his final visit as Colonel of the Regiment, a perfect excuse for an enormous regimental family weekend. Accompanied by the chairman of the Regimental Association and the regimental secretary, Jenkins and his wife Annie were put to a severe test of stamina, taking in a keenly contested family sports afternoon, two dinners, two dances, a brace of lunches, a church service and a full regimental parade, for which music was provided by the Pipes and Drums and the band of the Brigade of Gurkhas led by *Winston*. At one of the dinners the commanding officer paid heartfelt tribute to the Colonel, an occasion which also foretold Andrew Cuthbert's own farewell, since at the end of the year he was due to hand over to Lieutenant Colonel David Labouchere. A Squadron's tour in Cyprus was uneventful, mirroring that of previous deployments on the island and, because of a partial draw-down of the UN's contingent, it was cut short by a couple of months, enabling them to be back in Sennelager at the end of January 2005.

David Vetch, a former 4th Hussar, had long had a dream: to make a pilgrimage to the long valley near the little port of Balaklava in the Crimea to see for himself the ground over which on 25 October 1854 the Light Cavalry Brigade had charged for over a mile while under murderous bombardment on three sides from Russian artillery and continuous small-arms fire. The year 2004 marked the 150th anniversary of this epic catastrophe, and Vetch had a plan. If he could persuade a contingent of members of the serving regiment and the Regimental Association to join him, what better company could there be? Those consulted needed little persuasion: the Colonel of the Regiment, now Major General Arthur Denaro, and the chairman of the Regimental Association were enthusiastic, and in no time some 120 had signed up for the trip, including six serving officers, the Pipes and Drums and a number of wives. The Colonel-in-Chief heard about it and announced that he, too, would come and would stay at the hotel in Yalta that was to form the expedition's base. The two Davids, Vetch and Innes-Lumsden, the regimental secretary, flew out to Ukraine on a reconnaissance, and on 21 October the whole party left from Stansted airport.

The first full day in Yalta was taken up with a tour of the Lividia Palace, where in February 1945 Winston Churchill, Colonel of the 4th Hussars and Prime Minister of the United Kingdom, attended the peace-brokering conference with the leaders of the USA and the USSR. The palace had recently created a Churchill Room stuffed with memorabilia of the great man to which the party added by presenting four framed pictorial illustrations of Churchill's medals and decorations. Each evening thereafter there was a briefing on the Crimean battlefields to be visited the next day, the first being Balaklava. Thanks to the initiative of retired Major Tony Duff, a former Irish Hussar (and father of the guidon parade's pink panther), more than thirty horses had been hired and were waiting at the point where, in 1854, Lord Cardigan had assembled the Light Brigade. For the next hour, those who had volunteered to ride down the valley had an unforgettable experience, seeing from the ground just how narrow the valley was and marvelling that any of the brigade had managed to survive. Days walking the battlefields of Sevastopol, Alma and Inkerman followed, the Colonel-in-Chief displaying an impressively detailed knowledge of all the actions. The week also included a service on 25 October at the Balaklava Memorial, during

which Prince Philip laid a wreath. The Pipes and Drums led the procession
to the memorial and also gave impromptu concerts in the hotel and in the
streets of Yalta, during which they suffered (feeling absolutely no pain) the
close attention of a gaggle of excited and admiring young ladies. The week
finished with a regimental dinner in the Lividia Palace.*

David Labouchere's first year in command and Mark Cubitt's early
tenure as Regimental Sergeant Major was unusual in the sense that no
squadron was to disappear from Athlone Barracks on some independent
deployment. The regiment was able at last to become reacquainted with its
tanks and concentrate on its armoured role – a staggering statistic being
that A Squadron crews had not spent a night with their tanks since 2003.
Live firing took place, as usual, on the Bergen-Hohne ranges, while Poland
was the destination for field training, a series of deployments for individual
squadrons being followed by a regimental battlegroup exercise with C and
D Squadrons while A and B were attached for similar manoeuvres to
1st Battalion Light Infantry (1LI) and 1PWRR respectively. A more
unusual exercise took place in July in the shape of Exercise Pink Hussar,
when thirty wives took to the Sennelager Training Area for a weekend of
military activities which included fire and movement, orienteering,
Challenger 2 driving, command tasks and formal drill. The happiness
and welfare of wives and children has always had an important place in regimental priorities, and this chance to mimic and practise some of the things
that the men got up to was much appreciated and rated by the participants
as 'a fantastic weekend'.

In October the regimental trustees held one of their twice-yearly meet-
ings at Athlone Barracks and were pleased to see that the building of new
single men's accommodation was progressing well. Once complete, un-
married soldiers would each have an en suite room of their own, a development eagerly anticipated but which had been a long time in gestation.
The visit ended with a formal parade at which it had been planned that the
Op Telic medals would be presented. Sadly, the medal office did not come
up to scratch – failing to deliver on time. Sad too was the fact that this
parade marked *Winston*'s second and last retirement from regimental duty.

---

* A full account of this expedition can be found in David Vetch's book, *Balaklava – 150 Years
On*, with a foreword by HRH The Prince Philip, Duke of Edinburgh. A shorter account
appears in *The Crossbelts* (2004), Vol. 2, No. 6, the journal of The Queen's Royal Hussars
(The Queen's Own and Royal Irish).

He had not been quite himself for some time and in spite of careful nursing and veterinary attention he collapsed in January 2006 and had to be put down. He was to be replaced in 2008 by *Alamein*.

The deployment to Iraq on Op Telic 8 (by this time it was understood by the soldiers that Telic stood for Tell Everyone Leave Is Cancelled) dominated 2006, and once again the regiment had to reorganize into three enhanced squadrons, at the expense this time of the unfortunate Black Pigs, who provided troops to each of the other three. The British element of the Multinational Force (MNF) was again 20 Armoured Brigade, and the regiment arrived in station in April and May, having been cheered considerably by winning the Cavalry Cup football for the first time since 1998. RHQ, C Squadron, Headquarter Squadron and two companies of infantry deployed to Camp Abu Naji near Al Amarah, while A Squadron, as part of a 1LI battlegroup, were in Basra, and B were grouped with their old friends 1PWRR to provide the MNF reserve based some 7 miles south-west of Basra at Al Shaibah, a former RAF airfield which in 1956 had been handed over to the Iraqis. B and C Squadrons both had two troops worth of Challengers and all squadrons were equipped with heavy-duty-chassis wheeled Snatch vehicles and more orthodox Land Rovers, neither of which provided much protection for crews – and protection proved to be very much needed. The security situation in Basra and the surrounding areas had markedly deteriorated since 2003. Shiite militias, of which the so-called Mahdi Army of Muqtada al-Sadr was both the biggest and most lethal, had extensively infiltrated the Iraqi security forces and were leading the attacks on the multinational force as well as targeting oil facilities, reconstruction projects, the minority Sunni population of Basra and Iraqis working with the government or the MNF. Basra city had largely come under the control of the militias, to a point where the governor of the city declared that 'Our society is changing, becoming more religious.' He did not add, as well he might, that this had been achieved by armed coercion.

For the first four months C Squadron's home at Abu Naji was their base for patrolling by day and night in both tanks and wheeled vehicles, securing the airstrip so that re-supply flights could land, and guarding the camp. Forays into Al Amarah by tanks and armoured infantry Warrior vehicles in search of heavy weapons with which the insurgents attacked regularly proved largely unproductive, while, on the other hand, the long-range desert patrols to the Iranian border area gained positive results in terms of ammunition finds and friendly liaison with remote police stations and Iraqi army units. Abu Naji was the name given by Iraqis to the British and could be translated as 'Father of the Nation', an affectionate term which did not, however, prevent frequent long-range assaults on the base, mortar and rocket attacks occurring by day as well as night; during one such day over fifty missiles arrived within fifteen minutes, causing a number of injuries. In August the decision was made to hand the camp over to the Iraqis, after which, with much relief, the battlegroup settled into its new role, living off its vehicles in desert camps and releasing the infantry back to brigade head-quarters to reinforce Basra. So free were they of incoming mortar bombs and rockets that in ten weeks in the desert they were only attacked twice as they moved among the people they were there to help, earning in some measure the trust and consent of the population. In contrast, Abu Naji, destined to be a police training camp and defended only by an Iraqi infantry company, was overrun by insurgents, bent on looting, within five hours of the regiment leaving.

A Squadron in Basra had been disappointed to learn that they would have no tanks. Tasked with securing the 1LI battlegroup base at the Shatt al Arab Hotel (was there ever a more un-hotel-like hotel?) in one of the most lethally violent areas of the city, they were, however, remarkably successful in reducing the threat by patrolling aggressively and managing to avoid damage from some of the most accomplished roadside bombing teams in the country. Strike operations in the form of raids on the premises of suspect individuals were frequent and often yielded results, the most spec-tacular being a sortie to the home of reputedly the most proficient and prodigal of bomb-makers in which a cache of technically advanced equip-ment was seized in such quantity that it could not all be carried in the squadron's vehicles. This led to a noticeable diminishing of the frequency of roadside explosive devices for the next three months and the undoubted saving of many British lives. Intelligence gained on this raid also led to the locations of bombs already planted and the eventual death of the terrorist technician in a fire-fight. After two months of intensive action, a review of troop levels in Iraq led to the squadron being relieved by infantry and moved to a tented camp at the logistics base at Al Shaibah, which was theirs alone. There they settled in with their own cooks and administrative support, the only downside being that tents provided no protection from rocket attacks – a point taken up by a young trooper who asked the visiting Chief of the Defence Staff, Air Chief Marshal Sir Jock Stirrup, why they were not better protected. This pertinent inquiry was answered by Sir Jock, the most senior British serving officer, saying that he was certain there must be a good reason but he couldn't think what it might be.

At the airfield, A Squadron had a number of tasks: guarding the 8-mile perimeter of this huge base, manning the guard towers and providing a quick reaction force within the camp should it be attacked. This allowed plenty of time for continuation training and live-fire exercises. But the most challenging assignment was the provision of convoy escort to the thirty or more supply vehicles travelling four times a day to Kuwait and back – a task which required at least two troops. Near-misses with recklessly driven Iraqi trucks were a common hazard, while less frequent but equally lethal were shots fired at the escort by dissidents which, while inflicting no serious damage, often resulted in the death of the assailants.

B Squadron were fortunate to occupy concrete-clad containers at Shaibah, but they, too, were often on the road, deploying troops to Al Amarah to reinforce the regiment's battlegroup and even further afield to remote police stations, escorting agencies engaged in assessing the efficiency of the incumbents. Desert patrols were always popular, as were those to the Iranian border, where the endless sand and rocks gave way to welcome greenery. A promising tip-off by an ancient villager that arms had been hidden in his backyard turned out to be fiction – a plot by the wizened informer aimed at getting his estranged wife into trouble. One troop spent a week with an Iraqi army unit and found it was getting no response to its efforts to train them, other than sullen faces and low attendance at lectures. Restricting the instruction periods to an hour and a half in the morning and again in the late afternoon after five hours for lunch – the preferred schedule for the Iraqi military day – brought a marginally keener audience.

Towards the end of the tour both A and B Squadrons were involved in Operation Sinbad, an attempt by the MNF to improve the living conditions of those civilians living in the least salubrious areas of Basra and the surrounding villages. Several days would be spent collecting rubbish and removing tens of tons of raw sewage, while trying to encourage the locals, who steadfastly refused to join in unless they were paid. One young man who presented Squadron Sergeant Major Bushell of A Squadron with a black bag full of rubbish demanded 'dollar' as he did so. When told that 'dollar' would not be forthcoming he emptied his bag over Bushell's feet. Providing everyone present with a good laugh could not disguise the sad fact that the mindset of the villagers seemed entirely alien – they seemed to care nothing for efforts made to improve their environment. While engaged on Sinbad, 2nd Troop of B Squadron were deployed to help extricate soldiers of the Light Infantry who had been ambushed. Two tanks were able to engage the enemy, and such was their weight of fire that the extraction route was quickly made secure. The troop relished the fact that not only had they been engaged in a job well done but they had done so in their primary armoured role.

In common with the other British units, the regiment attracted a number of high-profile visitors during its tour: politicians, diplomats and senior military officers from a number of allied nations came, saw, were complimentary and went away. None, however, was so welcome as the Colonel-in-Chief, who arrived on 22 October. Accompanied by the Colonel of the Regiment, and wearing desert uniform and his tent hat, Prince Philip toured all the squadrons, including the hard-working and far-flung elements of HQ Squadron: the quartermasters, the motor-transport troop and the Light Aid Detachments (LAD) from the Royal Electrical and Mechanical Engineers (REME) made up of vehicle mechanics, recovery specialists and other tradesmen, without whose support and expertise no squadron could hope to survive. Showing a keen and knowledgeable interest in the various operations in which the regiment had been engaged and in the sometimes arcane equipment, HRH's visit, secret in the planning and wide-ranging in execution, demonstrated once again how involved he was in regimental affairs and how much his presence was appreciated by all ranks. In November the regiment was back in Athlone Barracks: casualties had been taken, some serious but none of them life-threatening. The families breathed a heartfelt sigh of relief as the celebrations began. For his leadership of the battlegroup, David Labouchere was awarded the OBE, while Staff Sergeant Christopher Lyndhurst of the LAD, for his outstanding bravery while recovering a broken-down Challenger under fire, won a Military Cross.

CHAPTER TWELVE

IRAQ AGAIN AND AFGHANISTAN

He who has a thousand friends has not a friend to spare. But he who has one enemy will meet him everywhere. (Ali ibn-Abi Talib)

The regiment had now been in Athlone Barracks for upwards of nine years, but in 2007 came the news that a move to Tidworth – still as an armoured regiment – was likely in the near future. This prediction was to be repeated at intervals, but without substance, for another ten years. Within the regiment, however, changes were rampant. No sooner had D Squadron and Recce Troop been reconstituted in the wake of Op Telic than C Squadron was warned that it was its turn to go into suspended animation later in the year in order that three full squadrons could go to BATUS in 2008, followed by another probable Telic deployment later in the same year. B Squadron, having been reunited with their Challengers and having fired them successfully on the ranges, were told that 'higher authority' had decreed that they should re-role to medium armour – that is, Scimitar reconnaissance vehicles – for an unspecified task. Retraining of drivers and gunners began immediately, only for the squadron then to be informed that they would not be required after all and could return to their Challengers to exercise with the regimental battlegroup in Poland. A Squadron, which imagined it, too, was to go on exercise in Poland as a component of a regimental battlegroup, was in the event left behind on the Sennelager Training Area to conduct extensive trials on a new Army-wide radio communication system known as Bowman. Only the Black Pigs sailed through untroubled by the turbulence around them, firing on the ranges and exercising in Poland as planned, where they were joined by Major HRH Prince Hamzah, who sportingly assumed for a few days the role of a troop corporal. At the top of the regimental tree David Labouchere handed over to Lieutenant Colonel Christopher Coles, while Mark Cubitt was commissioned into the regiment and Ian Hammond became RSM. One of the new team's first responsibilities was to organize a parade in Birmingham where, in May and at the invitation of Mike Sharpe, the Lord Mayor, a former Queen's Own Hussar and member of the Regimental Association, the regiment exercised its right to march through the city with bands playing, bayonets fixed and guidon flying, a magnificent sight which was followed by lunch for all ranks provided by the city council.

Despite the many 'overcoats on – overcoats off' vicissitudes to which the regiment was subject, it not only managed an impressively high attainment in gunnery and a well-reported-on performance in Poland, but found time and space to send groups and individuals on a variety of sporting activities and adventurous training, including a cricket tour to India and a seven-a-side rugby tournament in Slovenia, as well as producing the Army Wake-Board Champion in Trooper Tizard and a World Powerlifting Champion in Sergeant McConnell. The Pipes and Drums went to Cyprus, and there were battlefield tours to Arnhem and Nijmegen as well as an expedition, described somewhat mendaciously as 'cultural', which took in the Munich Oktoberfest! The major disappointment was the regiment's failure to retain the Cavalry Football Cup, won the previous year much against the odds during the Telic deployment.

It has been the habit over the years for commanding officers to claim, usually in their contribution to the regimental journal, that not only have they had the busiest of years but are looking forward to an even more action-packed twelve months ahead. Chris Coles sensibly ducked this issue when he invited readers to judge for themselves the events of 2008. The regiment had been warned that all its squadrons would exercise in Canada in one role or another during the summer, and that this would be followed by deployment to Iraq on Op Telic 13 in the late autumn. The year began with two pleasurable occasions – a visit by the new commander of 20 Armoured Brigade in January and an old comrades' visit, led by the Colonel-in-Chief, to celebrate St Patrick's Day. Visits by the Brigadier were, of course, routine – 20 Brigade Headquarters was in near-by Paderborn – but this visit was special in the sense that the Brigadier was Tom Beckett, who had been both an Irish Hussar and a Queen's Royal Hussar (in which he had led C Squadron), before commanding a parachute battalion. The Colonel-in-Chief's St Patrick's Day parade marked the fact that, according to the (admittedly fragile) forecast of events, it was the last time the regiment would be together until the summer of 2009. His Royal Highness headed a team of 200 old and bold drawn from all twelve Regimental Association troops led by their new chairman, Major Peter Pusinelli, who had taken over when Robin Rhoderick-Jones retired after twenty-five years as a regimental trustee. The familiar routine characterized by unbounded generosity and faultless organization kicked off on Friday, 14 March with an all-ranks regimental party in a marquee housing the thousand or so who attended. The highlight of the following day was travel through a 'time-tunnel' erected in a tank hangar in which the actions of the regiment and its immediate antecedents since the Second World War were depicted. Tableau followed tableau: scenes from Malaya, Korea, Aden, Borneo, the Inner German Border, Cyprus, Northern Ireland, Zimbabwe, the Balkans, Kuwait and Iraq followed one another in evocative detail – a product of immensely hard work and a highly developed dramatic awareness. The Colonel-in-Chief, indeed all the guests – not to mention the families – were in turn astonished and delighted.

The regimental parade the following day saw the regiment and the old comrades, a little jaded perhaps after parties in the various messes the night before but immaculately turned out, receive the shamrock from Prince Philip aided by a phalanx of retired commanding officers. Music came from the band of the Parachute Regiment and the Pipes and Drums led by *Alamein*, ridden by Sergeant Karen Povey of the regiment's staff and personnel support troop (SPS) – a triple whammy: a first parade for the drumhorse; the first time any drum-horse had paraded with a female on board; and the first time that the rider had come from the Adjutant General's Corps – although it must be stressed that the SPS, like the LAD, the doctor, the padre and the cooks were always, despite sporting different cap-badges, very much part of the regimental family. As the regiment and the Regimental Association marched past the Colonel-in-Chief, the heavens opened and there was no lingering on the square, everyone making for the bars and the lunch marquees with all speed. Regimental Sergeant Major Ian Hammond was well pleased with the drill and the steadiness on parade as he began the task of herding the officers, the members of the warrant officers' and sergeants' mess and the corporals in three different directions to have the traditional photographs taken with Prince Philip. It was then that his world fell in. Despite the splendid party in his mess the night before, he had had an early night (about 0530!) and, although feeling a little fragile, had travelled from his home to the office in good time to get into his parade No. 1 Dress, gold crossbelt, sword and scabbard. What he had not noticed, what the Commanding Officer would not notice, what the Colonel-in-Chief would not notice and what none of the eagle-eyed old comrades had noticed was that Mr Hammond had put on his crossbelt over the wrong shoulder. Only after the parade did one of his predecessors, now commissioned into the regiment, urgently point out to him his mistake. Ian Hammond did not buy any photographs of the parade.*

A fine win in the Cavalry Cup final restored the RSM's equilibrium, and in rugby, new ground was broken by a tour to Dublin, during which a great deal of Guinness was consumed, some of it in a clubhouse next door to a hall in which Sinn Fein was holding a meeting, causing one young trooper who failed to see what all the fuss was about to ask innocently, 'Who is this Sean Fane?' The summer saw a deployment of practically the whole regiment to Canada, a QRH battlegroup providing OPFOR, the opposing force or enemy for those battlegroups being tested. OPFOR was mainly made up of B Squadron personnel, who provided a tank company and a recce company, together with a company from 5th Battalion The Rifles (5 Rifles), the whole being equipped with a variety of armoured vehicles peculiar to BATUS. This force remained in Canada for three months while A Squadron under command of the Rifles battlegroup and D Squadron with 1PWRR were there for about half that time, providing the backbone of their respective groupings in the simulated battles, while OPFOR proved to be an opposition difficult to overcome. It was not until August that the regiment, having performed admirably in its various guises, came together again in Athlone Barracks and began the comprehensive training which preceded deployment on Op Telic 13. Most of this took place in and around Sennelager and covered topics that, until the fracas in the Balkans followed by the invasion of Iraq, had played no part in the training of an armoured regiment. These included familiarization with special weapons, language training, cultural awareness, air-land integration and, most importantly, introduction (or re-introduction) to the numerous complement of vehicles specially developed to meet the challenges presented to an occupying force in a country elements of whose population were at best far from supportive and at worst violently hostile.

Operations in Northern Ireland over two and a half decades had required armoured regiments to mothball their tanks and take instead either to light vehicles or to their feet. But such tours were the exception, and the main

---

* It is to Ian Hammond's great credit that he was the source for the account of this incident.

business continued to be maintaining the consistently high standard of performance in their primary role necessary to provide, as a part of NATO, a credible deterrent to any encroachment on the territory of a member nation. But now, for the Queen's Royal Hussars, leaving their tanks behind had become a way of life. Few had been required on operations in the Balkans, fewer still in Iraq and, worse, there was only a bare minimum available at home. While not infantry, the officers and soldiers of the regiment were increasingly in demand in an infantry role, and the inherently flexible mindset of the cavalry soldier – the product of his armoured training – ensured that they performed with distinction, often to the barely concealed surprise of senior officers brought up in other arms. There was a danger that this success might give rise to the questioning of the long-term future of the regiment and its like within the Royal Armoured Corps, and this was recognized with some concern by Christopher Coles and his fellow cavalry commanding officers. For the moment, though, like their predecessors at Balaklava, theirs was not to reason why.

Op Telic 13 was the last such operation in southern Iraq and was to see the draw-down of British troops in the country. Led by Brigadier Tom Beckett, 20 Armoured Brigade, as always, established its headquarters in Basra. Around half of A Squadron provided force protection for the US Army point-of-entry teams engaged in training Iraqis to take control of border crossings with Iran and was based at the Minden forward operating base at Shalamcheh, a main such crossing place. The other half began its tour manning the Challengers at the Contingency Operating Base (COB) in Basra as part of a quick reaction force. In the event, no quick reaction was called upon, leaving plenty of time for maintaining the tanks and taking part in the oxymoronic 'fun-runs' organized by Brigade Headquarters. These invariably began at an extremely unsocial hour of the morning, and the free T-shirts which were awarded at their conclusion were considered by members of the squadron to fall far short of a proper definition of 'fun'.

B Squadron's area of operations was the major port area of Umm Qasr and the eponymous town nearby. Located only 3km away was a large contingent of Americans guarding Iraq's biggest detainee prison which meant that the squadron had access to a variety of American goodies and dietary alternatives. There were also Americans within the port area mentoring Iraqi customs officials, and the squadron was constantly engaged in reconciling the often conflicting demands of the British, US and Iraqi chains of command. But perhaps the most important personage (and rapidly becoming the richest) with whom the squadron dealt was a flamboyant Turk with a huge lifter-crane engaged in clearing the waterway of wrecks and restoring the port to its former pre-eminent status. The importance of Umm Qasr was reflected in the number of high-ranking visitors with which B Squadron had to deal – in military terms a total of eighty-two stars, the equivalent of a brigadier every other day. After five and a half months and at the conclusion of a five-year British presence, the squadron handed over its responsibilities to the US 10th Cavalry.

For the Black Pigs the first four months were spent in providing military transition teams to mentor the headquarters and battalions of the Iraqi 51st Brigade in Basra and the nearby camp at Az Zubayr. Their accommodation in Basra was, to say the least of it, austere, the facilities often revolving around open sewers and boil-in-the-bag food. At Az Zubayr things were better, and there 1st Troop was able to enjoy hot showers and even walk (relatively safely) to work. In March the squadron finished this task, concluding that 51st Brigade, while not yet an adequately equipped or trained fighting machine, was generally effective in a gendarmerie role. Time was to prove this assessment a trifle optimistic. The British withdrawal now got underway, convoy after convoy heading for Camp Buehring in Kuwait, each escorted and protected by troops of D and A Squadrons mounted in heavily armed and armoured Mastiff six-wheeled vehicles and Snatch Land Rovers. These journeys, fully loaded on the road south and empty on return, took two consecutive nights to complete and were extremely testing for the troops involved. Every convoy was delivered safely, and the Colonel of the Regiment appeared in Kuwait to congratulate the crews. The thirteenth Op Telic was complete and the regiment – the last ground-holding British battlegroup to serve in Iraq – began its journey home, staging in part in Cyprus before returning to Germany for a period of normalization.

Not all the soldiers of the Queen's Royal Hussars had gone to Iraq. There was the usual stalwart rear party looking after the barracks and, above all, the families, but there was also a body of twenty-eight men led by Captain Gerald (Gez to his friends) Kearse, who had deployed to another even more dangerous theatre of operations. In the summer of 2008 the regiment had been ordered to provide an enlarged troop to supplement the Armoured Support Group Royal Marines (ASGRM) in Afghanistan. To prepare them for this, a package of special training was necessary, not least familiarization with the rubber-tracked, low ground-pressure, all-terrain vehicle known as Viking. The Viking, with its crew of two and carrying a further ten fully equipped soldiers, proved no problem for men now used to converting to all manner of ground vehicles with little notice. Training took place at Bovington and then moved to the Royal Naval Air Station at Yeovilton in Somerset to integrate with the Royal Marines and form a squadron-sized unit. Deployment took place in early December, and almost immediately the ASGRM, as part of a brigade operation, began clearing out the Taliban fighters from the area west of Lashkar Gah, the capital of Helmand province. The Support Group was organized in three troops, each with a mixture of Marines and QRH, one of them being led by Captain Kearse. Having cleared the ground, a series of patrol bases were to be built at key junctions to influence the neighbouring population. Routes to these were a magnet for IEDs and, together with constant enemy small-arms fire, roadside bombs were encountered on a daily basis. The Viking was much in demand, its manoeuvrability being hugely appreciated during, for example, the escorting of lengthy logistical convoys carrying supplies to the battle-groups holding ground in Helmand. Much common knowledge was shared between Hussars and Marines and, during the frequent situations of serious adversity, they became virtually indistinguishable. In June 2009 as the ASGRM prepared to leave the theatre of operations it was at a manning level 20 per cent below that when it deployed – a significant proportion had been lost to enemy activity. Two young lance corporals of the regiment had been wounded but, after a spell in the military's medical rehabilitation centre at Headley Court near Epsom in Surrey, were to recover. Two Royal Marines in Kearse's troop had lost their lives.

During the summer of 2009, Darren Potter, long a stalwart of the regimental football team, became RSM, almost his first task being to oversee the preparation for homecoming parades in Warwick, Worcester and Coleraine. All were attended by appreciative crowds on the street, and the entertainment provided by the three municipalities was uniformly generous. In September C Squadron re-formed, drawing officers and soldiers from all the other squadrons and the Viking troop, and spending the period before Christmas ensuring that its equipment was fit, its soldiers were reacquainted with armoured tactics and could shoot straight. October saw the retirement of Arthur Denaro from the colonelcy, the occasion being marked by a full regimental Balaklava parade, medal presentations and a march-past with music provided by the Band of the Welsh Guards and the Pipes and Drums, led by *Alamein* with Sergeant Karen Povey once again in full regalia.

Denaro was succeeded by Brigadier Andrew Bellamy who, sixteen years earlier, had been the regiment's first commanding officer. In November, Chris Coles, having presented the Pipes and Drums with his personal pipe banner, gave up command to Lieutenant Colonel Ian Mortimer, and soon afterwards the Christmas festivities began.

Hybrid Foundation Training (HFT) is a term invented to describe a year in which brigades of the British Army structure and train their battlegroups with a full spectrum of available military assets, rather than allowing regiments to focus exclusively on special-to-arm skills. Training solely for general war against a traditional enemy such as the old Warsaw Pact armies has, within HFT, to be supplemented by, among other skills, counter-insurgency and peacekeeping expertise. This was the lot of the regiment as it embarked on its programme for 2010. The first major engagement was firing on the ranges at Bergen-Hohne, where the crews achieved a pass rate of over 97 per cent against a standard of 80 per cent – the best result within the Royal Armoured Corps since that standard was formalized. From then on, the HFT concept took over, so that by the time the QRH battlegroup deployed to BATUS in October its sub-units had trained, first separately, and then together as a whole. The diversity of HFT is best illustrated by the composition of the battlegroup as it embarked on its exercises against an enemy on ground which now saw not just armoured vehicles operating across 'good tank country', but villages, an oil refinery and tunnel complexes, with insurgents, indigenous security forces and a hostile population – many parts being played by Afghans. Ian Mortimer's force was made up of A Squadron in Challengers, C Squadron mounted in BV206, a tracked, articulated, all-terrain vehicle carrying up to seventeen troops (six in its front half and eleven in the rear), Recce Troop in its Scimitar CVR(T)s, C Company 1PWRR as armoured infantry in Warrior, C Company 2nd Battalion Royal Regiment of Fusiliers (2RRF) as light infantry, Y Company 1PWRR equipped with Javelin 'fire-and-forget' anti-tank weapons, mortars and snipers, a battery of gunners, a squadron of Royal Engineers and elements of a Royal Artillery ISTAR (information, surveillance, target acquisition and reconnaissance) unit, Royal Military Police and Air Manoeuvre Planning. As if this was not enough, the battlegroup was joined for the second half of the exercise period by a Jordanian infantry company, who found the temperatures (sometimes down to $-20°C$) not at all to their liking. As a span of command, Ian Mortimer's battlegroup would have been unrecognizable to a cavalry commanding officer fifteen years earlier.

B Squadron, grouped with 5 Rifles, and the Black Pigs with 1PWRR, both squadrons in Challengers, were trained similarly and also went to BATUS in the summer, enjoying weather very much more to their taste than had the bulk of the regiment.

The Iraq deployment and the subsequent intense HFT made it difficult to put first-choice sports teams together in both 2009 and 2010, but there were successes in football (British Army Germany Champions and finalists in the Cavalry Cup) and skiing, at which the alpine team proved itself to be the best in the Royal Armoured Corps. After a few fallow years, a young polo team showed promise for the future, and there were sound hopes for better times in rugby, cricket, golf and sailing. The Pipes and Drums had a busy and high-profile year, performing at two royal tattoos (Windsor and Edinburgh) and one non-royal tattoo in Berlin, and coming fourth in the World Pipe Band Championships – a great credit to Pipe Major Nicholas Colwell and his men.

The military focus now changed to Mission Specific Training (MST), the preparation for deployment to Afghanistan where, as a battlegroup, the regiment was to form Combined Force Lashkar Gah (LSK), the first armoured regiment to undertake this role. Lashkar Gah is the capital of Helmand, the largest province in the country with an area only slightly smaller than the Republic of Ireland, encompassing 1,000 villages and a population of 900,000, most of whom are Pashto-speaking Sunni Muslims. Helmand is the world's largest opium-producing region, far outstripping Myanmar (Burma), the next largest, and its southern border with Pakistan, as well as being endemically porous, is among the most dangerous in the world. By 2011 British involvement in Afghanistan as a part of the NATO-led International Security Assistance Force (ISAF) had been extant for nine years. The enemy, chiefly the Taliban who had been driven out of government by the United States in the aftermath of the 9/11 atrocity in New York, had regrouped to launch a formidable insurgency using a variety of tactics including the employment of suicide bombers and IEDs as well as direct fire attacks on ISAF patrols and forward operating bases. The first British soldier to be killed in Afghanistan died in 2004, after which the toll escalated alarmingly, both 2009 and 2010 claiming over 100 British lives. Helmand province, long a stronghold of the Taliban, was the British army's operational area and here had been constructed Camp Bastion, an 8-square-mile base which at its peak housed 40,000 personnel and operated an airfield ranked as the fifth busiest of the United Kingdom. Bastion supported the Main

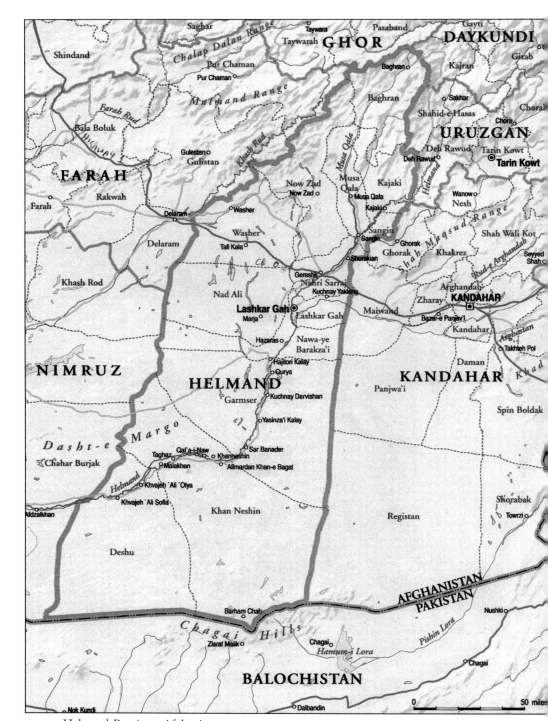

Helmand Province, Afghanistan.

Operating Base at Lashkar Gah, a city with a population of 250,000, in which was stationed Task Force Helmand, for which 20 Armoured Brigade, now under the command of Brigadier Patrick Sanders, was to become responsible in late 2011.

The regimental battlegroup was to deploy as Combined Force (CF) Lashkar Gah and was to operate principally in Babaji, the only one of the nine precincts of the city which had not transitioned (a state in which lead security authority had passed from ISAF to the Afghans), and was to be supported by the Afghan Uniformed Police (AUP), while also acting alongside the police and Afghan National Army (ANA) units in the other precincts. For this task the regiment was required to find a light role infantry company, a Warthog squadron, a Kandak (Afghan Army infantry battalion) Advisory and Training Team (KATT) and a police monitoring team known as an Operational Coordination Centre – District (OCC-D), while also under Ian Mortimer's command would be two infantry companies, one from the 1st Battalion The Yorkshire Regiment (1Yorks) and one from 5 Rifles, the latter being mounted in Warrior. Within the regiment this required – as was now usual – a radical reorganization. A Squadron went into suspended animation, C became an infantry company and D provided the Warthog Squadron, while the rest of the regiment was to man a number of smaller and sometimes complex sub-units.

MST was a new way of describing pre-deployment training and was broken down into individual and collective phases. Individual officers and soldiers had to learn and develop personal skills and specialist knowledge to enable them to operate in this new environment. Some 160 courses were provided, ranging from commanding, driving and maintaining the plethora of special-to-theatre vehicles to language training in Pashto and Dari (the language spoken most widely by the Afghan National Army) and a variety of Train the Trainer (T3) modules learning skills such as counter-IED, patrol, search and compound clearance. On completion, these newly qualified T3 instructors returned to Sennelager to cascade their knowledge downwards to all and sundry within their sub-units. And all this in addition to the annual training tests, of which there were nine, including fitness and shooting, undergone by everyone as a matter of routine, and the extensive briefings at all levels on what might be expected during the deployment. Sport, too, was far from neglected: the Cavalry Cup was won with a nail-biting 1-0 victory over the Royal Dragoon Guards, and a young polo team triumphed in the captains' and subalterns' tournament, while the more sedentary but equally skilful golfers gathered a number of trophies.

Woven into the MST was the complexity of turning C Squadron into an infantry company, for which it metamorphosed into C (Coriano) Company – Coriano being a 4th Hussar battle honour. Troop Leaders and some NCOs attended relevant courses at the infantry battle school in Wales, and individual training built up into company exercises – live-firing and tactical – conducted at Castlemartin, the Brecon Beacons, Thetford in Norfolk, Otterburn in Northumberland and Salisbury Plain. The men of Coriano Company were rarely in their quarters at Athlone, and neither were the Black Pigs. D Squadron made the transition from Challenger ('From Black Pig to Warthog') with relative ease, their Op Herrick role incorporating the firepower, mobility and protection skills endemic to armoured warfare. Warthog, a 22-ton articulated, amphibious, tracked vehicle had replaced the Viking, being better protected especially against mines and other IEDs. The front cab carried the commander, gunner and the vehicle's armament, which was similar to that provided with Viking, while the rear compartment had the capacity to carry eight fully equipped and armed infantry soldiers. D Squadron's first task (in addition, it must be emphasised, to the MST training) was to learn all about this new vehicle, and for this, in batches of thirty, the squadron went to Bovington and Lulworth. The Black Pigs' progression also involved exercises at Castlemartin, Thetford, Otterburn and Salisbury Plain.

During this quite extraordinarily busy year there were also highlights of a non-MST nature. Darren Potter retired and Colin Davidson became RSM. The Colonel-in-Chief visited on 29 July to learn all about the regiment's forthcoming tour, having to leave in the evening for his granddaughter Zara Phillips' wedding in Edinburgh. This was particularly fortuitous timing for Lieutenant Jimmy Hamilton, who was also due in Edinburgh, as Prince Philip was able to give him a lift in his private aircraft. An extraordinary achievement of which the regiment was hugely proud was the award of the Queen's Gallantry Medal (QGM) to Corporal Jason Robinson. In 2010 Jason had been placing a bet in a bookie's shop in Solihull when an armed robber ran in and demanded cash. Robinson ordered him to stop and confronted the assailant, who tried to shoot him (the gun fortuitously failed to work). The man fled, jumped into a car and tried to run the chasing Robinson down. Nevertheless, Jason took the registration number and reported it to the police, and eventually the man was caught and jailed for nine years.

Corporal Robinson's total disregard for his own safety in pursuit of an armed criminal was in the highest traditions of the regiment and of the Army. He was presented with his QGM at Buckingham Palace on return from Afghanistan in 2012.

The fifteen members of B Squadron's KATT arrived at Camp Bastion in mid-September, joining a number of similar teams which made up the Brigade Advisory Group, whose role was to advise and mentor the 3/215 Brigade of the ANA. B Squadron's team was to work with the 2nd Kandak, a battalion which had responsibility for the security of 60km of Highway 1, the country's major ring-road, to a depth of 4km either side. 2nd Kandak was made up of six *tolays*, or companies, of which four were deployed on the road at any one time. The battalion had an excellent record, security within its operational area was at an acceptable standard and improving, and it was clear that a transfer of full responsibility to it from ISAF was a not too distant prospect; the KATT's task was to ensure that this progress was maintained. It was important, too, that the locals could see that their own army was becoming increasingly less dependent on foreign support. An overriding component of KATT activity was relationship-building. This was achieved simply by spending time with the Kandak, hosting their commanders at suppers, drinking endless cups of tea with the *tolays* and playing cricket and football with their soldiers. A sort of routine was established, but often this also meant dealing with the unforeseen – acquiring sheep as presents for a feast, emptying the *tolay*'s septic tanks before disease broke out or dealing with the aftermath of attacks on standing patrols which had resulted in Kandak fatalities. Halfway through the tour 2nd Kandak was exchanged for another, 6th Kandak, led by an accomplished commanding officer who had just completed a tour in a most testing part of Helmand. The new battalion took the lead in a number of successful clearance operations in which elements of both the Warthog Squadron and Coriano Company were involved. As the tour came to an end, an agreement was signed informally transferring the lead for security on that section of Highway 1 to 6th Kandak with only minimal support from ISAF elements. B Squadron's KATT had made a real difference, and this was reflected in two members of this small team receiving much deserved commendations.

C (Coriano) Company was deployed to Patrol Base (PB) Attal in the Nahri Saraj district and found it agreeably comfortable, with its flushing loos, running water, good food and a well equipped gymnasium. The company's activities were also focussed on a road: Route 601, which connected

Lashkar Gah to Kandahar to the east. Coriano's area of operations included thirteen checkpoints manned by the Afghanistan Uniform Police (AUP) and the notoriously Taliban-supporting village of Popalzay. The company was supported by a plethora of attached units, including the recce platoon of 1PWRR, a detachment of REME fitters, a regimental medical officer and his team, a sprinkling of Royal Engineers, including those qualified to destroy IEDs, and a variety of Royal Artillery target-acquisition, intelligence and surveillance systems, as well as 105mm Light Guns. Coriano's platoons were broken down into multiples – a term invented early in British army counter-insurgency operations to describe a body of 10–12 soldiers led by a young officer or senior NCO. Almost as soon as they arrived at Attal, multiples were despatched to a variety of patrol bases, leaving only one platoon (three multiples) and the recce platoon *in situ*.

Coriano Company played a major role in a battlegroup operation in November 2011 aimed at pushing the insurgent line of enemy troops away from Route 601 in the area near Popalzay, so to allow a greater freedom of movement (fewer IEDs) to local nationals. A Royal Engineers bomb disposal team was tasked with locating and destroying existing IEDs in the area while being protected by soldiers of the battle group. A huge volume of intelligence had been generated over several Op Herricks, so enough information existed to enable accurate targeting. The lead was to be taken by the Afghan security forces (ANSF), who would search compounds and other sensitive areas before first light, allowing battlegroup sub-units to link with them in daylight, fight a close battle if that proved necessary and also target insurgents in depth. Conducted in this way, it was hoped (believed) that the locals would respond positively and that the less fanatical insurgents among them would re-integrate back into a government-supporting society. As the operation got underway, Popalzay emptied of women and children and C Company was soon being engaged by direct fire. The engagement lasted all day without British casualties; seven IEDs were destroyed and one insurgent – a practised layer of bombs – was arrested. This challenging operation was a success, combining as it did the well worked cordon-and-search operation by the ANSF in the dark and so many elements of the battlegroup and its supporting arms. It was followed by a dramatic reduction in IED emplacements on the road and also gave C Company some much needed space in which to influence the local population. It boded well for a future in which the ANSF would have full responsibility for security.

The Black Pigs did not deploy as part of the regimental grouping but joined a brigade reconnaissance force under the wing of the Queen's Dragoon Guards which also included elements of 1Yorks and a number of specialist sub-units concerned with intelligence, electronic warfare and un-manned aerial systems. D Squadron was organized into a small head-quarters and two large sabre troops and for the first two months was based at Bastion, although their intensive schedule of operations meant that they barely saw it, spending most of their time bouncing from one ISAF or ANSF base to another. The squadron's most frequent operation was cordon and search: troops would be inserted into the target area by both helicopter and Warthog, and then the latter would provide direct fire support to those on the ground. One major operation involved an eight-hour drive through the desert to launch, in conjunction with a heli-borne force, an assault on a target north of an area which the ANSF wished to clear of insurgents. The plan envisaged that this deception would draw off the enemy, and it worked perfectly. For two days, often under fire, the Warthogs held a perimeter, while 8km to the south the ANSF conducted their clearance operation and constructed a number of command posts with very little interference.

During their six-month deployment the Warthogs operated over the whole of the brigade's area of operations, often without returning to base for weeks at a time. One base – the most popular with the Black Pigs – was owned by the Danish army, an immensely hospitable battlegroup whose excellent food was just what was required after two weeks living off the vehicles. In common with the rest of the battlegroup, D Squadron received heart-warming support from their wives and comrades back in Sennelager and from families, friends and old comrades in Northern Ireland and the Midlands – Christmas and St Patrick's Day in particular triggering a deluge of goodies. The amazing ladies of the Women's Institute in Braunston in Northamptonshire organized upwards of twenty parcels a week during the tour.

The Queen's Royal Hussars battlegroup recovered to Germany in April and May 2012 and it was time to count the cost. There had been a number of life-changing injuries, including those suffered by Lieutenant Will Smethurst, Lance Corporal Matthew Whisken and Trooper Andrew Davies, and eight fatalities, seven of them infantrymen, six of those occurring when the Warrior in which they were travelling was caught in an IED explosion. The eighth was Corporal Jack Stanley of Coriano Company who, while on patrol near Popalzay on 3 February, stood on an IED which injured him so severely that he was to die in the Queen Elizabeth Hospital in Birmingham two months later. Jack Stanley, a leading member of the regimental football team that had won both the Army Cup and the Cavalry Cup was an outstanding soldier of whom his company commander said:

> *His enthusiasm, sense of humour and professionalism were infectious and his subordinates had a clear sense of loyalty to him. We have been deprived of one of the Army's finest soldiers and he will be dearly missed.*

Corporal Stanley was the first soldier of the regiment to be killed in action since Korea.

It is usually invidious to single out individuals from what on Op Herrick 15 was essentially a team effort, but the commanding officer said of Regimental Sergeant Major Colin Davidson:

> *No words will ever explain the depth of the relationship I had with him. Quite simply he was the right man for that time in the regiment's long and distinguished history.*

The regiment's padre, Peter King, had become known throughout Helmand for his blend of compassion and robustness. On his return to Sennelager he wrote:

> *It was a privilege to deploy with the regiment as chaplain on a tour when I experienced the best and the worst of humanity. Sorrow and joy melded on Herrick 15, leaving me a wiser and sadder priest, appreciating more the sanctity of life, the significance of loved ones and the intrinsic value of others. In the deaths within the battlegroup of eight fine young men, among them Corporal Jack Stanley, the ultimate sacrifice was paid. Even then, in the heart of darkness, in our grief and pain, a profound love was evident amongst QRH soldiers: in their compassion, in their care for one another and in their unfailing courage in going back on the ground in the aftermath of trauma.*

While the regiment was deployed it was superbly well supported by two organizations based on Headquarter Squadron: the Rear Joint Operations Centre, fewer than 20-strong under the command of HQ Squadron Leader, was based in Camp Bastion, its role being to sustain the battlegroup throughout the tour with food, water, ammunition, fuel, stores and equipment, as well as sorting and distributing over 3,000 bags of mail. In Athlone Barracks the Rear Operations Group, under the quartermaster, looked after the families, the infrastructure and, most importantly, organized and administered the best possible support for the wounded and their distressed families and friends, all of this illustrating comprehensively the ethos of a truly family regiment. The head of that family, the Colonel-in-Chief, came in May to hear all about it and present the campaign medals; most poignantly, he also presented the Queen Elizabeth Cross to Corporal Stanley's mother. Prince Philip's visit was followed by the handover of regimental command from Ian Mortimer to Lieutenant Colonel Jamie Howard and the re-forming of A Squadron.*

On 27 June a simple but memorable service was held at the National Memorial Arboretum near Lichfield in Staffordshire to unveil the Queen's Royal Hussars monument in the presence of both serving soldiers and old comrades. In the moving words of padre Peter King:

> [*This monument*] *speaks of the unity and deep bonds that exist between brothers-in-arms. It represents over three-hundred years of the collective histories of our antecedent regiments and the individual stories of thousands of Hussars. Here, at the heart of the nation, in an arboretum planted to mark the third millennium of the Christian era, we stand (in the words of the regimental collect) mindful of former valour. This memorial bears witness to a glorious heritage.*

* An account of Op Herrick 15 is given in pp. 8–74 of the QRH journal, *The Crossbelts*, Vol. 4, No. 4, 2012.

CHAPTER THIRTEEN

WHAT NEXT?

I never think of the future. It comes soon enough. (Albert Einstein)

The London Olympic Games of 2012 required a vast security operation which saw, for example, anti-aircraft missiles sited on the roofs of tall buildings, warships in the Thames and fighter aircraft on standby at airfields within easy reach. The government had planned that the armed services would be required to provide only certain specialist teams (search, IED detection and explosive ordnance disposal, for example) to supplement the private security company G4S, which was to provide the bulk of hands-on security. The first warning order, intimating that G4S was going to need a great deal more help than had been anticipated, arrived when RHQ was at Lashkar Gah and laid down that the regiment was to provide a squadron of 150 soldiers, which would include some 40 drafted in from the Royal Corps of Signals and half that number from the Royal Logistic Corps. C Squadron, still at that time Coriano Company, was given this task, and no sooner had its proper designation been restored back in Germany than it was changed again: for the duration of the Games it would be called 'Churchill Squadron' and supplemented not only by the signallers and logisticians but also from within the regiment. As recent deployments went, this one was cautiously welcomed by the soldiers, but it turned into a buzz of excitement when it was learned that among the events for which the squadron would provide security was women's beach volleyball, described by one young officer as probably the greatest of all Olympic sports – although there were those that argued that the Dutch women's hockey team also provided good entertainment.

The squadron's base in London was an erstwhile Territorial Army barracks in Southall, and the full scope of its assignment was to provide security for the Horse Guards venue, which not only hosted beach volleyball (for men as well as women) but was also a key location for the road-cycling, speed-walking and marathon events. The squadron was at first subject to training devised by G4S but soon found that the programme they were

supposed to follow broke most of the basic tenets of sound management and
was also far too elementary in its treatment of subjects in which the soldiers
of Churchill Squadron were well versed, for example dealing with incidents,
first aid, counter-IED and vehicle search – the last being of prime importance. If G4S training methods did not measure up, then its operational
plan was even more woeful, making no allowance for any form of leadership
or the management of personnel. Churchill Squadron scrapped it and sub-
stituted its own. The logistical support, however, was good: the accommodation was reasonably comfortable, the food, prepared at all hours of day
and night to suit various shifts, was in the hands of Gurkha chefs and was
unfailingly excellent, while the laundry arrangements were reminiscent of
the twelve-hour turnaround still found occasionally in the best hotels.
Women's beach volleyball lived up to expectations, as witnessed by the
20,000 people who turned up to watch the four two-hour sessions every day,
each one of whom had to be searched. The up-side was that seats were
always reserved for off-duty members of the squadron.

As the shortcomings of G4S became apparent, the regiment was tasked to
send to London another 100-strong squadron and a small RHQ. The Black
Pigs, having shed their Warthog structure and re-formed, now found
themselves, as the main providers of this new force, reorganizing once again
and adopting as their designation, 'Imjin Squadron'. RHQ, led by the commanding officer, took under its wing not just Imjin but also similar-sized
sub-units from the Queen's Dragoon Guards, 5 Rifles and 35 Engineer
Regiment. The role of this *ad hoc* force was to provide security for the
67-acre (27-hectare) Olympic Village in East London. What promised to be
rather a dull deployment proved to be anything but. Accommodation in
Tobacco Dock, a disused shopping centre, turned out, if anything, to be
slightly superior to the TA Centre, having a gym and even a bar; and a
rotation system allowed for a lot of time off in which to explore London, an
adventure made even more attractive by being able to travel the capital free
of any charges on the production of a military identity card. The task for
Imjin and its three sub-unit colleagues was threefold: first, the operating of
a vehicle search area at the main entrance to the village, second, a similar
operation at the tradesman's entrance and third – by far the most popular –
manning the athletes' pedestrian search area which allowed much interaction with a lot of famous names, numerous selfies and the collection of a
wide range of sometimes esoteric souvenirs. One Troop Leader managed to
acquire a golf-buggy, which a number of competitors flagged down in the

mistaken belief that it was some sort of military taxi service. No one was turned away, but after one tent-hatted joyride too far, the buggy was confiscated. A young Lance Corporal earned a ticket for the opening ceremony as a reward for exceptional vigilance (a number of others were able to see the rehearsals), and a Trooper was nominated to attend both the closing ceremony and a reception given by the Prime Minister. By the middle of August the Olympic adventure was over, and after summer leave the regiment settled down to retraining itself on Challenger. In September a seventy-strong party of old comrades, under their chairman, Lieutenant Colonel Phil Nunn, invaded Athlone Barracks and were, as always, wonderfully well looked after. In 1993 Phil Nunn had been the regiment's first quartermaster and was the first Regimental Association chairman to have served in The Queen's Royal Hussars. In the New Year, Colin Davidson was commissioned into the regiment and handed over the RSM's blackthorn to Matt Campbell-Wild.

The year 2013 was that in which Jamie Howard was determined to focus all ranks of the regiment on returning to its core operational role: combined arms manoeuvre on Challenger 2 – 'Return to the Core', as it soon became known. That this was an urgent necessity can be illustrated by the fact that 2013 was the first time C Squadron had live-fired Challengers since the summer of 2007; one member of the squadron had been away from tanks for so long that he needed conversion from Challenger 1 to Challenger 2! The high point of the squadron's training year was Exercise Bavarian Charger in May and June, which required it to deploy as part of a 5 Rifles battlegroup to an American training area in southern Germany. The exercise culminated in ten days of fighting in country a lot closer than that experienced at BATUS against a permanent OPFOR who knew the ground intimately, the final 72 hours being non-stop. C Squadron received high praise from its battlegroup commander and from the officer commanding OPFOR, who cited the squadron's ability to pop up in unexpected places as the best he had seen during his three years in post.

For RHQ, A and B Squadrons the focus was BATUS, to which they would deploy as a battlegroup in June for six weeks – the former in Challenger and the latter now configured as a command and reconnaissance squadron. After live firing, followed by tactical exercises up to battlegroup level on the Sennelager training area, the move to Canada began in July, when the QRH element was joined by two armoured infantry companies, a predominantly airborne light-role infantry company, together with the appropriate artillery, engineer and other support units. D Squadron also went to Canada to bolster OPFOR and spent their entire time trying to kill A Squadron leader, who not only survived but had the last laugh in comprehensively defeating the enemy in the final exercise. Since the time that the Queen's Own Hussars and the Irish Hussars had first sent battlegroups to the prairie in the 1970s, BATUS had evolved to incorporate the inexorable march of technology, providing some of the best and most arduous training a soldier could experience. In the early days the training area was, apart from half a dozen trees, featureless – ideal tank country and a considerable challenge to map-reading skills. Technological advances and the demands made of armoured soldiers to adapt to a different kind of warfare, notably counter-insurgency and fighting in built-up areas, have resulted in the appearance of a plethora of man-made structures including an entire town. One aspect, however, has been unchanging, and that is the opportunity offered for adventurous training once the formal exercises have been concluded. A wide variety of expeditions was available in 2013, ranging from trekking on horses and parachuting, to the more physically demanding mountaineering, rock-climbing and glacier-walking. For the less adventurous, expeditions across the Rockies in hired cars have always been unfailingly popular, the generosity of the people in small lakeside villages in both Alberta and Montana in the United States seemingly inexhaustible, even after four decades of being invaded by British soldiers looking for a party.

Shortly after the return from Canada, the award of Duke of Edinburgh's Squadron for the next twelve months went, after ten months of keen competition, to A Squadron after a series of competitions including the testing of various key military skills, equipment care, regimental knowledge, the Astley Cooper cross-country running cup and a specific challenge set by the commanding officer. For many years this feature of regimental life had been perforce in abeyance, squadrons regularly being scattered on a variety of commitments, causing the playing field to be constantly uneven. It says much for the intense will to win that the sabre squadrons were so close in points in the resurrected competition that only in the last event, a log-run, did the winners emerge. A squadron also broke new ground in emigrating *en masse* for Remembrance Sunday to Ecot, a small village in Normandy in whose churchyard is the beautifully kept and tended grave of Lance Corporal Alfred Raymond Hope of the 8th Hussars, who died there not long after D-Day 1944 – an event still remembered by the older inhabitants. The squadron took the opportunity of organizing a short battlefield tour around this incident, the tour guide being, fittingly, Nicholas Haines, a retired officer of the Queen's Own Hussars and father of A Squadron's leader.

At the beginning of the year the regiment was warned that in 2014 it would deploy as a battlegroup on Op Herrick 20, the final Afghanistan deployment before the British government's planned withdrawal of all combat troops from the theatre. In the months that followed, the regiment's commitment was scaled down and it became clear that only C Squadron would go and that they would configure as the Warthog Group, in the role carried out by the Black Pigs in 2011 and 2012. The squadron began its MST in September together with the two platoons of 5 Rifles, who were to be their dismounted infantry. D Squadron had enjoyed a turbulent year, the exigencies of the demands made upon their commanders resulting in a turnover of three squadron leaders, two squadron sergeant majors, three seconds-in-command and a bewildering array of troop leaders. They had fired on the ranges in Challenger, provided OPFOR at BATUS in CVR(T) and then began to train as infantrymen for Exercise Jebel Storm in Oman, on which they were to embark in early 2014 and for which they were to be joined by troops from B Squadron. Changes elsewhere in the regiment included the commissioning of Matt Campbell-Wild after an unusually short tour as RSM and the promotion of Neil Rudd to take his place. Rudd had the distinction of being the first purely QRH RSM, not having served in either the Queen's Own Hussars or the Irish Hussars.

Producing winning sports teams was again difficult, but the football, rugby, polo and ski teams all had their moments. A revival of inter-squadron boxing revealed such unsuspected talent that six went on to compete for Royal Armoured Corps titles, two becoming champions. In November, history had its moment when a commanders' dinner was held in the officers' mess and attended by every Challenger tank commander, both to commemorate the battle at El Alamein and to learn a little of the parts played in it by the 3rd, 4th and 8th Hussars. A short presentation by a squadron leader, extracts from the written accounts of some of those who had been present delivered in period military dress, and a talk by the commanding officer on 'The Montgomery Way' preceded the meal, after which the occasion became a general celebration of regimental life. It was a rare opportunity for all the tank commanders to eat together and gave the more junior of the non-commissioned officers a valuable insight into the grandeur of the mess.

Yet another splintered year began as elements of HQ Squadron travelled to Thetford for MST and C Squadron deployed for the same purpose to the Sennelager Training Area and then went on to Castlemartin, followed by Thetford. Most of the remainder fired both Challenger and CVR (T) on the ranges, and this was followed in mid-February by the departure of the Black Pigs for Oman, at a strength of 140 having been joined by soldiers from B Squadron. The first mistake made by the Army (in order to 'save money') was to was to use civilian flights for the deployment, either forgetting or ignoring the fact that the kit carried by soldiers far exceeds the weight allowed by any airline, an error compounded on arrival in Oman by the baggage being confiscated by the authorities as being suspicious! Once this was sorted out, the joint training with the Omani Jebel (Mountain) Regiment could begin, a period of low-level training culminating in a battalion-sized exercise against an enemy provided by the squadron's old friends, 5 Rifles. Finally, there was an extended period of adventurous training encompassing diving and sailing, led by the Black Pigs, and rock-climbing, abseiling and mountain-walking led by Omanis, culminating in a desert feast featuring a range of meat courses absent from the menus produced by the chefs in Athlone Barracks. Everyone returned at the end of March with an impressive tan.

April saw C Squadron, now heavily immersed in the final stages of their MST, becoming Duke of Edinburgh's Squadron, and confirmation that the regiment was to deploy a battlegroup to Glasgow in July to carry out security duties at the Commonwealth Games. A Squadron's year was a microcosm of what now was becoming the norm for the ever-shrinking number of Army units left in Germany. After its successful firing period the squadron disintegrated into penny packets, producing manpower and training support for the Duke of Edinburgh's Squadron and the Black Pigs for their overseas deployments, manpower for the battlegroup going to Glasgow and providing the bulk of a force protection platoon for the British Army Training Unit in Kenya. To an extent, B Squadron was also fractured, providing, among other small-scale commitments, a mentoring force at Westdown Camp on Salisbury Plain for an infantry company from Jordan who were to deploy on Op Herrick 20. The Jordanians, although fixated primarily on depriving all the supermarkets in Salisbury of chocolate, demonstrated a high level of competency, their earlier experiences of Afghanistan standing them in good stead. Operation Comet, as the Glasgow commitment was known, saw the commanding officer and his team leading a composite squadron from the regiment, based on D Squadron, a company of Irish Guards, another from 1st Battalion Royal Anglian Regiment, and a myriad of attachments from the Army Reserve, the Royal Navy, and the RAF. The bulk of this force was based not in Glasgow but in Edinburgh, in accommodation the soldiers found to be comfortable but about which the Navy and Air Force reservists complained incessantly – inviting not a little scorn from those who had experienced living conditions in Afghanistan and Iraq. On the job training was fascinating, the main planks in enforcing security at entrances being '*If your name isn't down here, you're not coming in*' and the unravelling of the mysteries of scanning machines used at airports. The work was not onerous: over-reacting to the early experiences at the Olympic Games, the authorities had erred on the side of caution, so that soldiers had plenty of time off to watch events.

The Duke of Edinburgh's Squadron left for Helmand in June, part of the last British manoeuvre battlegroup to deploy to Afghanistan. The Warthog Group, together with two platoons from 5 Rifles, numbered 220 soldiers with 33 vehicles, and was tasked with protecting Camp Bastion by interdicting the Taliban in depth. During their three-month tour, the squadron conducted ten operations of up to six days in duration, suffered four IED strikes and were in contact with the enemy on 170 different occasions. After eight cycles of Op Herricks the Warthog fleet was more than a little tired, and often it became a race against time to put enough vehicles on the road to carry out a task. On one mission a troop came under heavy fire whilst refitting a thrown track, and two REME vehicle mechanics, Craftsmen Cooke and Hollingsworth, sustained gunshot wounds, both of them being speedily evacuated to Birmingham, where they both made full recoveries, enabling them to return to duty. 'A sprint not a marathon' was how the tour had been described to the Group at its outset, and C Squadron were not disappointed. Their deployment had been busy, challenging, exciting and, above all, successful. They returned to Sennelager in October, and the following month the Colonel-in-Chief came to present them with their medals. Hot on His Royal Highness's heels came the news that the regiment had been granted the Freedom of Worcester. Lieutenant Colonel Alex Porter, who had become commanding officer in September and was the first who had not served in either parent regiment, was able to look forward to a pleasurable addition to the forecast of events when in 2015 the regiment would exercise that Freedom for the first time.

As was now becoming depressingly familiar, the year had proved a difficult one in which to produce sports teams which could harness continuity.
Nevertheless, the footballers reached the final of the Cavalry Cup before
becoming unstuck at the hands of the Light Dragoons, and the golfers (the
game no longer the prerogative of old – or at least older – stagers) did
creditably well, even winning a piece of silverware in the Army's inter-corps
championships. Once the regiment had gathered together again, proper
teams were easier to put together and winter sports were particularly
popular: alpine ski, bobsleigh, skeleton bobsleigh and Cresta teams all drove
south (the nordic ski team went to Norway) for competitions, gaining both
experience and, in the case of those engaged in sliding down runs of unfor-
giving ice, a spectacular collection of bruises. To commemorate the 1914
Christmas Truce, a football team from 20 Brigade, for which the regiment
provided the captain and another key player, took on the 21st Panzer
Division and beat them comfortably. Commemoration of the Great War
also resulted in 'The War Horse Ride', an event in Flanders which remembered the Cavalry Division of the British Expeditionary Force which went
to France in August 1914. This adventure, which received national newspaper coverage, commemorated the fifteen regiments which had made up
the Division, each being represented by a serving or retired officer or soldier
from the present-day successor units. The 3rd Hussars were represented by
Michael Cunningham, a retired Queen's Own Hussar and current trustee of
the regiment, who had travelled with his horse all the way from North
Wales, while Cornet Benjamin Fyfe, dressed and kitted out as a trooper,
represented the 4th Hussars.

The regimental trustees held a meeting in Athlone Barracks in March
2015 under the chairmanship of the new Colonel of the Regiment, Lieutenant General Tom Beckett, who had taken over a few months earlier from
Andrew Bellamy. They left Sennelager – probably wisely – a couple of days
before the St Patrick's Day celebrations which, as usual, began with 'gun-
fire' – a mixture of tea and whiskey served by the officers and senior ranks to
the soldiers and junior NCOs. This was followed by the parade, at which
shamrock was presented to all ranks by the commanding officer and squadron leaders and this year incorporated the finale of a Potential Junior Non-
Commissioned Officer Cadre and the promotion of the top three students
to Lance Corporal. The traditional highlight of St Patrick's Day (certainly
for spectators) is the inter-squadron bed race, in which an officer lying in
a loose approximation of a bed is manoeuvred round a 1½-mile obstacle

course while being attacked from all sides by marauders from rival squadrons armed with eggs, flour and a range of other non-lethal missiles. The celebrations concluded with parties in the messes and squadron bars at which a Guinness or two were despatched. Thereafter the regiment began to disperse, squadron by squadron, on its various tasks for the year. When Captain Robbie Thorne arrived back in the regiment in June to become operations officer after a period away at Lulworth, he walked round the regimental lines to catch up on all the news and was surprised to find only one squadron present and of that only one troop remaining intact. The year had, however, begun with relative cohesion, all squadrons carrying out firing on the Bergen-Hohne tank ranges (having performed miracles in improving the parlous state of the tanks collected from TFSU), where the commanding officer excelled himself in achieving one of the best results in the regiment. The main item in the 2015 programme was a considerable exodus to Canada in April, when RHQ, B, D and hefty elements of HQ Squadron were to act as OPFOR for the first battlegroup exercise, while on subsequent BATUS exercises the regiment was to provide the OPFOR tank company in the shape of first D and then C Squadron. Meanwhile, A Squadron started on a range of Regular Army Assistance Table (RAAT) tasks, providing the armoured component of training delivered to units and establishments throughout the United Kingdom, chiefly in support of courses run at the Land Warfare Centre at Warminster – the former School of Infantry. In May the squadron handed over its vehicles in Athlone and took up residence at Knook Camp on Salisbury Plain, a temporary barracks (it had been first built during the Second World War!) with an Army-wide reputation for extreme discomfort and providing, according to one troop leader, '*Luxury beyond our wildest expectations, some of the accommodation even having cold showers and others a rat population so quiet that it was possible to have uninterrupted sleep as often as two or three times a week*'.

The Challenger fleet taken over by the squadron proved to be refreshingly functional: only once in six weeks did a tank fail to make it back to base under its own steam. Often acting as a *de facto* battlegroup headquarters with a company of infantry and a reconnaissance squadron under command, A Squadron's drills at both troop and combat-team levels benefited to an extent not now easily available in Germany, and the occasional bouts of dismounted training in the urban environment of the purpose-built village on Copehill Down provided interesting diversions – as did the unenviable task of providing an enemy for a Special Air Service exercise. There was, however, time to broaden individual horizons: an exchange of visits with the crew of the Royal Navy frigate HMS *Iron Duke* and with an engineering company which restored and maintained classic racing cars, and a tour of HMS *Victory* (ending with a different sort of tour of Portsmouth's nightlife) all provided life-enhancing experiences. At the end of June the squadron returned to Germany.

The deployment to BATUS concerned not only the provision of OPFOR but a fifty-strong commitment to support the winter repair programme and to provide temporary staff for eight months. Providing the enemy for large-scale exercises is always popular, and never more so than in Alberta, where the wide-open spaces and the fact that OPFOR have been on the ground well in advance of the visiting battlegroups give a certain advantage. The regiment built on that by producing a propaganda news-sheet, *The Prairie Oyster*, which lost no opportunity to make fun of the units from the armoured infantry brigade which provided the battlegroups under test. 'Armoured Infantry' had in 2012 under the future design for the army announced as 'Army 2020', replaced 'Armoured' as the qualifier for brigades which included tanks and infantry borne in armoured vehicles. This curious nomenclature, imposed by an infantry Chief of the General Staff, seems to have been introduced either to reflect the fact that such brigades were infantry-heavy or perhaps to make it easier for politicians with no military experience to understand how the infantry was deployed. HQ and B Squadrons returned home in June, followed by D Squadron in August and finally C Squadron and the temporary staff in November.

The Freedom of Worcester was exercised on 27 June, a contingent of 200 officers and soldiers marching with bayonets fixed, drums beating, band playing and the guidon flying through enthusiastic, street-lining crowds and followed by 100 old comrades drawn from all the Regimental Association troops. Two receptions followed, including lunch for 500 of the regimental family on the racecourse. The day was a huge success, illustrating the deep support given to the regiment by the people of Worcester. It also marked the impending commissioning into the regiment of the RSM, Neil Rudd, who was preparing to hand over his blackthorn of office to WO 1 Darren Grinsell in August. The remainder of the year passed in a relatively prosaic manner as squadrons returned home. Sports teams had, yet again, been difficult to assemble with any degree of continuity, and silverware was hard to come by. The rugby team, determined to make the most of an otherwise not hugely distinguished season, sent a team to Jersey to play beach rugby and another to the Dubai Sevens at the end of the year – the first regular Army regiment to be invited to the International Social Men's section of this event.

January 2016 saw the beginning of a designated Training Year, a precursor to the Readiness Year which was to be the regiment's lot in 2017. It was also the commanding officer's last full year in the appointment and he could hardly have asked for a more successful one. Morale was high: the manning situation was improving and the quality of both the young soldiers and of the officers emerging from Sandhurst was of the highest. The regiment was now becoming used to accepting only the best – a gratifying situation ascribed by Alex Porter in large part to being based in Germany and being one of only two Challenger regiments left in the Army. What he might have added was that the Queen's Royal Hussars was a happy family unit in the widest sense, embracing wholeheartedly not just its families and those attached from the specialist corps within it, but the network of loyal old comrades embodied by the Regimental Association.

In the dark months of a German winter the regiment went *en bloc* to carry out annual live-firing on the Bergen-Hohne ranges, surpassing themselves in the percentages achieved. A Black Pig troop won the Churchill Cup – given annually to the best performing troop in gunnery – for the second year running and, despite austerity in military expenditure, a German range warden was heard to remark that one squadron had fired more rounds on their last day than a Bundeswehr tank company had managed in two weeks. The connection with Winston Churchill – 'the greatest Hussar of them all' – continued to be cherished by the regiment, its newest manifestation being through the International Churchill Society. Founded first in 1968 as the Churchill Centre, the Society seeks to educate new generations in 'the leadership, statesmanship, vision, courage and boldness' of Sir Winston and sponsors an annual conference as well as periodic lectures in which prominent world figures apply Churchill's experiences to today's issues. Curiously, both the Irish Hussars and the Queen's Royal Hussars seem to have been outside this loop until in 2016 the regiment was represented by Lieutenant Barnaby Spink at that year's conference held at the National Churchill Library and Center in Washington DC. Speakers over the three days included the British historians Sir David Cannadine and Andrew Roberts, the current chairman of the American Joint Chief of Staffs, James Baker, a former Republican Secretary of State and Barry de Morgan, the Irish Hussar officer who had commanded the bearer party at Churchill's funeral. The regiment resolved to continue this representation annually, while perhaps wondering why it had not done so before. Within the serving regiment, however, the connection with the great man has become highly visible in that 'Churchill's Own' has become a popular, unofficial, self-imposed nickname and is found emblazoned on tracksuits and other items of sporting dress as well as being emphasised as a marketing ploy in recruiting literature.

The most important military training manoeuvres of the year took place at BATUS, to which the whole regiment deployed in various groupings, beginning with D Squadron which provided the heavy armour element of 5 Rifles battlegroup, followed by C (Duke of Edinburgh's) Squadron with 1PWRR. Last to go was a regimental battlegroup, led by the commanding officer with B Squadron (Command and Recce Troops) and A Squadron (which had taken to calling itself 'The Devil's Children' – a nickname bestowed upon the 3rd Hussars by the Sikhs in 1846) in its Challengers, together with the now usual and formidable collection of armoured and light infantry companies, gunners, sappers and smaller sub-units from various corps. Each exercise period (now known as Prairie Storm) lasted for thirty-one days and took every soldier and crew through the full tactical spectrum – almost every mission being conducted at night, on radio silence and against an accomplished OPFOR which as the summer progressed had got to know the ground intimately. Every squadron was well reported on, with the QRH battlegroup being graded the best of the BATUS season.

The Prairie Storm experience was particularly important for The Duke of Edinburgh's Squadron as it was to be in 2017 a part of a 1PWRR battlegroup providing a NATO body called the Very High Readiness Joint Task Force (Land), prepared to deploy anywhere in the world at five days' notice. As part of the preparation for this supremely important role, the battlegroup spent three weeks in September on the Sennelager Training Area for Venerable Gauntlet, an exercise designed to test its readiness, together with other components of the Task Force drawn from Poland, Norway, Romania, Spain and Denmark. Shortly after the squadron's return to barracks, the Black Pigs left Athlone and travelled to Salisbury Plain to provide the armoured element for the live-firing Land Combat Power Visit (a firepower demonstration) which had two highlights: the squadron hit all its designated targets first time and on every day, and there was the long anticipated debut appearance of the Ajax reconnaissance vehicle, destined to replace CVR(T) in Recce Troop. During their three weeks on the Plain the squadron lived at Westdown Camp, like the infamous Knook a 75-year-old temporary accommodation barracks, but happily rodent-free.

The Pipes and Drums had a fractured year, its members being scattered with their parent squadrons in Germany, Canada and the United Kingdom. Despite the difficulties, they managed a number of engagements, including one in Dublin where, like the rugby team before them, they were made hugely welcome. Soon afterwards, Pipe Major Colwell, after ten distinguished years, left on promotion for the Royal Irish Regiment, to be replaced after a short interregnum by Pipe Major Gary Grant from the Scots Guards. The regimental sports world, having had no chance of continuity for most of their teams, saw an innovation in the holding of an inaugural Sports Awards evening, during which colours were presented to players who had represented the regiment with distinction, a number of them having gone on to represent the Royal Armoured Corps, the Army and even the Combined Services. The climax came with the award of 'QRH Regimental Sports Personality of the Year' to Lance Corporal Daniel Webb, who had developed and coached not only the regimental rugby team but the RAC team as well, and a 'Lifetime Achievement Award' to Major Mick Burgess, who had played golf for the regiment for over twenty years and had won just about every title possible in Army golf. The alpine skiers provided the most high-profile team success, winning both the RAC and Divisional championships and going on to provide two competitors (out of nine) for the Army team that won the inter-services cup. But it was the regimental boxing evening in December which set the regiment buzzing. The last of eleven closely contested bouts was a middleweight contest between, in the red corner, the adjutant, Captain George Trypanis, and in the blue, RSM Darren Grinsell – surely a first, not only for the regiment but, in all likelihood, for the Army. The RSM secured the verdict – perhaps just as well for his credibility with all ranks!

The year also saw two major events within the wider regimental family. The first arose from a Ministry of Defence decision that it would no longer fund more than one museum for each regiment: the Queen's Own Hussars museum in Warwick and the Irish Hussars museum in Eastbourne would have to become one. Neither premises lent itself to expansion so it was decided to buy a building in which each collection could be housed and displayed, together with the artefacts already accumulated during the relatively brief life of the Queen's Royal Hussars. After much debate the trustees decided that the new location should be Warwick, in the heart of the regiment's Midlands recruiting area. A major fund-raising effort spearheaded by Brigadier Andrew Bellamy (still ongoing as this account is written) had by 2016 raised enough money to buy suitable premises in Trinity Mews in the town and to enable the necessary interior redesign and refurbishment to get underway. Warwick and its castle are popular tourist attractions, particularly among Americans, and the soubriquet 'Churchill's Own' will be useful in advertising the museum.

The second notable occasion was the retirement of Major David Innes-Lumsden from the post of regimental secretary after seventeen spectacularly successful years – sixteen more than he expected to serve when he first took on the appointment! He was not, however, to be entirely lost, as the Colonel of the Regiment invited him to be a trustee and (jointly with Lieutenant Colonel Andrew Ledger) deputy chairman of the Regimental Association, now chaired by Colonel Andrew Cuthbert. Cuthbert, who had taken over from Phil Nunn – another appointee who had enjoyed a hugely successful tenure – had commanded the Queen's Royal Hussars, and this heralded the advent of a new generation at the head of the Association. The trustees, accompanied by their wives, marked David Innes-Lumsden's departure with a formal lunch and presentation at the Cavalry and Guards Club in April, attended by the Colonel-in-Chief. Major Jim Austin, a former Irish and Queen's Royal Hussar (he had commanded HQ Squadron at Camp Bastion during the regiment's last tour in Afghanistan) became the new regimental secretary and immediately scored when, after a gap of many years, he managed to penetrate the defences of a hitherto uncooperative civil service and secure the employment of an assistant secretary in the form of Sean (known as Seamus) Hamilton, another former Irish Hussar with a degree in IT and Computing – a strong team indeed.

The final full year of this story saw command of the regiment pass to Lieutenant Colonel Nicholas Cowley and confirmation – after a decade of rumour, counter-rumour and broken promises – that in 2019 the regiment would indeed move to Tidworth, where it would be one of only two Challenger regiments left in the army. Cowley's declared priority on arrival was to ensure that the regiment was ready for war at any time through achieving excellence in leadership at every level and in physical fitness. A formal development programme was initiated which aimed to allow soldiers and officers of all ranks to study and think formally about leadership for an hour a week. Guest speakers from industry, higher echelons of the armed forces and sport were invited to talk, including Arthur Denaro, who shared with Cowley extensive experience of the Special Air Service. Physical fitness assumed a high profile, and a Churchill Troop was formed in which soldiers who were recovering from injury or who were unfit for other less dramatic reasons were exercised twice a day under the supervision of a physical training instructor and the regimental nurse, the aim being to rehabilitate them fully.

The principal military manoeuvre of the year was Exercise Saber Junction (American spelling), in which a QRH battlegroup deployed to Hohenfels, a densely forested and hilly training area in Bavaria to join the United States 2nd Cavalry Regiment – a brigade-size unit in which QRH provided one of three battlegroups. The 2nd Cavalry would be opposed by an OPFOR (*pace* BATUS) type force which had been in post for three years and had come to know the 63 square miles (163 square kilometres) of the training area well. The regimental battlegroup was formed from A, B and HQ Squadrons together with an Italian company equipped with tank-killing guns and a Polish mechanized infantry company. Inter-operability (talking to three allied nationalities) initially posed problems, as did the presence of enemy drones, constantly employed on reconnaissance tasks. Despite the European Union regulation which demanded that drivers of all vehicles (including military) should have six hours unbroken sleep in every twenty-four, the exercise offered as realistic a simulation of conventional warfare as possible, and the Challengers demonstrated once more their usefulness in difficult terrain, allowing crew commanders a great deal of flexibility and consequently the ability to prove that their tanks remain a battle-winning asset.

Another important, but smaller-scale, deployment took place in early spring when a D Squadron troop joined a 5 Rifles battlegroup in Estonia in a move designed by NATO to demonstrate solidarity with the Baltic states should they be threatened by foreign incursions. Again, in forested terrain, the Challenger demonstrated its capability as a decisive asset in the battlegroup's manoeuvres, and the troop was commended by the battlegroup commander for its performance. After four months it was replaced by another from the Black Pigs, who continued the good work and were visited by the British Prime Minister, Mrs Theresa May.

On 19 August history was made in the person of Lieutenant Leah Bertram who, since the government had made it legally possible for women to serve in ground close-combat roles, became the first woman officer to be commissioned into the Queen's Royal Hussars. Leah was, however, no stranger, since for two years she had been, as an officer of the Adjutant General's Corps, the detachment commander of the twenty or so soldiers of the staff and personnel support troop responsible for the human resources and financial support of everyone in the regiment. Women officers in the SPS role, in command of the Light Aid Detachment REME and as regimental medical officer, had frequently been attached in the past, as had female soldiers in these sub-units, but Bertram was the first to be cap-badged and take her place as a troop leader in a sabre squadron. She is unlikely to be the last, and it is expected that female soldiers as members of a tank crew will soon follow.

The year was a stellar one for the regiment's sportsmen. Following disappointments in both the Cavalry Cup football and inter-regimental polo (losing semi-finalists in both), the cross-country, cricket, tennis and golf teams were all champions of British Army (Germany), the golfers sweeping the board. The alpine skiers also excelled themselves, carrying off eleven trophies and providing three members of the Army team including the captain. Football and rugby teams played in Cyprus and Munich respectively, while there was an adventure training trip to Malta. The horsemen redeemed themselves by winning the captains and subalterns polo tournament.

The Queen's Royal Hussars entered 2018, their silver jubilee year, with a new Regimental Sergeant Major in the person of WO1 Guy Hepple (Darren Grinsell having been commissioned into the regiment) and with much to look forward to. With the regiment scheduled to deploy to BATUS as OPFOR and to provide a squadron as a manoeuvre force for exercises on Salisbury Plain, this so-called 'Committed Year' promises as always to be busy. Recruiting of officers and soldiers was buoyant and the regiment won a cash prize for the highest retention rate in the Army.* On present planning, a change from Sennelager would come about in the summer of 2019 with a move to Tidworth. What appeared to be certain, as an Army restructuring plan known as 'Army 2020 Refine' is implemented, is that the regiment when in Tidworth will retain its Challengers as part of 20 Armoured Infantry Brigade and, with the Royal Tank Regiment, become one of only two Challenger regiments. This reduction in heavy armour capability by a third would make the United Kingdom Army one of the most tank-light in the

---

* Retention is the term used when a soldier elects to stay in the Army rather than leave at the end of his (or her) current engagement.

world and may turn out to be possibly the worst politico-military decision ever made, even if – as has been forecast by some military analysts (optimists?) – each regiment was to be enhanced by the addition of a further Challenger squadron, thus turning them into four sabre squadrons each of eighteen tanks arranged into four troops of four with two within each squadron headquarters.

Another debate, still unresolved as this history is published, is the question of how long Challenger 2 will remain in service and with what (if at all) it should be replaced. A life-extension programme is mooted, probably with the aim of retaining it until 2035. After that, in line with the perhaps somewhat fanciful plans for civilian road vehicles, an unmanned tank may take its place in the order of battle. Whatever the outcome, the soldiers and officers of the Queen's Royal Hussars will still be needed and, like their predecessors, they will do their duty with professionalism, flair and fun. *Mente et Manu*.

APPENDIX A

COLONELS-IN-CHIEF AND REGIMENTAL COLONELS

Her Majesty Queen Elizabeth, The Queen Mother
Colonel-in-Chief, 7th Queen's Own Hussars   1947–1958*
Colonel-in-Chief, Queen's Own Hussars   1958–1993
Colonel-in-Chief, Queen's Royal Hussars   1993–2002
  (The Queen's Own and Royal Irish)

His Royal Highness The Prince Philip, Duke of Edinburgh
Colonel-in-Chief, 8th King's Royal Irish Hussars   1953–1958
Colonel-in-Chief, Queen's Royal Irish Hussars   1958–1993**
Colonel-in-Chief, Queen's Royal Hussars   2002–
  (The Queen's Own and Royal Irish)

Her Royal Highness The Princess Margaret
Colonel-in-Chief, 3rd The King's Own Hussars   1953–1958

* When appointed, Her Majesty was King George VI's consort and as such was The Queen. She became Queen Mother in 1952.
** From 1993 to 2002 His Royal Highness The Prince Philip, Duke of Edinburgh, was Deputy Colonel-in-Chief of the Queen's Royal Hussars (The Queen's Own and Royal Irish).

* * *

3rd The King's Own Hussars
Duke of Somerset's Regiment of Dragoons
1685–1687   Brigadier General Charles Seymour, 6th Duke of Somerset
1687–1688   Colonel Alexander Cannon
1688–1694   Major General Richard Leveson

The Queen Consort's Own Regiment of Dragoons
1694–1695   Colonel Thomas Fairfax
1695–1703   Major General William Lloyd
1703–1732   Lieutenant General George Carpenter, 1st Baron Carpenter

The King's Regiment of Dragoons (from 1714)
1732–1743   General Sir Philip Honeywood
1743–1752   Lieutenant General Humphrey Bland

3rd (King's Own) Regiment of Dragoons (from 1751)
1752–1755   Field Marshal James O'Hara, 2nd Baron Tyrawley
1755–1772   Lieutenant General George Keppel, 3rd Earl of Albermarle
1772–1797   General Charles Fitzroy, 1st Baron Southampton
1797–1799   General Francis Lascelles
1799–1807   General Charles Grey, 1st Earl Grey
1807–1821   General William Cartwright

3rd (The King's Own) Regiment of (Light) Dragoons (from 1818)
1821–1829   Field Marshal Sir Stapleton Cotton, 1st Viscount
            Combermere
1829–1839   Lieutenant General Lord George Beresford
1839–1855   General Lord Henry Manners
1855–1866   General Peter Latour

3rd (King's Own) Hussars (from 1861)
1866–1872   General Henry Hankey
1872–1884   General Sir George Lockwood
1884–1891   Lieutenant General Edward Cuertyon
1891–1909   Lieutenant General Edward Howard-Vyse
1909–1912   Major General Richard Blundell-Hollinshed-Blundell
1912–1924   Field Marshal Sir Julian Byng, 1st Viscount Byng of Vimy

3rd The King's Own Hussars (from 1921)
1924–1926   Major General Alfred Kennedy
1926–1946   Brigadier General Philip Kelly
1946–1955   Brigadier George Younghusband
1955–1958   Lieutenant Colonel Sir Douglas Scott Bt

4th Queen's Own Hussars

The Princess Anne of Denmark's Regiment of Dragoons
1685–1688   Brigadier General John Berkeley, 4th Viscount Fitzhardinge
1688–1689   Colonel Thomas Maxwell
1689–1693   Brigadier General John Berkeley, 4th Viscount Fitzhardinge
1693–1710   Lieutenant General Algernon Capell, 2nd Earl of Essex
1710–1713   Field Marshal Sir Richard Temple, 1st Viscount Cobham

1713–1735   General William Evans
1735–1768   Field Marshal Sir Robert Rich Bt

4th Regiment of Dragoons (from 1751)
1768–1770   Field Marshal The Hon. Henry Seymour Conway
1770–1788   General Benjamin Carpenter

4th (Queen's Own) Regiment of Dragoons
1788–1797   Field Marshal John Griffin, 4th Baron Howard de Walden
1797–1802   General Sir Robert Sloper
1802–1808   General Sir Guy Carlton, 1st Baron Dorchester
1808–1836   General Francis Hugonin

4th (Queen's Own) Regiment of Light Dragoons (from 1818)
1836–1841   General Lord Robert Somerset
1841–1847   Lieutenant General Sir James Dalbiac
1847–1861   General Sir George Scovell

4th (Queen's Own) Hussars
1861–1865   General Sir James Grant
1865–1874   General William Fitzgerald de Ros, 23rd Baron de Ros
1874–1880   General Lord George Paget
1880–1881   General William Parlby
1881–1904   General Alexander Low
1904–1919   General Sir Alexander Moore

4th Queen's Own Hussars (from 1921)
1919–1941   Major General Sir Reginald Barnes
1941–1958   Colonel Sir Winston Churchill

7th Queen's Own Hussars

The Queen's Own Regiment of Dragoons
1690–1696   Brigadier General Richard Cunningham
1696–1707   Lieutenant General William Kerr, Marquess of Lothian
            (Lord Jedburgh)
1707–1709   Colonel Sir Patrick Hume, Baron Polworth and 1st Earl
            Marchmont
1709–1714   Lieutenant General The Hon.William Kerr
1714   *Regiment disbanded. Reformed in 1715*

The Princess of Wales's Own Regiment of Dragoons
1715–1741   Lieutenant General The Hon William Kerr,

The Queen's Own Regiment of Dragoons (from 1751)
1741–1760   Lieutenant General Sir John Cope

7th (The Queen's Own) Regiment of Dragoons (from 1751)
1760–1763   General John Mostyn
1763–1779   Field Marshal Sir George Howard
1779–1795   General Sir Henry Clinton

7th (or Queen's Own) Regiment of (Light) Dragoons (from 1783)
1795–1801   General Sir David Dundas
1801–1842   Field Marshal Henry Paget, 1st Marquess of Anglesey

7th (The Queen's Own) Regiment of (Light) Dragoons (Hussars)
(from 1807)
1842–1846   Lieutenant General Sir James Kearney
1846–1864   General Sir William Tuyll

7th (Queen's Own) Hussars (from 1861)
1864–1866   General James St Clair Erskine, 3rd Earl of Rosslyn
1866–1873   General Sir John Scott
1873–1879   General Charles Hagart
1879–1884   General Henry Benson
1884–1896   Lieutenant General William Dickson
1896–1907   Major General Robert Hale
1907–1924   Major General Sir Hugh McCalmont

7th Queen's Own Hussars (from 1921)
1924–1946   Major General Alexander Cambridge, 1st Earl of Athlone
1946–1948   Colonel Geoffrey Fielden
1948–1952   Colonel Thomas Thornton
1952–1958   Major General Ralph Younger

8th King's Royal Irish Hussars

The Regiment retained the tradition of serving under the name of its Colonel until 1751 (i.e. Killiigrew's Dragoons, Pepper's Dragoons etc.)

1693–1706   Major General Henry Conyngham
1706–1707   Major General Robert Killigrew
1707–1714   Major General John Pepper
1714   *Regiment disbanded. Re-formed in 1715*
1715–1716   Major General John Pepper

1716   *Regiment disbanded. Re-formed in 1719*
1719–1722   Major General Phineas Bowles
1722–1725   Brigadier General Richard Munden
1725–1731   Field Marshal Sir Robert Rich
1731–1733   Major General Charles Cathcart, 8th Baron Cathcart
1733–1736   Brigadier General Sir Adolphus Oughton Bt
1736–1740   Lieutenant General Clement Neville
1740–1755   Lieutenant General Richard St George

8th Regiment of Dragoons (from1751)
1755–1758   General John Waldegrave, 3rd Earl Waldegrave
1758–1760   General Sir Joseph Yorke, 1st Baron Dover
1760–1787   General John Severne

8th (The King's Royal Irish) Regiment of (Light) Dragoons
(from 1777)
1787–1789   General Sir Charles Grey, 1st Earl Grey
1789–1797   General Francis Lascelles
1797–1798   General Sir Charles Grey, 1st Earl Grey
1798–1804   General Sir Robert Laurie Bt
1804–1818   General Sir John Floyd Bt
1818–1833   General Sir Banastre Tarleton Bt

8th (The King's Royal Irish) Regiment of (Light) Dragoons (Hussars)
(from 1822)
1833–1839   General Sir William Grant
1839–1840   Lieutenant General Sir Joseph Straton
1840–1843   Lieutenant General Philip Philpot
1843–1855   General Sir John Brown
1855–1865   Field Marshal George Bingham, 3rd Earl of Lucan

8th (The King's Royal Irish) Hussars (from 1861)
1865–1868   General John Lawrenson
1868–1875   General John Gibson
1875–1880   Lieutenant General Rudolph de Salis
1880–1886   General William Forrest
1886–1887   Lieutenant General Sir James Sayer
1887–1895   Lieutenant General Sir Charles Crauford Fraser Bt
1895–1910   Major General William Mussenden
1910–1930   General Sir Thomas Mahon

8th King's Royal Irish Hussars (from 1921)
1930–1948   Brigadier John van der Byl
1948–1958   Air Marshal Sir John Baldwin

Queen's Own Hussars
1958–1961   Major General Ralph Younger
1961–1965   Colonel Sir Douglas Scott Bt
1965–1969   Brigadier Hugh Davies
1969–1975   General Sir Patrick Howard-Dobson
1975–1981   Colonel Marcus Fox
1981–1986   Lieutenant General Sir Robin Carnegie
1986–1993   Brigadier James Rucker

Queen's Royal Irish Hussars
1958–1965   Colonel Sir Winston Churchill
1965–1969   Lieutenant Colonel George Kidston Montgomerie of
             Southannan
1969–1975   General Sir John (Shan) Hackett
1975–1985   Major General John Strawson
1985–1993   General Sir Brian Kenny

Queen's Royal Hussars
(The Queen's Own and Royal Irish)
1993–1999   Major General Richard Barron
1999–2004   Major General David Jenkins
2004–2009   Major General Arthur Denaro
2009–2014   Brigadier Andrew Bellamy
2014–   Lieutenant General Sir Thomas Beckett

BATTLE HONOURS

3rd The King's Own Hussars

WAR OF THE AUSTRIAN SUCCESSION: **Dettingen.**

NAPOLEONIC WARS: **Salamanca, Vittoria, Toulouse, Peninsula.**

INDIA: **Cabool 1842, Moodkee, Ferozeshar, Sobraon, Chillianwallah, Battle of Goojerat, Punjaub.**

BOER WAR: South Africa 1902.

THE GREAT WAR: Mons, Le Cateau, **Retreat from Mons, Marne 1914,** Aisne 1914, Messines 1914, Armentières 1914, **Ypres 1914–15,** Gheluvelt, St Julien, Bellewaarde, Arras 1917, Scarpe 1917, **Somme 1916–18, Cambrai 1917–18,** St Quentin, Lys, Hazebrouck, **Amiens,** Bapaume 1918, Hindenburg Line, Canal du Nord, Selle Sambre, **France and Flanders 1914–18.**

SECOND WORLD WAR: Sidi Barrani, **Buq Buq, Beda Fomm,** Sidi Suleiman, **El Alamein, North Africa 1940–42, Citta della Pieve,** Citta di Castello, Italy 1944, **Crete.**

7th Queen's Own Hussars

WAR OF THE AUSTRIAN SUCCESSION: **Dettingen.**

SEVEN YEARS WAR: **Warburg.**

FRENCH REVOLUTIONARY WAR: **Beaumont, Willems.**

NAPOLEONIC WARS: **Orthes, Peninsula, Waterloo.**

INDIA: **Lucknow.**

BOER WAR: **South Africa 1901–02.**

THE GREAT WAR: **Khan Baghdadi, Sharquat, Mesopotamia 1917–18.**

SECOND WORLD WAR: **Egyptian Frontier 1940, Beda Fomm, Sidi Rezegh 1941,** North Africa 1940–41, **Ancona,** Rimini Line, **Italy 1944–45,** Pegu, Paungde, **Burma 1942.**

Battle honours in **bold** were emblazoned on the Guidon of the **Queen's Own Hussars.**

4th Queen's Own Hussars

WAR OF THE AUSTRIAN SUCCESSION: **Dettingen**.

NAPOLEONIC WARS: **Talavera, Albuhera, Salamanca, Vittoria, Toulouse, Peninsula**.

INDIA: **Ghuznee 1839, Affghanistan 1839**.

CRIMEA: **Alma, Balaklava, Inkerman, Sevastopol**.

THE GREAT WAR: **Mons**, Le Cateau, Retreat from Mons, **Marne 1914**, Aisne 1914, Messines 1914, Armentières 1914, **Ypres 1914–15**, Langemark 1914, Gheluvelt, St Julien, Bellewaarde, Arras 1917, Scarpe 1917, **Somme 1916–18, Cambrai 1917–18, Amiens**, Hindenburg Line, Canal du Nord, Pursuit to Mons, **France and Flanders 1914–18**.

SECOND WORLD WAR: **Gazala**, Defence of the Alamein Line, Ruweisat, **Alam el Halfa, El Alamein, North Africa 1942, Coriano**, San Clemente, Senio Pocket, Rimini Line, Conventello-Comaccio, Senio Santerno Crossing, Argenta Gap, Italy 1944–45, **Proasteion**, Corinth Canal, **Greece 1941**.

8th King's Royal Irish Hussars

INDIA: **Leswarree, Hindoostan, Central India, Afghanistan 1879–80**.

CRIMEA: **Alma, Balaklava, Inkerman, Sevastopol**.

BOER WAR: **South Africa 1900–02**.

THE GREAT WAR: **Givenchy 1914, Somme 1916–18, Cambrai 1917–18, Bapaume 1918**, Rosieres 1918, **Amiens, Albert 1918**, Beaurevoir, Pursuit to Mons, **France and Flanders 1914–18**.

SECOND WORLD WAR: Egyptian Frontier 1940, Sidi Barrani, Buq Buq, Sidi Rezegh 1941, Relief of Tobruk 1941, **Gazala**, Bir el Igela, Mersa Matruh, **Alam el Halfa, El Alamein, North Africa 1940–42, Villers Bocage**, Mont Pincon, Dives Crossing, Nederrijin, Best, Lower Maas, **Roer, Rhine**, North-West Europe 1944–45.

KOREAN WAR: Seoul, Hill 327, **Imjin**, Kowang San, **Korea 1950–51**.

Queen's Royal Irish Hussars

LIBERATION OF KUWAIT: Gulf 1991, Wadi al Batin.

Battle honours in **bold** were emblazoned on the Guidon of the **Queen's Royal Irish Hussars**.

The Queen's Royal Hussars
(The Queen's Own and Royal Irish)

The Queen's Royal Hussars (The Queen's Own and Royal Irish) carry all the accumulated battle honours of their predecessors. Forty-four battle honours are emblazoned on the regiment's guidon, presented on Friday, 13 June 1997, by the then Colonel-in-Chief, Her Majesty Queen Elizabeth the Queen Mother. These are:

Obverse

Dettingen	Warburg
Leswarree	Hindoostan
Albuhera	Salamanca
Orthes	Toulouse
Peninsula	Waterloo
Affghanistan 1839	Moodkee
Ferozeshah	Chillianwallah
Balaklava	Sevastopol
Central India	Lucknow
South Africa 1900–02	Imjin
Korea 1950–51	Gulf 1991

Reverse

Mons	Marne 1914
Ypres 1914–15	Givenchy 1914
Somme 1916–18	Cambrai 1917–18
Amiens Khan	Khan Baghdadi
Villers Bocage	Rhine
Buq Buq	Beda Fomm
Sidi Rezegh 1941	Alam el Halfa
El Alamein	Citta della Pieve
Ancona	Coriano
Italy 1944–45	Greece 1941
Crete	Burma 1942

A photograph of the guidon can be found in the colour plate section in the centre of the book.

THE VICTORIA CROSS

The Victoria Cross is the highest ranking award in the United Kingdom's honours system and is given for 'gallantry in the face of the enemy'. The medal is made from metal taken from artillery pieces captured by the British in the Crimean War and is inscribed '*For Valour*'. It was first introduced in January 1856 by Queen Victoria (who played a major personal part in its design) to honour acts of outstanding gallantry in the Crimea. Private Samuel Parkes of the 4th (Queen's Own) Regiment of Light Dragoons (later the 4th Queen's Own Hussars) was one of the first recipients.

The medal has been awarded 1,358 times to 1,355 recipients. Only fifteen have been awarded since the Second World War: eleven to soldiers of the British Army, including one in Iraq and three in Afghanistan, and four to soldiers of the Australian Army (all in Vietnam).

Eight members of the ancestor regiments of the Queen's Royal Hussars (The Queen's Own and Royal Irish) were recipients.

4th (Queen's Own) Regiment of Light Dragoons
Private Samuel Parkes (Crimea, October 1854)
Private Samuel Parkes, sometimes described as the colonel's rollicking orderly, was not at the roll-call at the conclusion of the charge of the Light Cavalry Brigade at Balaklava on 25 October 1854, having had his horse shot from under him. Beginning to make his way back on foot he saw Trumpet-Major Hugh Crawford, who by then had neither horse nor sword, being attacked by two mounted Cossacks. Having driven off the Russians, Parkes and Crawford, now joined by a third man, tried to rescue the badly wounded Major Halkett who ordered them to leave him and save themselves. More Russians arrived, and Parkes, continuing to fight, was shot in the hand before he and Crawford were taken prisoner. The third man, Trooper Edden, escaped, but Parkes and Crawford remained in captivity before being returned to the regiment exactly a year later. Parkes was presented with the Victoria Cross by the Queen in Hyde Park in 1856.

7th (The Queen's Own) Regiment of (Light) Dragoons (Hussars)

Cornet William Bankes (India, March 1858)

On 19 March 1858 during the Indian Mutiny, desperate fighting was taking place in the Musa Bagh district of Lucknow where a troop of the 7th had charged a strong force of rebels who were intent on capturing British guns. The troop leader and his second-in-command were put out of action and Cornet William Bankes took charge, although wounded in head, arm and leg. Under his leadership the troop drove off the attackers, but not before he had collapsed, bleeding from eleven wounds. He later died and was awarded Victoria Cross posthumously.

Major Charles Crauford Fraser (India, December 1858)

On the last day of 1858 the 7th were fighting a strong force of rebels under the notorious Nana Sahib, driving them into the River Rapti, which rapidly became a seething mass of horses and men. During the melee an officer and two private soldiers who could not swim were stranded on a sandbank, exposed to enemy fire. Major Charles Crauford Fraser of 1st Squadron, although wounded himself, dismounted into the water and managed to bring all three men to safety. For this action he received the Victoria Cross from the Queen in 1859. It is of interest that, as a Lieutenant General, Sir Charles Crauford Fraser Bt was Colonel of the 8th Hussars from 1887 to 1895.

8th (The Kings Royal Irish) Regiment of (Light) Dragoons (Hussars)

Captain Clement Walker-Heneage (India, June 1858)
Sergeant Joseph Ward (India, June 1858)
Farrier George Hollis (India, June 1858)
Private John Pearson (India, June 1858)

Captain Clement Walker-Heneage, Sergeant Joseph Ward, Farrier George Hollis and Private John Pearson were all serving in A Squadron of the 8th (The King's Royal Irish) Regiment of (Light) Dragoons (Hussars) during the Indian Mutiny, as they charged several hundred of the rebel army of Tatya Tope before the fort of Gwalior in June 1858. After routing the enemy they were attacked by a new force emerging from the fort and again put the rebels to flight, effectively ending resistance at Gwalior. For this action Major General Sir Hugh Rose, commander of the Central India

Field Force, awarded the squadron four Victoria Crosses, ordering that one should go to an officer, one to a senior rank and two to corporals and below. Walker-Heneage, Ward, Hollis and Pearson were elected by their comrades to receive the honour – the first instance of its kind.

Troop Sergeant Major James Champion (India, September 1858)
Troop Sergeant Major James Champion of D Troop of the regiment won his Victoria Cross on 8 September 1858 when both officers of his troop were disabled and he assumed command as they pursued a rebel force at Beejapore, some 50 miles south-west of Gwalior. Despite being severely wounded by a ball through his body he continued to lead the charge, always going forward and disabling several of the enemy with his pistol. By so doing he was deemed responsible by his leadership and personal courage for the destruction of over half of a force of 800 sepoys.

APPENDIX D

REGIMENTAL MUSIC AND NICKNAMES

MUSIC

Quick March. The Quick March of the Queen's Royal Hussars (The Queen's Own and Royal Irish) is a combination of Light Cavalry (from the Queen's Own Hussars) and St Patrick's Day (from the Queen's Royal Irish Hussars).

Slow March. There are four: The 3rd Hussar Slow March; Litany of Loretto (4th Hussars); In the Garb of Old Gaul (7th Hussars); March of the Scottish Archers (8th Hussars).

Trot. Encore.

Canter/Gallop. Bonnie Dundee.

The Regimental Song. Sung by all ranks at all types of gatherings, formal and informal, and also during the march past the saluting base on Cavalry Memorial Sunday in Hyde Park in May each year. The tune is the second part of the regimental Quick March and the lyrics are:

I'm a soldier of the Queen's Army,
I'm a galloping Queen's Hussar.
I sail the ocean wide and blue,
I'm a chap who knows a thing or two.
Been in many a tight corner,
Shown the enemy who we are.
I can ride a horse, go on a spree and sing a comic song,
And that denotes a Queen's Hussar.

NICKNAMES

3rd The King's Own Hussars
Bland's Dragoons. From 1743 to 1752 The King's Regiment of Dragoons were known as *Bland's Dragoons* after their Colonel, Lieutenant General Humphrey Bland.

Moodkee Wallahs. As the 3rd Light Dragoons, the regiment fought in the Sikh Wars of 1845–46 and 1848–49. At the Battle of Moodkee (or more properly Mudki) in December 1845, the Sikhs called them *Moodkee Wallahs* and also *Shaitan-ke-Bacheche* (The Devil's Children). *Moodkee Wallahs* stuck for a century.

4th Queen's Own Hussars
Paget's Irregular Horse. Colonel Lord George Paget commanded the 4th Light Dragoons in the Crimea and, as effectively Lord Cardigan's second-in-command, commanded the second line in the Light Brigade's charge at Balaklava. Paget was an eccentric who ran his regiment on a very loose rein, so much so that it became known as *Paget's Irregular Horse.* He smoked a cigar throughout the charge and later went on to command the brigade.

7th Queen's Own Hussars
The Strawboots. After the Battle of Warburg in 1760 the 7th (The Queen's Own) Regiment of Dragoons spent a miserable couple of years in Germany, where they were neglected by the commissariat to the extent that when their boots wore out they had, when mounted, to bind straw to their legs. *Strawboots* was short-lived as a nickname.

The Saucy Seventh. The indignities suffered after Warburg were set aside half a century later when the smartness of their uniforms and the generally high standard of turnout was exemplary This transformation dates from 1807, when the regiment first became Hussars as the 7th (The Queen's Own) Regiment of (Light) Dragoons (Hussars), and *The Saucy Seventh* was established as the Prince of Wales's second favourite cavalry regiment after the 10th (Prince of Wales's Own) Regiment of (Light) Dragoons (Hussars).

The Lillywhite Boys. The new hussar uniforms acquired between 1807 and 1811 had predominantly white facings to jackets and pelisses, and this short-lived nickname seems to have been acquired then and was used on recruiting posters. *Lillywhite Boys* has been the nickname of many a cavalry and infantry regiment down the years but did not stick long to the 7th Hussars.

8th The King's Royal Irish Hussars
The Crossbelts. At the Battle of Almenara in 1710, Pepper's Dragoons overthrew a corps of Spanish cavalry and equipped themselves with the sword-belts of the fallen enemy and wore them across their own, becoming

known almost instantaneously as *The Crossbelts*. This nickname lived on in the Queen's Royal Irish Hussars as the title of the regimental journal and is also the name of the journal of the Queen's Royal Hussars.

The Queen's Own Hussars and the Queen's Royal Irish Hussars

Neither the Queen's Own Hussars nor the Queen's Royal Irish Hussars acquired nicknames during their thirty-five years' existence, although the latter were generally known as *The Irish Hussars*. Both were sometimes referred to by the politically incorrect (and the jealous!) as respectively *Queers on Horseback* and the *Queerest Regiment in History*.

The Queen's Royal Hussars (The Queen's Own and Royal Irish)

During its first twenty-five years the Queen's Royal Hussars has not had a nickname bestowed upon it by outsiders. Within the regiment, however, *Churchill's Own* has recently been unofficially adopted. It will be interesting to see whether this catches on in the wider world.

COMMANDING OFFICERS AND REGIMENTAL SERGEANT MAJORS

OF THE QUEEN'S ROYAL HUSSARS (THE QUEEN'S OWN AND ROYAL IRISH)

Commanding Officers

1993–1994	Lieutenant Colonel Andrew Bellamy
1994–1996	Lieutenant Colonel Nigel Beer
1996–1998	Lieutenant Colonel Nicholas Smith
1998–2000	Lieutenant Colonel Christopher Vernon
2000–2002	Lieutenant Colonel David Swann
2002–2004	Lieutenant Colonel Andrew Cuthbert
2004–2007	Lieutenant Colonel David Labouchere
2007–2009	Lieutenant Colonel Christopher Coles
2009–2012	Lieutenant Colonel Ian Mortimer
2012–2014	Lieutenant Colonel James Howard
2014–2017	Lieutenant Colonel Alexander Porter
2017–	Lieutenant Colonel Nicholas Cowley

Regimental Sergeant Majors

1993–1995	WO1 (RSM) Brian Nicholl
1996–1998	WO1 (RSM) Tom Hamilton
1998–1999	WO1 (RSM) Mark Butler
1999–2001	WO1 (RSM) Kenneth Sparkes
2001–2003	WO1 (RSM) John Nutt
2003–2005	WO1 (RSM) Euan Johnston

2005–2007	WO1 (RSM) Mark Cubitt
2007–2009	WO1 (RSM) Ian Hammond
2009–2011	WO1 (RSM) Darren Potter
2011–2013	WO1 (RSM) Colin Davidson
2013–2014	WO1 (RSM) Matthew Campbell-Wild
2014–2015	WO1 (RSM) Neil Rudd
2015–2017	WO1 (RSM) Darren Grinsell
2017–	WO1 (RSM) Guy Hepple

AFFILIATED REGIMENTS
(as at 2018)

British Army Reserve Affiliations

B (Staffordshire, Worcestershire and Warwickshire Yeomanry) Squadron, Royal Yeomanry

B (North Irish Horse) Squadron, Scottish and North Irish Yeomanry

Commonwealth Affiliated Regiments

Canada
- The Sherbrooke Hussars
- The Royal Canadian Hussars
- 8th Canadian Hussars (Princess Louise's)

Australia
- 3rd/9th Light Horse (South Australian Mounted Rifles)
- 2nd/14th Light Horse Regiment (Queensland Mounted Infantry)
- 4th/19th Prince of Wales' Light Horse Regiment
- 3rd Battalion The Royal Australian Regiment

New Zealand
- Queen Alexandra's Mounted Rifles

South Africa
- The Natal Mounted Rifles
- The Umvoti Mounted Rifles
- 1st Light Horse Regiment